User Experience Design

A Practical Playbook to Fuel
Business Growth

SATYAM KANTAMNENI

WILEY

For general information on our other products and services or for technical support, please contact our Customer Care Department within the United States at (800) 762-2974, outside the United States at (317) 572-3993 or fax (317) 572-4002.

Wiley also publishes its books in a variety of electronic formats. Some content that appears in print may not be available in electronic formats. For more information about Wiley products, visit our web site at www.wiley.com.

Library of Congress Cataloging-in-Publication Data

Names: Kantamneni, Satyam, author.
Title: User experience design: a practical playbook to fuel business growth / Satyam Kantamneni.
Description: Hoboken, New Jersey: Wiley, [2022] | Includes index.
Identifiers: LCCN 2022008654 (print) | LCCN 2022008655 (ebook) | ISBN 9781119829201 (paperback) | ISBN 9781119829379 (adobe pdf) | ISBN 9781119829386 (epub)
Subjects: LCSH: User interfaces (Computer systems)—Design. | Design—Human factors.
Classification: LCC QA76.9.U83 K3257 2022 (print) | LCC QA76.9.U83 (ebook) | DDC 005.4/37—dc23/eng/20220308
LC record available at https://lccn.loc.gov/2022008654
LC ebook record available at https://lccn.loc.gov/2022008655

Cover Design and Images: UXReactor / Diana Ximena Sánchez Sánchez
SKY10032993_032922

PRAISE FOR USER EXPERIENCE DESIGN
A Practical Playbook to Fuel Business Growth

"Satyam shares his extensive expertise in UX leadership, design, and business strategy through an actionable series of playbooks. These playbooks will help organizations transform their approach and leverage best practices in user-centric design and experience strategy. This is a valuable reference no matter what stage of user experience design maturity your organization has reached."

—Amy Lokey, SVP and Global Head of Design, ServiceNow

"Satyam brings a holistic business perspective to the concept of design and has written a highly entertaining, insightful, and practical guide for how the best companies leverage design to drive disproportionate returns. The book is expertly illustrated, making it easy to read, and contains a treasure trove of anecdotes, case studies, and practical examples to help you on your journey. This book is a shining example of a product designed for its users!"

—Lewis Black, CEO, Actian Corporation

"I first met Satyam in 2014 and was struck by his passion for and insights in user experience design. He was ahead of the times in recognizing the strategic importance of good user experience for business and anticipated the movement towards consumerization of enterprise applications. This book should be a required reading for business leaders—even a cursory reading of this book will influence their mindset and help them realize that investment in superior customer experience could be a significant and long-lasting strategic advantage."

—Venk Shukla, General Partner, Monta Vista Capital

"A treasure trove of experience frameworks, best practices, plays, and insights for enhancing design impact to the next level. I wish I had these experience frameworks early on in my career. A must-read for all design and business leaders. Absolutely priceless."

—Arin Bhowmick, Chief Design Officer and Group Vice President, IBM Products

"Satyam strikes a perfect balance between demystifying experience strategy and elaborating its practical application in this book. A must-read for not only UX professionals but also for executives of all functions. And I can see how this book will be equally helpful for early career employees and seasoned leaders. Why has nobody else written about this before?"

—Bora Chung, Chief Experience Officer, Bill.com

"The PUX™ plays in this book provide a disciplined and practical approach that teams can use to make better design decisions across the customer journey. By focusing on bv.d, teams can scale up and maintain a focus on creating ongoing customer value."

—Thomas DeMeo, VP of Product Management, Coupa Software

"As experience continues to become more central to the value that organizations create and deliver, it becomes even more important to teach people at every level in the organization how to design the right experiences. With that being the case, this is one of the most important books to be published in the last decade and will certainly help you (and your organization) understand how to employ the right mindset in everything you do."

—Justin Lokitz, business model and strategy expert and coauthor of the bestselling books, *Design A Better Business: New Tools, Skills, and Mindset for Strategy and Innovation,* **and** *Business Model Shifts: Six Ways to Create New Value For Customers.*

"Satyam Kantamneni outlines a set of extremely practical best practices that will help teams and organizations deliver services to their customers that they will value and love. The book is essential reading for business leaders who want to understand how better UX unlocks business growth."

—Greg Petroff, SVP of Research and Product Design, Compass

Dedicated to my wife, Gayatri, and wonderful daughters, Veda and Mantra, who have unconditionally supported my entrepreneurial journey, which has made this playbook possible.

PART I
PLAY TO WIN

27 PLAYS TO PRACTICE

PART 3

GAMETIME

GAME
PLANNING

READY,
SET, GO

ABOUT THE AUTHOR

Satyam is the founder of UXReactor together with his brother, Prasad. Under his leadership, UXReactor has become the fastest-growing specialized user experience design firm in the US, with a team of 60+ employees spread over three continents.

Before starting his entrepreneurial journey, Satyam served as managing director of product design at Citrix in San Francisco, where he played a crucial role in growing the product design team from four members to more than 100 practitioners. Satyam was instrumental in building PayPal's Global Design Center in India while leading a design team in Silicon Valley.

He is a perpetual learner with educational background representing a unique trifecta in engineering, human-centered design, and business. He is an alumnus of Harvard Business School's famed General Management Program, studied design thinking at Stanford University, and holds a master's degree in human factors from Wright State University.

While at Harvard, Satyam realized that most businesses aren't leveraging the full power of user experience (UX) design as an engine for strategic growth. Companies either don't have the in-house design expertise or relegate design to a support role—even when hiring external UX agencies.

Satyam resolved to change that. Through UXReactor, Satyam is demonstrating that UX can and should drive enterprise-wide innovation and business outcomes. UXReactor has enabled clients to generate multiple hundreds of millions in additional revenue from user-centered innovation.

Satyam has also advanced the UX discipline by developing and curating the PragmaticUX™ framework: a consistent, replicable, measurable, and scalable approach to innovation in a digital world. UXReactor relies on this proven framework to lead user experience and product innovation for multiple Fortune 500 companies.

He lives in Dublin, California, with his wife and two daughters.

Linkedin

ABOUT uXreactor

To win and keep market share, businesses need to differentiate on experience. It's no longer enough to upgrade your features or platform design. Your buyers demand intuitive, seamless solutions that make users better and more powerful, with less effort.

When you can do that, you can earn untouchable loyalty.

We specialize in transforming experiences for complex B2B organizations. Most UX design agencies avoid the complexity of enterprise systems. And they aren't prepared to navigate the organizational silos in large B2B firms.

UXReactor thrives on those very UX challenges. We're at our best creating seamless experiences out of complexity. That's why enterprise software companies and leaders across industries choose UXReactor.

We help organizations

→ Discover new markets and validate new or existing products so you get from innovative ideas to remarkable profits faster;

→ Design user and customer experiences that give your firm a competitive advantage;

→ Build experience transformation capacity inside your firm so you can innovate on demand and design experiences that magnetize more loyal customers.

Every engagement we lead is focused on improving the metrics that matter most. UXReactor's experience design work is a force multiplier for greater adoption, retention, CLTV (customer lifetime value), satisfaction, efficiency, engagement, revenue, and more.

For clients such as ServiceNow, Tekion, Nokia, Actian, Extreme Network, and CloudKnox, UXReactor has helped them reach significant business milestones and win coveted awards. Recently, we celebrated CloudKnox's acquisition by Microsoft, who came to us with a back-of-the-napkin idea; Tekion's hyper-growth and a valuation of $3.5B in five years; and a 100% increase in customer growth rate within one year for one of the UK's largest cell phone service providers.

Founded by executives who have led innovation and design at some of the most iconic tech companies in the world, the firm has codified proven techniques based on decades of industry experience.

Our diverse team of 60+ includes experience design strategists supported by specialists in user research, interaction design, and visual experience design—all aligned around UXReactor's proprietary PragmaticUX™ framework; this playbook is a treasure trove of some of those leading techniques.

And UXReactor is truly global. We're headquartered just an hour outside San Francisco, in Pleasanton, California, with offices in Hyderabad, India, and Medellin, Colombia.

Learn more

PREFACE

The story of this Playbook started in late 2012 when I was a design leader at a large software company leading the centralized design group responsible for the user experience (UX) design for most of the company's leading products. At that point, I had spent close to six years in UX design leadership in two separate organizations, starting as associate UX manager before being promoted to managing director of design.

As part of my career planning conversation with my manager, the topic of aspirations came up. I was itching to transition my role from design leadership into business leadership, where I felt that I could make a more holistic impact in the organization. As a result of this conversation, the company sponsored me to attend Harvard Business School's famed General Management Program, an executive education program designed for senior leaders to get an end-to-end management training. The program was a transformational experience for me, as I was surrounded by more than 100 accomplished leaders who had achieved a lot and were now in the similar pursuit of gaining more formal business learning.

There were two key takeaways for me here: First, I learned the power of frameworks; the professors would consistently iterate and set up simple frameworks that students could understand, teach, and replicate. From SWOT analysis, to the "Five P's of Marketing," to the Balanced Scorecard, I built an appreciation for the power of frameworks and have used the same approach as we share the plays later in the book.

Second, as I engaged with each of my peers, I recognized that the designer's toolkit I had been exposed to could solve a multitude of business problems. Rapid experiments, a cornerstone to a designer's toolkit, could be adapted to increase innovation. Journey mapping users and their processes could help an organization unlock efficiency. And conducting user research could validate product-market fit.

My thoughts were overflowing with possibilities. Interestingly, most of my fellow students would never have considered engaging a "designer" like me to solve their business problems. This was primarily because all the designers (marketing, interior, industrial, graphic, or UI) they had previously worked with were skills-based contributors.

At the end of the program, I had made up my mind that I was going to double down on continuing on the design leadership path. I knew that I—and the larger design profession—still had a lot of impact to make.

My inspiration in this pursuit was an accounting professor in Chicago by the name of James McKinsey, who in 1926 founded a small firm with a similar vision that the accounting practice could be a key factor in creating business value. The rest is history, as he went on to generate significant value for every company that engaged his firm. As part of his body of work, McKinsey is credited with establishing budget planning as a management framework that is still used in business today.

I spent the next year and a half looking at ways to elevate design as a business driver; however, it was easier said than done. I still remember a conversation I had with one of the general managers who was responsible for a product suite that generated more than half a billion dollars in revenue. I shared my opinion that good design is good business and that we should invest more effort on design to make the product suite more usable and seamless. The candid answer I got was, "Why would I do that? I can put that $1 in sales (boots on the ground) and it will give me $10 back."

Unfortunately, I didn't have a rebuttal for his insight, because I couldn't really articulate how $1 in design could deliver value in return. While I believed in the power of design, I struggled to show its impact in a consistent manner. There was always something getting in the way: Sometimes it was the organizational priorities, sometimes it was the designers' capabilities, sometimes it was lack of tools and processes; there were myriad reasons.

On further analysis, I could root the challenge in four key areas: the attitudes (mindsets), the people (or lack of), the process (or lack of), and the organizational environment. This was a much deeper problem than I had anticipated.

I subsequently decided to spend the next phase of my career trying to get back to the drawing board and look at it afresh through an "experimental medium" we called UXReactor. Fundamentally, we focused on the four key variables (mindsets, people, process, and environment) that we wanted to experiment with. For the next seven years, we hypothesized, experimented, iterated, and evolved our learning into an internal playbook called the PragmaticUX™ Playbook.

Over this time, we had built more than 100 frameworks (plays) around practitioner intents, such as how to plan strategic investments, how to prepare for a design kickoff, how to ensure the whole organization has deep empathy for the user, how to conduct a design interview, and even how to summarize the weekly status as a report. We had frameworks for everything. Everything that could be codified with better ways to handle the mindsets, people, processes, and environment—we studied them all.

With this Playbook as our backbone, UXReactor has grown and helped our client partners create millions of dollars in value and impact. At the same time, we've gained recognition for our work, including the 2019 FastCompany Innovation by Design Award, as well as being named the fastest-growing specialized user experience firm in the US on the esteemed Inc. 5000 list for two consecutive years.

As we engaged within various contexts and client-partners, we got better at updating and evolving the plays in the Playbook. Soon, we were fielding inquiries from prospective clients about the Playbook itself, in addition to our consulting services. Interestingly the alumni (ex-teammates) of UXReactor would also report back that they were adding way more value in their new organizations than peers with twice their experience because they were trained by our Playbook. Universities also started approaching us to include our plays as part of their graduate-level curriculum.

We realized that it was time to publish this to the wider world so that more business and design leaders and practitioners could leverage these plays to help fuel their own business growth.

Writing this book was, in itself, a user experience design process. Our intent is that it becomes a reference and an accelerator for anyone who intends to drive their business by leveraging the power of experience design.

It was not an easy task, because we had to solve four specific design problems in order to produce the book that you're now engaging with:

→ First and foremost, we had to find **how to make it easy for the reader (you) to read and navigate.** This is why we use a lot of illustrations for ease of scanning, remembering, and leveraging. The book is written so you can jump among the various plays and themes if you choose. If you don't read it cover to cover, that's okay.

→ Second, we had to figure out **how we can teach you to "fish"** without giving specific recommendations that may not be relevant to you and your business context. We did this by introducing the Mindful Canvas that is common across all the plays. Our aim is that it will help you be mindful about the variables in the context of the problem you are looking to solve with the play.

→ Third we had to envision **how might we make it useful and desirable,** while keeping five different reader personas in mind. We were advised to cut down the number of personas—but that was a difficult ask because it truly takes the full ecosystem to make an impact, and for that we needed each persona in the system to take away something relevant. Chapter 12 is the fastest way for you to know which plays to focus on based on the persona you identify with.

→ Fourth, we had to address **how might we make it relatable to you.** We did this by including ample anecdotes, examples, and case studies. In Part 3 of this book, we also share various game plans where we bring the various plays together in a simulated (inspired from real life) context for each reader persona.

I am confident that we've taken a solid stab at solving these four problems. Like everything user-centered, the user's input is essential. So I and my team would love to hear from you—please do not hesitate to connect with me through the resources available to you at www.UXDPlaybook.com. It's also important to note that as my team and I put this Playbook together, we have taken great care to uphold the confidentiality of our clients and/or situations that we have been privy to. We have done this by using fictitious company names, by changing names of individuals, or adjusting the context of the data. We did this while ensuring that the relevant facts and insights were not lost.

Finally, I hope that this book will provide you with the mindset, the mindfulness, and the tools to create 10X value in every organization that you are part of. I can wish nothing but the best as you pursue a goal of making the world a better place—one experience at a time.

PLAY TO WIN

"If you don't play to win, don't play at all."
– Tom Brady

BUSINESS × TECHNOLOGY × DESIGN

> "It is in Apple's DNA that technology alone is not enough—it's technology married with liberal arts, married with the humanities, that yields us the results that make our heart sing."
>
> – Steve Jobs

CASE STUDY OF ALTEDUKATION
Going digital is not the sole determinant of great outcomes

AltEdukation[1] (a fictional company inspired by real life) was a well-established company providing after-school enrichment programs to K–12 students across the West Coast. By 2019, after decades of growth, the organization was operating 20 locations in California, Oregon, and Washington, working with more than 4,000 paying students at any given time.

The company grew its revenue by more than 40% in 2019. Then, in early 2020, the COVID-19 pandemic erupted. By March, state governors were issuing shelter-in-place orders. Unfortunately, all of AltEdukation's in-person sites shut down for an extended period.

Upper management quickly convened a meeting to determine how to move forward. They had to transform to survive, so they asked their small but effective design, technology, and education teams to digitize all training and to find tools enabling their enrichment programs to go fully virtual. It was imperative that the current programs not stop due to the shelter-in-place orders. Otherwise, the company would need to refund students' fees en masse, which would set the business back significantly.

For the next month, the team worked hard to select and transition to various online tools and platforms. They digitized booklets and tests; integrated tools for student collaboration, curriculum tracking, and online payments; and chose a web conferencing tool for instructors to use. Everyone at AltEdukation felt good about all they had achieved in such a short time.

But to their surprise, satisfaction scores and enrollment rates dropped dramatically over the next few months. Students found it difficult to navigate different tools, locate course material, and collaborate

---

[1]AltEdukation is a real-life-inspired company created to illustrate the problem that businesses and their users are going through while digitally transforming. If you are intrigued by AltEdukation's predicament and curious about what the CEO should have done differently, go to Chapter 45.

with their peers, while instructors struggled to adapt to the new pedagogical approach required by online teaching.

Although these digital tools allowed the programs to proceed, the experience was not the same. Students felt that all they were doing was watching instructors lecture via web conferencing software. Since AltEdukation was not providing an enhanced learning experience, students might as well watch YouTube or Khan Academy videos instead—at least those were free.

Upper management knew that they had to act fast to save the company, but they had no idea how to move forward.

→ Where should they **start**?
→ What should the **business strategy** be?
→ Who should **lead** the effort?
→ Who should be on the **team**?
→ What kind of **investment** was needed?
→ Should they focus on the **instructors** or the **students**? And what about the **parents**?
→ What new **tools and features** should they incorporate?
→ Could they do this?

There were more questions than answers for AltEdukation's leadership team.

The Systemic Magnitude of the Problem

Why was going digital not enough? To understand that, let's deconstruct AltEdukation's digital ecosystem.

Students learning from home were expected to navigate and master multiple digital systems:

→ One for assessment;
→ One for online learning;
→ One for tracking their progress and grades;
→ One for asynchronously communicating with their classmates;
→ One for scheduling;
→ One for email or structured communication.

What's more, these systems didn't account for the different needs between kindergartners and high schoolers.

Meanwhile, parents were expected to support their children in multiple digital systems:

→ One for checking grades;
→ One for tracking class projects;
→ One for making payments;
→ One for communicating with the teachers and staff;
→ One for communicating with other parents;
→ One for coaching their kids at home.

Teachers/instructors had to master and deliver curriculum in multiple digital systems:

→ One for creating content;
→ One for managing class curriculum;
→ One for communicating with students and parents;
→ One for working with their state's Department of Education tools.

And finally, customer support teams had to develop and administer multiple digital systems:

→ One for tracking and managing student payments;
→ One for tracking and managing student access and passwords;
→ One for communicating with parents, students, instructors, and administration;
→ One for working with their vendors and partners.

The Shifting Paradigm

AltEdukation was not alone in this situation. In fact, this exact scenario has been playing out throughout the rest of the world and across very different industries. Businesses were expected to rapidly transform to ensure viability or risk becoming obsolete.

Judges, lawyers, and plaintiffs litigating on a web conferencing tool;

Medical and mental health appointments being handled via a mobile app in the comfort of home;

Million-dollar real estate bought through 3D walkthroughs and online notarizations;

Business-critical brainstorming sessions via online collaboration tools, with limited face-to-face activity;

Candidates interviewed and offered roles to work remotely without even having met a single coworker in person, then working from home and interacting entirely via digital tools.

Every facet of every business now was being run by multiple, disjointed digital systems in the garb of digital transformation. While these business transformations were being put in place, the contrast of users' expectations between their personal applications and their work/business applications became increasingly stark.

What became clear was that consumers, having been immersed in technology for nearly two decades, are no longer willing to accept disjointed digital experiences.

The pandemic brought to the forefront a critical insight for many businesses: Going digital was not enough. The user's experience was the new problem to solve.

> **Users were no longer willing to accept disjointed digital experiences.**

INTRODUCTION
Merging roles of business, technology, and design

A study by Design Management Institute (DMI) found a 228% differential between design-centric companies and the S&P 500 Index. Corporations that made the list include Apple, Coca-Cola, Ford, Herman-Miller, IBM, Intuit, Newell-Rubbermaid, Procter & Gamble, Starbucks, Starwood, Steelcase, Target, Walt Disney, Whirlpool, and Nike.

In a separate 2018 research study of the business value of design by McKinsey, the data also showed that top design-centric companies were outperforming their competition by as much as a 2X multiple.

> **Design-centric companies were outperforming their competition by as much as a 2X multiple.**

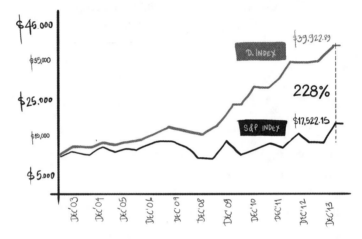

DESIGN MANAGEMENT INSTITUTE: DESIGN VALUE INDEX

At the same time, the beginning of this millennium brought technology and digital systems front and center in people's work and life. It's not surprising that eight of the 10 most valuable companies in the world today are technology companies. Technology is revolutionizing everything, and the world is getting rapidly digitized. Can the same emphasis on design continue to propel organizations forward? The answer is: It depends.

An updated playbook is needed to merge the dynamic nature of technology with traditional design practices. Differentiated digital experiences that are created when digital tools are built and deployed thoughtfully by user-centric design can yield a market share gain between 1 and 5 percentage points. This data is from a 2019 McKinsey report detailing various digital growth strategies and how industrial companies can sustainably outgrow their peers. To clarify, we're talking percentage points, not basis points (1/100th of a percentage), so this can easily convert into millions or even billions of dollars in business value.

Differentiated digital experiences don't just magically happen. They must be deliberately designed. And organizations that fail to recognize this are not playing to win.

It's not a fluke that digital companies such as Apple, Amazon, Uber, Nest, and Airbnb are so successful in generating business value. They understand and harness the union of technology and experience design to fuel growth. They are category leaders not just because they have the best technology but rather because they understand their users and create awesome experiences for them each and every time.

The Nest thermostat is a case study in the power of a superior digital experience: In just four years, the company leveraged that competitive advantage to build a $3.2 billion business that Google acquired in 2014. Not only did they build a beautiful, well-designed physical thermostat, but they also designed the multiple user experiences that went with it: the ordering experience, the unpacking experience, the installation experience, the configuration experience, the scheduling experience, the monitoring experience, and the mobile experience. Again this value was created by deliberate user-centered design.

> **Differentiated digital experiences don't just magically happen. They must be deliberately designed.**

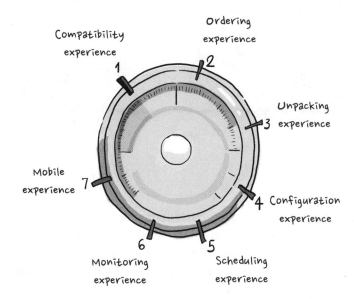

Even though organizations and leaders understand the power of designing differentiated digital experiences, it is fairly evident in my two decades of experience (the majority of it leading and supporting organizations in Silicon Valley) that most are not able to leverage this to fuel business growth.

There are different reasons and challenges, and my goal (via this book) is to unpack them and provide a mindful framework for business leaders, design leaders, design practitioners, and design collaborators to achieve the full potential of the union of design and technology.

THE USER EXPERIENCE PROBLEM
Understanding this problem is half the battle

56% of users of digital services stated that they are dissatisfied by the user experience.

Global market intelligence leader International Data Corporation (IDC) predicts an investment of $6.8 trillion for a three-year period ending 2023 to transform organizations into digital-at-scale enterprises (organizations that build and grow through significant investment in technology). At the same time, 56% of users of digital services stated that they are dissatisfied by the user experience, according to a 2021 McKinsey Global Digital Sentiment Insights survey.

In other words, businesses are "sinking" staggering amounts of money into digital products and services that people (users) don't find usable, useful, and desirable. For that investment, some businesses will generate growth, but most will lose trillions of dollars simply because they don't understand the new problem where the user's experience directly affects current and future business outcomes.

The User Experience Problem

In simple terms, the experience problem means ensuring that each user that engages in the business ecosystem gets what they want, when they want it, where they want it, and how they want it, every time they experience the digital product or service.

Every company is now a technology company, either because it offers technology products or has made (or will make) immense technology investments for internal operations. To thrive, companies must create the best user experience for all users engaged in their business ecosystem. This includes (but is not limited to) their direct users, their employees, and any partners and vendors who are part of the system.

Companies need to recognize that they are not creating value[1]—and in fact are losing value—by doing the following:

→ Not understanding users and their context to build a relevant solution;
→ Forcing users to engage with multiple products/services to get their work done;
→ Shipping features that user(s) cannot find easily;
→ Having capabilities that require training;
→ Delivering a digital product or service that is not aesthetically pleasing.

Conversely, users today are making decisions based on attributes such as:

→ How fast they can **learn and onboard** the product;
→ How **easy** it is to find information in the product;
→ How **intuitive** the product is;
→ How easy it is to **navigate** through the product;
→ How **desirable** the product is aesthetically;
→ How well customer support is **integrated** with the product;
→ How the product makes them **feel**;
→ How well it enables **collaboration** with other users in the product;
→ How **seamless** is the overall experience engaging with the business;
→ How **connected** it is with their existing systems.

A Clear and Present Risk

According to research by Credit Suisse, the average age of an S&P 500 company is now less than 20 years, down from 60 years in the 1950s. Researchers directly attributed this shift to the disruptions caused by technology transformation. Blockbuster vs. Netflix, Nokia handsets vs. Apple iPhone, Borders vs. Amazon—examples abound of companies that perished while competitors thrived.

Businesses today do not have the luxury to sit around and slowly evolve, as the competition is just a click away. With the cost of technology innovation exponentially decreasing, competitors can easily and quickly launch a better alternative. Consider that it took eBay years to build an e-commerce platform that can now be launched in minutes on Shopify.

Leaders who understand and leverage the power of user experience by constantly delighting their users with useful, functional, and desirable solutions will ride this wave to growth. That is the fundamental thesis of this Playbook. Those who do not will be left wondering what just happened and how they missed the opportunity of the decade.

[1]The best definition of value creation I have come across is from BusinessDictonary.com, where they define value creation as the performance of actions that increase the worth of the goods, services, or even the business.

EXPERIENCE VALUE CHAIN
Creating business value by solving the user experience problem

As businesses focus their investment in user-centered experience design across their digital ecosystems, they need to understand the various ways to create user and business value by understanding what I call the experience value chain.

There are three ways businesses can create value in the context of digital technologies and systems. The first is at the user interface (UI–Screen UX) level, the second is at the product user experience (Product UX) level, and the third is at the experience transformation (XT–Organizational UX) level, which represents a deliberate shift across every aspect of the organizational ecosystem.

To illustrate the differences between the three:

User Interface Design

Organizations operating at the user interface (UI) design level concentrate on value creation by designing the user interface for various digital modalities (mobile, desktop, web, over-the-top (OTT), interactive voice response, kiosk, tablet, etc.)

They focus on design tasks such as:

→ Optimizing the screen to ensure users intuitively take the desired action;
→ Designing the UI with an attractive look and feel;
→ Creating consistent visuals across the system;
→ Designing each screen by laying out the elements and iterating on screen hierarchy and layout;
→ A/B testing the screens for better conversion.

UI design is critical and is the minimum value that users expect in any digital system. While this is a foundational area of focus and expertise, most organizations unfortunately think this is all it takes to build a great experience, without realizing that they are just scratching the surface.

Product Experience Design

Organizations operating at the product design level foster deep understanding of the product and its system, while triangulating it with the user's intent. Their designers are trained and expected to think about the user and their context in the digital product before focusing on the UI, and they directly influence business planning and prioritization of the relevant design problems. This focus generates a whole new level of value creation.

In addition to performing screen level design tasks, UX designers focus on fundamental problems such as:

→ Optimizing the flow of the user's interactions across the product;
→ Ensuring that users' intent is addressed in multiple ways in the product;
→ Understanding how and why users behave to better inform the UI design;
→ Prototyping concepts for user testing based on user needs and pain points;
→ Understanding the user ecosystem so they can identify the right design solutions;
→ Working hand in hand with product engineering to catalyze the system that is being built.

Contrary to widespread misconception, UI and UX design are not equivalent (tip: stop using the moniker "UI/UX" while referencing the skill; it unfortunately shows a lack of understanding). Practitioners at this level operate as collaboration catalysts, ensuring that the entire product maintains a user-first approach.

Experience Transformation

Experience transformation (XT) builds on the critical foundation laid by the UI design and product UX design levels. XT ensures that each touchpoint in a user's experience has been carefully designed, orchestrated, and optimized across all departments. Whether the user is calling technical support, engaging with customer success, using the product, transitioning from another product, or working with a system integrator, their experience should be consistent, seamless, and above all, delightful.

To excel at this level, practitioners must be deeply focused on transforming the business, working across the whole organization to design and deliver the best experiences. In short, everyone from the board of directors to the newest intern should be aligned on leveraging the deep understanding of the user to unlock business value by doing things such as:

→ Building a deep portfolio of user insights and helping increase overall empathy for the customer across the organization by communicating and championing the insights;
→ Working with the M&A team to evaluate other businesses for acquisition based on how they can enhance the experience the company delivers as a whole;
→ Working with marketing to define the user audience and how to effectively communicate with them;

→ Working with the sales team to define how the offering should be designed from a user-centric experience perspective, and determine how to best get users to try and buy the product;

→ Reporting to the board of directors on the business impact of experience transformation (XT).

At the XT level, every aspect of an organization is centered on its users and their experiences. And because these experiences extend beyond the product itself to the entirety of the customer's engagement with the company, they would take competitors years to replicate, even assuming they are able to figure out the why behind all of the iterations. This is because XT change entails a fundamental shift in people, processes, mindsets, and culture—a shift that builds tremendous value.

The Journey Is Just Starting

Although the value proposition is immense, most organizations are yet in the early stages of figuring out how to design and build a user experience–centric world. After studying over 100 different organizations I have found the distribution along the experience value chain looks like this:

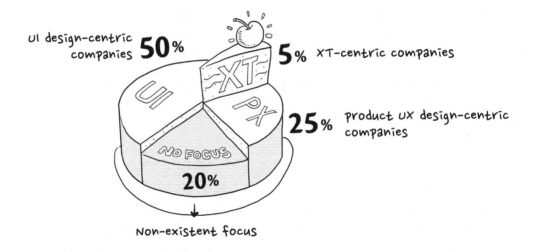

There's an enormous difference between the companies that get UX design and the companies that don't.

The goal of this Playbook is to enable the vast majority of organizations to deliberately and effectively navigate the experience value chain and unlock the immense business value.

Building an Economic Moat While Creating Value

Investment guru Warren Buffet has often stated the importance of an "economic moat" for businesses to succeed over the long term. Investopedia defines economic moat as "a business's ability to maintain competitive advantages over its competitors in order to protect its long-term profits and market share from competing firms."

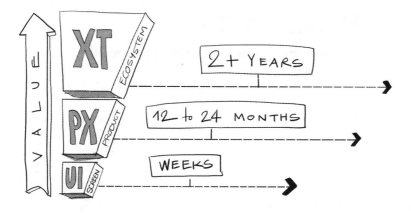

Interestingly a company's rise through the three levels of the experience value chain directly correlates to increased value and a deeper competitive moat. As we touched on above:

→ From a competitive standpoint, UI design can be easily copied by a reasonable competitor in a matter of weeks. They can examine your product or service and develop something similar.

→ But when you start looking at product UX design, it takes 12 to 24 months for a competitor to reach parity. That becomes a more significant investment.

→ However, when you start down the path of XT, you're creating a holistic customer experience that would take a competitor multiple years to replicate, because it requires a foundational shift in the organization's priorities, values, and skills.

→ Perhaps most important, in an XT organization, continuous improvement is built in as users and their needs change. Competitors are forced to constantly play catch-up. That is an economic moat.

BUSINESS INSANITY

Doing the same thing and expecting a different result

The following insanity plays out every day in the business world: In their pursuit of the best user experience, organizations are making the same mistakes over and over again, without realizing what they are doing wrong.

It's not uncommon to consistently see businesses hiring a couple of designers or a design agency or bring in a speaker and assuming they are on the right path of unlocking the business value that the business data is referring to. It takes a lot more than that, but to start with they need to understand the following.

User Experience Design: The Secret Is in the Semantics

"User experience design" (UX Design) is a deliberately structured term. "User" precedes "experience," and "design" is at the end. This ordering reflects best practices. However, most organizations jump to designing around the capabilities of their technology before considering either their users or their experiences.

Forty percent of products are developed without any input from end users. Not coincidentally, 35% of new ideas and start-ups fail due to poor product-market fit. Organizations burn through billions of dollars with no clear outcome, a waste compounded by lost time and opportunity cost. The modus operandi needs to change quickly if organizations are to be relevant and grow shareholder value.

Developing the wrong solution is costly. But companies that are mindful of the "user before experience before design" principle will build products that users actually want and need as the sequencing protects them.

Inside-First vs. User-First

In the pursuit of developing and shipping products quickly, most organizations make the mistake of innovating in the wrong direction. They approach the project "inside-first."

In **inside-first** organizations, internal stakeholders leverage their business instinct, technology, processes, and sales machines to try to design and engineer a solution for their end users. Typically, they frame the problem by stating:

→ We have a major release in a few weeks; can we clean up the user experience?
→ Our competitor just launched a mobile product; can we create one, too?
→ Our sales partners told us that our product looks old; how can we redesign it?
→ We have engineers ready to build; how quickly can you make the wireframes?
→ Can we build an analytics product like this other company's?
→ The CPO said we need to add these screens; can you design them?

The above statements demonstrate inside-first thinking—and no UX designer, design team, or UX design firm can truly add value in this context, as the goal here is to design and create artifacts—quickly.

In contrast, **user-first** organizations curate a collective, deep understanding of their users and their experiences before making any business, design, engineering, marketing, sales, or product decisions. They frame the problem by stating:

→ Can we research our users' needs that we aren't currently serving and include them in our strategic planning?
→ Our users are having difficulty with the onboarding experience; can we design and iterate further?
→ We've identified a user problem; can you help research further and prototype a solution we can test?

→ How can we align all our different departments' workflows so we can deliver a seamless user experience?

Effective innovation and marketplace disruption stems from organizations that are User-First. Unfortunately, too many organizations make the mistake of approaching innovation "Inside first", thereby making the same mistake every time while expecting different results.

Small Design vs. BIG DESIGN

As stated earlier, design is the trailing component of user experience design but important nonetheless. Too many organizations are caught up in the craft of design while neglecting the larger discipline of DESIGN. While craft is a critical element of the process, it's helpful to metaphorically think in terms of a biodiverse ecosystem: Consider the forest as a whole before focusing on the individual trees.

Visionary SpaceX founder Elon Musk uses the title of chief designer. It signals DESIGN: the realization that everything in this world, business or personal, from arranging a house party, to engineering a company reorganization, to transporting humans to Mars—everything is DESIGNED.

Organizations that are built for BIG DESIGN are destined to be more thoughtful and resilient than organizations that focus on small design craft because their larger pursuit is to deliver value to the user and their ecosystem by consistently understanding the user's intent, needs, and goals while connecting these dots with the business needs and outcomes.

Remember, that every system being designed has users and related ecosystems, with their related constraints and opportunities. Adopting a BIG DESIGN philosophy also sets the foundation for an egalitarian organizational culture in which DESIGN is the purview of every teammate who cares about users and their experience. BIG DESIGN thinks holistically about experiences.

HERE'S A TIP!

Take any object, thing, service, or system and apply the reverse-think technique: Identify all the possible user needs and problems the designer intended to solve to get to the solution you now have on hand. For example, what problems were DESIGNERS attempting to solve when they created:

Systems such as the US Constitution;
Physical objects such as the stapler;
Digital interfaces such as the login screen;
Artifacts such as the airline boarding pass;
A living object such as a butterfly.

Practicing this technique will help you master BIG DESIGN thinking. If anything, you will start appreciating that DESIGN is a mindset. Organizations that make this mind shift are able to unlock the full potential of creating value through user experience design.

Experience Debt: Death by a Thousand Cuts

In the pursuit of shipping a feature as quickly as possible, companies are frequently forced to make compromises. This often translates into not resolving all of the experience problems they've identified for specific users. Even when they've developed good solutions to the problems, time or technology constraints prevent them from building those solutions out.

Each deferred solution becomes a debt the business owes to the user. In most pragmatic organizations, this is acceptable and normal. However, when these debts start accumulating and compounding, it can become detrimental to the business as a whole.

Organizations carrying a high experience debt are easily disrupted by competitors, who have the advantage of observing the problems, starting from scratch, and building the product or service correctly. In addition, user loyalty is highly compromised; they become open to trying other products that offer a better experience.

Unfortunately, too many businesses are unaware that they are accumulating experience debt. The debt is a ticking time bomb that will explode even with the most well-intentioned user experience design goals.

CHAPTER 06

TWO CASE STUDIES OF EXPERIENCE TRANSFORMATION

Learning from the leaders

While it is important to understand the experience value chain and why most organizations are not able to fully unlock the value, some organizations have been able to successfully get there.

Let's take a closer look at two remarkable companies, Tesla and The Walt Disney Company. Each one has applied the myriad ideas and practices described in this Playbook, and each one has disrupted their respective industries (or in Disney's case, the world at large). Of course, experience transformation in the current business landscape is a never-ending journey—the way forward is one of constant evolution and adaptation without a finish line. Let these case studies be your guide.

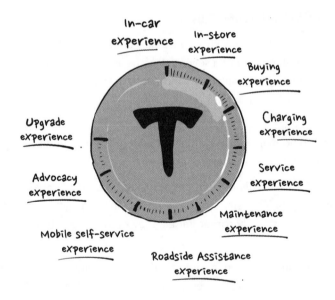

> **99% of automotive shoppers begin their purchase journey expecting to be frustrated.**

Tesla

It's not just electric motors that set Tesla apart as a car company. The relative newcomer successfully combined deliberate and thorough experience design efforts with disruptive technologies to gain a significant advantage over competitors. Despite the price premium on many models, the demand for Tesla's cars is so high that the company can't keep up with production—as of August 2021, there was a four- to six-week wait for the Performance Model 3 and a five- to six-week wait for the Performance Model X. But the sought-after cars are part of a much bigger experience that begins the moment the prospective owner starts considering the vehicles.

A Better Buying Experience

If ever an experience warranted a redesign, it would be buying a car. In the traditional scenario, tense, drawn-out negotiations with salespeople working on commission and against quotas leave consumers cold. A study by DrivingSales found that 99% of automotive shoppers begin their purchase journey expecting to be frustrated. It's an experience fraught with distrust: Half of consumers reported they will walk if the dealer requires a test drive before giving a price and 43% will bolt if they're required to give personal information upfront. By contrast, the same study reported that 56% of shoppers would buy more cars if the process were easier, and auto sales could rise about 25% if the experience were better.

> **Auto sales could rise about 25% if the experience were better.**

Tesla differentiates itself by alleviating the many pain points in car shopping. First, they sell directly to customers, rather than licensing products through independent dealerships. This gives them control over their customer-facing ecosystem—how they present their vehicles and how their employees express information about the company and their products.

When the customer is ready to purchase, they use an in-store digital design center, during which pricing is non-negotiable (read: no angst). A car can also be purchased remotely on Tesla's website, making the same customizations in a process that feels similar to buying a laptop online. Tesla has a delivery team responsible for guiding the customer through payment, document signing, and delivery. When the car is ready, the customer signs all the documents online and can pick it up at a dealership or if they choose, have it delivered to a convenient location.

This revitalized car-buying experience shows a deep understanding of several of the plays described in this Playbook—in particular, the user empathy play (Chapter 14: "User Empathy Play") and experience ecosystem play (Chapter 18: "Experience Ecosystem Play"), which allows organizations to build an intimate and binding understanding of their customers. That accrued empathy allows brand leaders to map a customer's optimal experience and design each touchpoint along the way. Tesla excels at fine-tuning each step, starting from the moment a prospect looks into buying a car and continuing through their experience as an owner.

Experience That Lasts a Lifetime

The Tesla experience doesn't end once the customer gets their new car. Rather, this is when the experience can really begin to take flight and delight. Leveraging technology to create better customer experiences enables Tesla to offer innovations such as at-home wireless software updates that other companies aren't even remotely equipped to match. Plus, approximately 80% of repairs can be completed remotely, free of charge—a huge incentive for anyone who hates spending time and money at the auto repair shop. When service center repairs are necessary, they're generally completed four times faster than at a conventional repair shop (as the same amount of care is spent in designing the experience for the dealership employees). Of course, technology alone didn't create these exemplary experiences—great experiences don't just happen, they are deliberately designed.

> **The Tesla experience doesn't end once the customer gets their new car.**

This deliberate design shows up immediately in the physical design elements of the cars. With the Model 3, the minimalism serves as both a reflection of the company's design aesthetic as well as a testament to Tesla's philosophy that cars shouldn't be complicated. Once inside, a large touchscreen replaces the conventional cluster of control knobs and buttons. (The only familiar button inside the vehicle is the control to activate hazard lights above the windshield.)

The more subtle elements of design show up in the experience of driving the car. There are a whole host of Easter egg features in the operating system that continue to delight customers. Take Chill Mode, for instance, which provides a smoother ramp-up to speed designed to help drivers avoid unintentionally exceeding the speed limit. There are also settings that allow parents to monitor the speed and location of teen drivers. And while the touch screen has many available shortcuts to make it easier to access certain controls, the temperature, music, and navigation can also be voice-activated. Because so much of the car is controlled by the operating system (OS), the driving experience improves with each update. This iterative approach was seeded early on. When Tesla released the Model S in 2012, they sold 100,000 units to early adopters, allowing them to gain deep and detailed insights from a contained cohort of drivers as they continued to iterate the innovative design of the car.

"We obviously cannot compete with the big car companies in size," CEO Elon Musk has said of Tesla, "so we must do so with intelligence and agility." That agility is reflected in the corporate culture he's created, which dictates that: "anyone at Tesla can and should email or talk to anyone else according to what they think is the fastest way to solve a problem for the benefit of the whole company. Moreover, you should consider yourself obligated to do so until the right thing happens."

This is indicative of the kind of organizational design thinking that has put the company in position to act on a broader innovation strategy that will allow consumers around the world to gather, manage, and store their own electrical sources

(something that's already underway with Tesla's home solar panels and batteries). This kind of thinking can be put into practice using the design problems and opportunities (Chapter 34: "Design Problems and Opportunities Play") , which helps identify the right problem to solve and then find a solution that benefits the organization and its customers. By eliminating outdated business hierarchies and focusing on solving problems both internally and for customers, Tesla has a distinct edge.

Good Design Is Good Business

Despite inconsistent profitability, quality problems in its luxury cars, and a slow production schedule, Tesla has quickly become the world's most valuable automaker. Their success has spurred competition in the electric vehicle space, but no other automakers have been able to compete (they have built an economic moat through engineering and experience design). Audi, Jaguar, and Porsche recently added new electric models, and there are more budget-friendly options such as the Chevy Bolt and Nissan Leaf, but combined they've barely made a dent in a US market dominated by Tesla.

According to Car and Driver, "Tesla's Apple-like 'one-stop experience' proved a huge plus for owners. Its ability to manage all aspects of EV purchase and ownership—sales, financing, service, fast charging, and route planning that incorporates fast charging—were cited by an overwhelming 91% of owners as a reason to buy another Tesla."

This "Apple-like" user experience is the kind of technology ecosystem that traditional automakers will find extremely difficult to replicate. The fact that Tesla's entire business model is built around using technology to design great ownership and driving experiences gives them a tremendous advantage over traditional automakers headed into the EV market. They also maintain a big leg up on like-minded newcomers Rivian and Polestar, whose head of US operations, Gregor Hembrough, recently conceded to The New York Times, "Right now, there's only one party in town."

The Walt Disney Company

There's a reason Walt Disney is often heralded as the world's first experience designer. According to historian Sam Gennawey, Disney had the ability to use technology effectively by letting it recede into the background so that the story or experience could shine through.

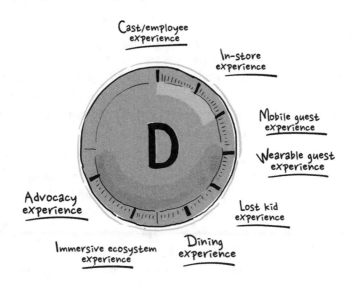

That remains one of the guiding principles of modern experience design. "The technology that works the best is the technology you never notice," Gennawey says. "[Disney] was one of the first people who found a way to do that."

Walt Disney expressed numerous tactics and traits that made him a keen experience designer and business leader. In fact, he employed nearly all of the crucial mindsets you'll read about throughout this book.

> **The technology that works the best is the technology you never notice.**

A Designer at Heart

One of the central ideas powering experience design is that technology that works for you without interrupting you is technology you will want to use. Another central idea is that in order to create technology that consistently rewards users, the technology must continually evolve as needs and behaviors change. This was something Disney understood well.

Back in 1966, Disney described the plan for Walt Disney World's Experimental Prototype Community of Tomorrow (or EPCOT) as "an experimental prototype that is always in the state of becoming, a place where the latest technology can be used to improve the lives of people." This line of thinking is central to the design mindset (Chapter 8).

Disney was always pushing technology as a means to enhance the ways users could experience a story. Before going into production on Snow White, for instance, Disney created a short film called The Old Mill that let artists test state-of-the-art techniques he wanted to use for creating water effects as well as a new multiplane camera that allowed animators to create depth of field.

He was also fixated on optimizing the mundane, which is where his systems mindset (Chapter 8: "Mindsets of a User-Centric Organization") was able to shine. "Think of process as a railroad engine," Disney said. "If the engine does not run properly, it does not matter how friendly the conductor acts or how attractive the passenger cars look, the train will still not move and the passengers will not pay their fares. Process is the engine of Quality Service." A well-defined process makes the whole system work, and when that process is attuned to deliver the optimal experience to users, great things can happen.

Insatiable Attention to Detail

When designing the groundbreaking theme park back in the early 1950s, Disney and his team of designers (or "imagineers") would obsess over every detail within the grounds. Disney understood good design and led by example. He was known for making contractors replace plastic with wrought iron for realism, counting the steps between trash cans to reduce the likelihood of guests littering, and touring the park incognito so that he could test experiences.

He was never completely satisfied. He always asked for more from his team. In his theme parks, this took the form of "plussing," incrementally improving details and elements of an experience. In modern terms, Disney was always iterating. He wasn't "adding more stuff"—which so many companies do—he was finding ways to make good experiences even better. Nothing was off limits: getting the sound effects on the Pirates of the Caribbean ride loud enough to rattle the riders; making sure that the animatronic Tiki Birds had dozens of different gestures, not just 10; sending friends and family on rides like Jungle Cruise before they opened to elicit feedback and fine-tune the experience.

This attention to detail is the lifeblood of an experience mindset (Chapter 8: "Mindsets of a User-Centric Organization"), and it persists in the parks today. According to "Be Our Guest," The Disney Institute's manual on perfecting the art of customer service, "... as you walk through Disney World, the volume of the ambient music does not change. Ever. More than 15,000 speakers have been positioned using complex algorithms to ensure that the sound plays within a range of just a couple decibels throughout the entire park. It is quite a technical feat acoustically, electrically, and mathematically." This ongoing attention to detail started with Walt Disney himself and continued on after his passing—his changes and ideas combining with the continual improvements born out of the design culture he created—creating a theme park ecosystem that is always growing and evolving.

An Ever-Evolving Theme Park Experience

MyMagic+ is a recent evolution in the theme park ecosystem, a massive $1 billion investment that overhauled the digital infrastructure of Disney's theme parks. Bob Iger, the then CEO, is not someone who shies away from making investments in technology. In fact, he held a vision of "embrac[ing] technology and us[ing] it aggressively to enhance the quality of Disney's product and thus the consumer experience" (Chapter 19: "Experience Roadmap Play"). Indeed, MyMagic+ would enable a fundamental shift, away from delivering a one-size-fits-all experience and "treating [guests] as a giant blob of people."

Around the time the investment got approved, a number of key guest experience metrics, such as intent to return, were falling (Chapter 28: "Experience Metrics Play"). Guests were experiencing a number of pain points, such as long wait time and high ticket prices. With MyMagic+, Disney hoped to use technology to improve the theme-park experience and encourage more return visits.

" **Wait time at the turnstile dropped by 30%.**

At the core of MyMagic+ were MagicBands, wearable wristbands with RFID chips that track guests' movement and store personal information. They allow guests to check in to hotels, enter the theme parks, and pay for food and merchandise with a simple tap against an RFID reader. After MagicBands were made available, wait time at the turnstile dropped by 30%; guests can now seamlessly enter the parks and go on their favorite rides sooner through FastPass+. Frictions resulting from pulling out their credit cards to pay for food and merchandise were eliminated. And, because MagicBand tracks guests' location and movement, Disney sensors allow Disney operations to know if an area is too congested and then act accordingly, either by sending character parades or open up FastPass availability. The result? 5,000 more guests can now enter the parks on the busiest days.

Underneath the magic of MyMagic+, an extensive ecosystem of cast members, organizations, systems, and technologies were involved (Chapter 18: "Experience Ecosystem Play"). On the back end, over 70,000 employees were trained on the technology and 28,000 hotel rooms were equipped with radio frequency–reading technology. Moreover, MyMagic+ has to be integrated into attractions throughout the theme parks so guests can, for example, customize the color, shape, and engine of their virtual car on the Test Track attraction at Epcot.

Making Profit by Creating More Value

Even some of Disney's close collaborators thought Snow White was going to ruin him. His first feature-length film came on the heels of many successful shorts with a bankable new star named Mickey, but the mouse was nowhere to be found here. The picture also went well over its initial budget and Disney had to mortgage his own house in order to finish it, with an eventual budget of $1.5 million. The reason he pushed himself and his team so hard was a hardwired desire to give audiences an experience they'd never had before. The film was a staggering success that went on to make $8 million internationally during its initial release.

" **A hardwired desire to give audience an experience they'd never had before.**

While producing the feature film Fantasia in 1940, Disney spent an estimated $200,000 to develop the first stereophonic theatrical sound system to give the audience an immersive viewing experience. The soundtrack was recorded across multiple audio channels and reproduced with "Fantasound," a revolutionary sound system Disney developed with RCA that was an early precursor to surround sound.

The business mindset (Chapter 8: "Mindsets of a User-Centric Organization") is all about making profit by creating business and user value, something Disney was always targeting. With his theme parks, his ceaseless behind-the-scenes work fine-tuned an experience so effortless that even wizened adults could suspend their disbelief and become part of an unfolding storybook journey through the park. Not only are these experiences that customers are willing to pay for, they are happy to pay more for them. In fact, Disney claims that 70% of first-time visitors plan to return to their theme parks (a figure they are actively trying to improve, no doubt).

Reimagined Disney Store Experience

In an era where customers are shopping more online, Disney invested $480 million to lure customers back into its brick-and-mortar stores. The company underwent a major redesign of its retail stores that made shoppers feel like they were on a Disney theme park vacation rather than shopping for merchandise. "We knew we needed to elevate and improve the experiences that we have both in stores and online as retail is changing," Paul Gainer, executive vice president of Disney retail, remarked in an interview.

In the newly designed stores, giant video screens (OTT) will stream real-time parades at Disney theme parks. Kids can battle Darth Vader or interact with characters from across the Disney franchise. Touch screens allow customers to select their own Disney music while a magic mirror makes it seem as if Disney's princesses are speaking to the kids who stand in front of it.

The high-tech makeover created a more enjoyable, interactive, and immersive experience for adults and kids alike. And it was a fruitful business investment. The store revamp has helped boost profit margin by 20%. Ninety percent of Disney Store guests in North America and Europe also felt more connected to the greater Disney brand that will undoubtedly have trickle-down effects across Disney's greater enterprise (e.g. retail, theme park, merchandise, entertainment)—a prime example of how business will reap financial reward by first creating value and delivering magical experiences to users.

GROWTH BY EXPERIENCE DESIGN

"You always reap what you sow;
there is no shortcut

– Stephen covey

GETTING THE SYSTEM RIGHT

Implementing four elements of a winning system

It's an ambitious goal: to radically reshape our organizations with a singular, unwavering orientation to the user experience—in order to keep competitors at bay and drive business growth. So how do we begin?

We start with a system that we at UXReactor call the bv.d system. It stems from the lessons I've learned in working with and observing some of the largest design groups and organizations in Silicon Valley. As I studied the variations between successful and unsuccessful teams, I discovered that the difference came down to four key variables. Successful teams embraced all four traits, and unsuccessful ones were weak in at least one of them.

$$bv.d = m.p.p.e$$

The bv.d System

Business value by design (bv.d) consists of four key factors that can make or break the intended outcome of becoming an experientially transformed organization:

→ The right mindsets;

→ The right people;

→ The right process;

→ The right environment.

Groundbreaking results happen when you have a group of effective and collaborative people following a rigorous process and working in a nurturing environment, all aligned on a shared set of mindsets.

Each attribute multiplies and builds upon the other, generating exponential business value. The opposite is also true: If one factor is missing or neglected, the entire system will falter. Let's examine each of these four essentials.

The Right Mindsets

Everything in the organization starts and ends with the mindsets of the people and the organization. An effective mindset can overcome most challenges, while an ineffective mindset can mess up even the best opportunities.

These five mindsets yield high bv.d:

→ Experience mindset;
→ Design mindset;
→ Outcome mindset;
→ Business mindset;
→ Systems mindset.

We'll dig more deeply into mindsets in Chapter 8: "Mindsets of a User-Centric Organization."

The Right Process

A high bv.d relies on a strong process that is replicable, understandable, sustainable, pragmatic, and, most important, effective in driving value for the business and its users. This process needs to be grounded in deep user empathy where variables such as strategic perspective, consistent ideation, design rigor, collaboration, implementation velocity, and above all, governance[1] are factored in.

More on process in Chapter 9: "The Experience Design Process."

The Right People

Like the adage that it takes a village to raise a kid, similarly, it takes two major groups of people to come together to accelerate business value.

The first is the practitioners (whom we call experience practitioners) who bring the necessary leadership, focus, skills, and accountability to the table. The second group is all the collaborators that work with the practitioners to ensure their work delivers the highest impact to the business and the users.

Read more about people in Chapter 10: "Getting the Right People Right."

The Right Environment

The last but not least factor for a high bv.d is the organizational environment that surrounds the system.

A highly effective environment is one that is centered on a collective empathy for the users. By nature, it's collaborative, diverse, and trusting. It shares a strategic vision and values a culture of experimentation. In a nurturing environment, people care about the outcome of their work, and user-centric ideas see the light of day more often.

In organizations that lack the right environment for people to thrive, BIG DESIGN quickly devolves to small design as teams focus more on product attributes than on user needs and expectations. A lack of true purpose becomes highly demotivating. More on this in Chapter 16.

---

[1]Governance: Investopedia defines governance as a system of rules, practices, and processes by which a firm is directed and controlled. Having a good governance process is the hallmark of a healthy and thriving organization.

CHAPTER 08

MINDSETS OF A USER-CENTRIC ORGANIZATION

What can we learn from a 15th century polymath

As organizations and practitioners evolve to catalyze business value through user experience design, their focus needs to shift to solving the user's problems by leveraging different perspectives, not simply applying one tool or another. In essence they need to think like holistic problem solvers.

What Does That Look Like? Consider Leonardo da Vinci, the 15th Century Italian Polymath.

Leonardo painted masterpieces such as the Mona Lisa and The Last Supper. He was a visionary inventor, drafting sketches of a flying machine and a parachute. He also understood human anatomy so well that he designed the Vitruvian Man, well known for its anatomical and mathematical accuracy.

Now here's someone who was always striving to learn new disciplines and explore new fields. No wonder he is known as a great artist, an engineer, a biologist, an astronomer, and a mathematician. He connected dots among seemingly unrelated fields like no one else. The other person in our generation who was able do this successfully was Steve Jobs who interestingly admired da Vinci's ability to see beauty in both art and engineering.

Five Mindsets to Master

To apply Leonardo's example to the digital renaissance we are now living in, practitioners and collaborators have to approach every problem differently. To be successful in today's fast-paced digital world, they need to cultivate five critical mindsets, which we mentioned in the previous chapter; we explain them in detail in the following sections:

→ Experience mindset;
→ Design mindset;
→ Outcome mindset;
→ Business mindset;
→ Systems mindset.

1. Experience Mindset: Moving from UI to Experiences

The first mindset to cultivate is the experience mindset, which is enabled by a profound belief that users care about experiences first, and the practitioner needs to deliberately craft and design every touchpoint of this experience. A great experience will delight the user and will make them appreciate how easy it is, how intuitive it is, and how it makes them feel valued.

The best experience is one where you don't even need to interact with a UI. The best experiences are like magic where the system and the designers take away all the heavy load from the user.

To adopt this mindset, you need to immerse yourself to understand:

→ **The user(s):** Who will be using the product or system your team is designing?
→ **Their journey:** What are the steps they will take to get to the desired outcome?
→ **Their needs:** What needs does the system address, and how does it move them along effectively?
→ **Their pain points:** What pain points do they have to address to get to their intended outcome?
→ **Their context:** What is the context in which they'll be using the product or system?

A deliberate shift a practitioner needs to make is to break departmental silos in an organization because these are the single biggest killer of great experiences. Users don't care how your organization is structured, how your departments are managed, or where the practitioner sits in the organization. All they care about is how they are engaging with your product and ecosystem and whether it is working for them. They expect you to earn their loyalty by thinking through every aspect of their experience.

HERE'S AN EXAMPLE!

Login Screen vs. Login Experience

To illustrate the experience mindset, you can conduct a simple test to have any practitioner design a login screen vs. a login experience. If the problem is framed as a login screen, we typically end up with a display of the standard username, password, forgot password, register, and so forth. On the other hand, when you think about a login experience, some of the best login experiences are about solving problems such as remembering the password and security question answers. In fact, the best user experience is one where the user doesn't even have to think about any of this. This is what Apple's design team considered when they created Face ID, the biometric authentication tool for mobile devices.

HERE'S A TIP!

Use the word "experience" with anything you plan on designing, and your mind will focus on things differently. Think about:

→ Dashboard screen vs. dashboard experience;
→ Restaurant menu design vs. restaurant menu experience;
→ Landing page vs. landing experience;
→ Onboarding process vs. onboarding experience;
→ Meeting agenda vs. meeting experience.

2. Design Mindset: Connecting Empathy to Experimentation

The design mindset is often misunderstood. For most people, the word "design" conjures the visceral (small design) aspects of design that put form above the user's need and context. On the contrary, the design mindset embraces design as a way to solve a specific problem by experimenting with every variable—both intrinsic and extrinsic to the system at hand.

This means the designer has to deeply empathize with the user, understand the problem that they are trying to address, and ideate and experiment around that problem before actually converging on a solution.

To have a design mindset, you need to:

→ Empathize with: The user(s); and their journey.
→ Frame the problem
→ Understand the variables at play in the system (intrinsic and extrinsic)
→ Experiment … experiment … experiment: Prototype, test, iterate

One huge shift that designers need to make is to stop thinking about screens and how the solution would look before truly understanding the needs of the user. Designers spend too much time designing to requirements, engineers spend too much time building features and enhancements to specification, and product managers spend too much time getting features to the market.

For every design problem, first, understand why the user needs a solution, and try to identify at least three ways for the user to get to their intended outcome.

The Saga of the Dashboard Screen

A great example of this mindset emerged when my firm was working with a Fortune 500 software company. We were given a requirement to design a dashboard screen, which we quickly reframed as a dashboard experience. As part of the client's requirements, we were provided with a lot of different data elements that needed to be showcased on this "screen."

If we approached this the traditional way (as they expected), we would have begun by manipulating that data on a design tool and playing with variables such as layout, hierarchy, typography, visualization, colors, and so forth.

But this approach overlooked key insights: Why did the target user need to see this information? Why do they care about this data? What are they looking for? What are they trying to do with the data?

Instead, we empathized with the users we were building this for. As we started going into the why by interviewing users, we realized that most of them didn't care about all the data or the dashboard screen. They cared about the outcome and the impact this system would enable for them. Ultimately, they cared about three things: the system's availability, its quality, and its impact. So we framed the problem as "How might we rapidly show the user the data that mattered to them in their context."

With this knowledge, we experimented with different ways of conceptualizing and presenting this data. We realized that if everything is going well in the system, then the target user just needs a notification email stating that all three variables are doing great and not a dashboard screen. As we wrapped up the engagement, we reframed everything from marketing collateral to screens to defining ROI for customers around these three variables.

While this added about eight more weeks to the project timeline, it gave the client a few years of value creation in comparison to their competitors.

The design mindset allowed us to leverage the empathy we had built for the user by reframing the problem and experimenting with various solutions, which helped us converge on a more effective solution.

HERE'S A TIP!

Always frame the design problem from the target user's perspective. Eliminate "solutioning" terms such as "screens", "browsers", "clicks", "forms", "navigation". For example: How might we understand that the system is delivering value to us?

3. Outcome Mindset: Focusing on Goals, Not Activities

The experience practitioner's unique role in the organization is to engage with customers, frame problems, ideate, and design solutions. Carrying this out requires experience practitioners to have an outcome mindset: taking accountability for solving the overall user experience and business problem, not merely the discrete activities they create along the way. In simple terms, if a user or business has a design problem, until that problem has been solved and verified, the outcome has not been achieved. It may take days or months to get there, but it is not done until the problem has been thoroughly solved.

The goal is not to design six screen variations that look impressive in a presentation. The goal is to solve a root problem, where users can intuitively navigate through complexity and achieve their intended goal each and every time.

To adopt the outcome mindset, a practitioner must articulate, visualize, and measure the outcome they plan to achieve for:

→ Your users;   → Your business.

In order to develop an outcome mindset, designers need to stop trying to measure impact by quantifying the hours they have worked and the screens they have created. Instead, the impact is achieved once they have verified and solved the user's problem.

Adopting this mindset can accelerate a practitioner's career in any growing organization.

who owns migration

One example of this mindset arose when I was working with a large software company redesigning their next-generation $1.5 billion product line. We spent nearly 18 months taking apart the various features and functionalities of the product and simplifying them.

When we released the product, we learned that users liked what they saw—but that they were not going to adopt it in the near future. This puzzled us. Upon further investigation, we learned that users had spent significant time getting the prior version up and running, and they were not excited about repeating the process for the updated version. We hadn't considered their migration experience; more important, we hadn't identified how we were going to achieve the overall outcome cohesively when we kicked off this initiative. Throughout the design and development journey, all practitioners were busy executing their part of the project, without understanding how the outcome of having happy users was being achieved overall.

In retrospect, this scenario could have been completely avoided. If we had designed the product with the outcome mindset as a team, we would have recognized the user's predicament well in advance of the product launch. And even though this was not in our scope of responsibility, we would have created migration workflows and cultivated integration partnerships to make it easy for users to adopt our streamlined and elegant next-gen product line.

4. Business Mindset: Show Me the Money!

The business mindset for practitioners is an acute understanding that businesses exist to make a profit by creating value for their users. If the experience mindset is the arrow, the business mindset is the target. And effective outcomes happen when arrow meets target.

In January 2007, Adobe launched a beta product for photographers. **User research** showed that many professional photographers were only using a small portion of the feature set in Adobe Photoshop. So Adobe launched a new product called Lightroom, which became a multimillion-dollar product line that, most important, customers loved.

Most practitioners don't fully understand the breadth of user-related challenges their companies face, from product adoption to customer satisfaction to long-term loyalty. A practitioner with the business mindset views any and all of these as an opportunity to create value in the system.

To utilize the business mindset, a practitioner must be able to:

→ Clearly articulate business goals and connect whatever they're doing to a business problem that matters; and

→ Articulate the business's value to its users.

The Genesis of a Billion-Dollar Product

An organization that was creating collaboration software conducted formative user research. The research team realized that a lot of medical practitioners were using the product, even though they were not the intended user group the product was being built for.

The researcher and her team applied the business mindset by asking what value could be created for these unexpected users. They further realized that medical staff was using the software to collaborate with other medical professionals across the globe in the absence of an existing solution. But one challenge was that the organization's product was not HIPAA certified. And through that came the idea of a line of a HIPAA-certified software with workflow enhancements specific to the medical field. The organization created a roadmap to build that product line as it opened up the opportunity to target an unmet need in a multibillion-dollar market.

5. Systems Mindset: Understand Complexity to Design Simplicity

The systems mindset is the philosophy and ability to understand any specific area of focus by understanding the system as a whole, through building a deep understanding of its components, interrelationships, patterns, and idiosyncrasies. As the complexity of technology and its capabilities continue to increase, the systems mindset helps practitioners understand it and tackle problems effectively.

To employ the systems mindset, the practitioner must consider all the:
- → Users in the system before thinking of one specific user to focus on;
- → Experiences in the system before thinking of one specific experience to focus on;
- → Workflows in the system before thinking of one specific workflow to focus on;
- → Screens in the system before thinking of one specific screen to focus on;
- → Patterns in the system before thinking of one specific pattern to focus on.

The Problem Is Not Always What It Seems

Early in my career, I was working on a project where the identified problem was to design a report UI for a specific business user, looking to understand their departmental performance in the product. As I started understanding their intent and expectations, a key question arose: How would they get to this business-critical report if they were not in front of the screen? Could they call customer service and get this data? Could they call one of their financial analysts to get this data?

As we broadened the problem, the product manager and I dug deeper into the system architecture to understand who owned this data and how it was compiled. We further realized that customer service also didn't have the data handy, while financial analysts who were actually supposed to be entering this data didn't have it either as they were simply typing in the numbers.

Our investigation made us think about all the systemic implications—which eventually led to multiple enhancements including the creation of a performance report, a new customer support workflow, and a report preview for the financial analysts. Not only did we improve the user experience by devising multiple ways to access the data, but we also reduced user error because the financial analysts could see how the data they entered affected decision-making in the department.

This is why it's important to always understand the system. Lacking a systems mindset, I could have followed this "small design" philosophy by creating a beautiful report without further thought.

Every UX practitioner should develop these five mindsets. Together, they establish a mental framework for empathizing with the user, ideating different solutions until you achieve the outcome, and driving clear business value across the system.

THE EXPERIENCE DESIGN PROCESS
Creating a structure that facilitates success

To drive effective business growth, a strong user experience design process is needed to consistently take business and user problems and convert them into effective solutions.

In one of the organizations I was associated with, the board of directors mandated that the organization adopt design thinking (similar to the design mindset) as a critical business discipline. And in order to accelerate change management, we sponsored design thinking training for multiple leaders across the organization over a two-year period. We partnered with a top business school to offer a design thinking boot camp for leaders from sales, HR, professional services, engineering, and customer support.

Despite the investment, it was becoming evident that while many people were getting attuned to and excited about the power of design thinking, the philosophy wasn't trickling down to the departments. There wasn't a process to deploy design thinking across the organization in a sustainable way across all departments and roles. This became a significant bottleneck to manage the transformation in the organization.

Unfortunately, many high-potential organizations have not invested in the process and therefore are never able to build momentum or sustainability in their design practice. In the absence of a cohesive process, it becomes a free for all, purely based on the individual experience and motivation of each practitioner.

Without established processes for strategic planning, product prioritizing, user research, and design, organizations struggle to produce high-quality experiences on a consistent basis.

We need a process that allows practitioners to maneuver and navigate the ambiguity and complexity of the various business and user problems being solved—at scale.

> **"Eighty-five percent of reasons for failure are deficiencies
> in the systems and processes rather than the employee.
> The role of management is to change the process rather
> than badgering the individuals to do better."**
>
> **– W. Edwards Deming**

A PragmaticUX™ (PuX) Playbook

From the beginning, my team at UXReactor looked to meet the process challenges of bringing the power of the design mindset and experience mindset to unlock business value at scale. And this effort required rethinking and experimenting with existing business processes to learn more about:

How might we...

→ Think about building a vision for the products and the experiences;
→ Hire a type of practitioner;
→ Design a team structure;
→ Integrate with existing product development and design processes;
→ Design complex, multi-user, multi-mode digital platforms;
→ Build traceability and curation of the iterative design process;
→ Discover great user insights at scale;
→ Curate and communicate the insights;
→ Measure success;
→ Build organizational culture on this philosophy.

Our team converted what we learned in asking these questions (and more) into plays as part of an internal guidebook we called the PragmaticUX™(PUX) Playbook. This living and evolving playbook has become the basis of the UXReactor practice, for the seven years of our existence.

The playbook was structured around four pillars:

→ Experience strategy: The process for building and sustaining an organizational focus on experience design;
→ User research insights: The process for building and sustaining an organization's empathy for its users;
→ Product thinking: The process for building and sustaining an organization's productization of great experiences;
→ Design doing: The process for building and implementing the experience design right.

The 27 plays included in Part 2 are a subset of the larger PragmaticUX™ Playbook.

The PuX™ Design Process

In the pursuit of creating **user and business value** as we go after various experience problems, we need a robust and rigorous process that allows us to tackle the challenges that come to understanding and focusing on the problems. The PuX™ design process was UXReactor's structured way to effectively do this.

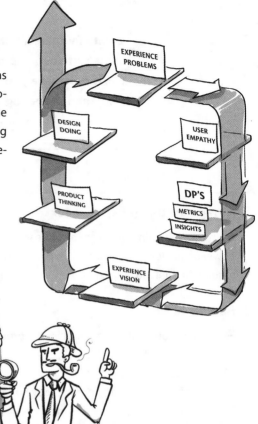

The first step to solve the **experience problems** is to start with building deep empathy for the user and why the experience problem exists. Specifically, understanding who the user is, what the problem is, what the intent is, what the journey is, and where they are in the process. This is done by leveraging the powerful plays of user research.

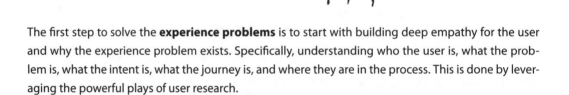

Through this research, three key elements should emerge. The first element is the **user insights**. Insights would include data such as, What is the user looking to achieve? What is the context? What are the pain points? What are the opportunities that we can go after? So there's a lot of insights that can be gained when you start understanding and studying and experiencing the problem for a specific user or a group of users.

The second element is a **collection of design problems that need to be solved** from the user's perspective for the experience problem to go away.

And finally, the third element is an understanding and identification of the **metrics of success** from the user's perspective if everything went well in their experience.

With this data a good experience designer should be able to **design and** ideally **prototype** a high-level vision of how the user's world would further evolve or be enhanced. A **vision** where a majority of the identified design problems have been solved and all the experience problem no longer exist; what would that world look like?

With a much clearer articulation of the vision for the user's experience, the next step is to **prioritize** which part of this vision is going to be productized based on the other business dynamics such as investment, technology capabilities, skills, and timelines, to name a few. Ideally this is a **collaborative** process where the intention remains to achieve the larger experience vision, although in pragmatically scoped phases.

Finally, based on the prioritized plan and scope, the project moves into the critical phase of structured, **detailed design.**

At the end of the detailed design phase, additional user research will be conducted to answer two fundamental questions:

1. **Have we solved the experience problem we intended to?**

2. **Have we made a measurable impact on the metrics we identified?**

If the answer to both is yes—awesome! We can now move on to other experience problems in the system and apply the same design process to them. However, if the answer is no, we need to retrace our steps one at a time, all the way back to the user research phase if needed, and identify the step that needs to be adjusted until the answer turns to yes. It's all about the power of iteration.

GETTING THE RIGHT PEOPLE RIGHT
Aligning skills, roles, and personnel in a user-centric organization

Inevitably the first action that every organization that understands the business value in being user experience–centric takes is to hire a designer or two and hope this will be the Holy Grail in their transformation. This unfortunately always turns out to be filled with angst both for the organization (wanting to see a transformation in the business) and the designer (wanting to be the change agent involved in strategic work), as they both end up not getting what they expected, at a huge opportunity cost of wasted time.

To understand what it takes, businesses need to understand two major people-related variables that make user experience design function effectively. The first is all the people that make up the user experience design practice, and the second is all the collaborators that work with this team to ensure the intended outcome.

A good design practice should consist of competent people with the skills needed to deliver a great user experience, as well as leaders who can help orchestrate the business outcomes by leveraging the individual practitioners, methods, and tools.

The Team of Practitioners

First, recognize that UI design and UX design are two distinct disciplines, as we discussed in Chapter 5. To assemble an effective team of practitioners, you need to understand the various types of expertise needed across the team. Specifically, four skills are must-haves for a mature design practice:

User experience researcher

This practitioner is accountable for gathering, curating, and communicating user insights across the organization. This person is an expert in research methods and provides the user data behind organizational decisions. Most organizations don't include this role; when they do, they only conduct validation user research (commonly called usability testing). This is the fastest way to nullify the power of user research because it concentrates on what you've decided to build rather than showing you what you could be building for your user.

Interaction experience designer

This practitioner is accountable for designing all interaction touchpoints for the system. They understand the various digital modalities (mobile, web, OTT, IoT, etc.) and their related technological flexibilities. This practitioner is an expert in system thinking and design tools. Most organizations do not create the environment to allow this practitioner to think end-to-end while designing the user's experience, thereby diluting the power they bring to the table.

Visual experience designer

This practitioner is accountable for all creative aspects of the digital interface. They're experts in color theory, typography, visual composition and hierarchy, and design tools. They're also known for extreme attention to detail that they leverage to bring the soul to any experience that is being designed. Given the visceral nature of the artifacts created by this practitioner, most organizations mistake this role and skillset to completely represent the user experience practice, thereby expecting every aspect of the practice (including research and interaction) to be handled by this "full-stack" designer.

Content experience designer

This practitioner is accountable for the content and its voice and tone throughout the system being designed, including labels, instructions, errors, emails, notifications, and so forth. This person is an expert in written communication and understands how to use copy to communicate with the user in their expected language, voice, and tone. This role is sometimes also titled as UX writer. Most organizations have "documentation specialists" or technical writers, but they are never included as part of the larger user experience practice.

The Leaders That Orchestrate the Magic

As the adage goes, in any organization "the attitude reflects leadership." A major challenge for many organizations that are looking to tap into the potential of user experience design is that they don't have effective leaders accountable for this transformation.

Two types of leaders help ensure the practice stays healthy and delivers the intended business outcomes: the **chief experience officer** (CXO) and the **experience strategist.**

Chief Experience Officer (CXO)

The typical business is a fragmented and siloed world, where multiple chiefs lead their individual domains—marketing, finance, revenue, HR, information technology, product, and so forth. Most organizations, however, do not have a CXO, a chief experience officer whose focus is on users and their experiences across all facets of the business regardless of internal structures or functions, a leader whose responsibility is to consistently think about the users, their journey, and their needs, and monitor whether the organization is going above and beyond expectations to wow users and win their loyalty.

In the absence of a CXO, this role usually falls to the overworked chief executive officer, who, on top of carrying out their regular responsibilities, is trying to ensure that every department consistently delivers on user experience. This is even more difficult because of the siloed structure of typical organizations. Ultimately, users feel the effects of not having a CXO when they deal with disjointed processes, systems, and tools created by siloed stakeholders as they interact with the organization through their offerings. In a business world catalyzed by experiences, the need for a chief experience officer is loud and clear.

Some organizations have a role called the chief customer officer (CCO), but traditionally the CCO focuses more on customer service, customer contact, and customer success. The scope needs to expand significantly to unlock the full potential of user experience design.

Some organizations hire design leaders and assume they will automagically evolve to play the role of CXO. While this can happen, it's uncommon. To transition to an executive role, the practitioner needs to master additional mindsets and skills beyond the craft of design, including business vision and change management. (Read more about the design leader's game plan in Chapter 46: "A Design Leader's Game Plan.")

What Does a Chief Experience Officer Do?

As a strategic leader, the chief experience officer is in charge of a broad scope of user-experience related activities:

→ Experience design strategy;

→ Experience vision;

→ Experience design;

→ User research;

→ Experience analytics and metrics;

→ Interviewing, recruiting, and supervising experience practitioners and teams;

→ Managing the people, processes, mindsets, and culture in the organization that directly affect the user's experience;

→ Influence organizational innovation;

→ Influence mergers and acquisitions related to users, journey;

→ Drive and manage the organization's empathy scale (Chapter 17: "Shared Empathy Play"), a measure of how much empathy the whole organization has for users;

→ Collaborate with other C-suite leaders such as the chief technology officer (CTO) and the chief product officer (CPO) to ensure a high level of alignment.

In other words, the CXO is in charge of initiatives across the entire business life cycle, from business strategy to user empathy and innovation to design and delivery.

This person is someone who has direct access to the CEO and has good functional relationships with the rest of the organizational leaders. They should have enough influence in the organization that can be leveraged for driving the synchronization of work and future strategy and be able to navigate the dynamics of a matrix organization.

How Is This Role Different from the CPO's?

The role of the chief experience officer is different from the emerging role of chief product officer (CPO). While they share the same intended business outcome, their accountabilities differ.

The CPO is accountable for products in the business. CPO has a product roadmap.

The CXO is responsible for the users and their experience in the business ecosystem. The CXO has an experience roadmap. (For more, see Chapter 19: "Experience Roadmap Play.")

Where Should This Person Be Hired From?

The CXO doesn't need to come from a traditional design background. It surely should be somebody who practices the experience mindset and believes that users care about experiences first and that experience design is the new currency of success.

In the absence of a CXO, organizations become inefficient, teams fail to collaborate, and the user is collateral damage. In these cases, the experience strategist can step into the role of micro-CXO leading initiatives on the ground.

Experience Strategist

The strategist is a grassroots leader accountable for orchestrating business outcomes while leading the various facets of experience DESIGN (yes, BIG DESIGN) for the scope of a project or product.

This person works with the CXO (when in place) and leads the day-to-day planning and execution of user experience design on the ground level. They are experts in catalyzing collaboration across the organization. They understand all aspects of the experience practice and can effectively collaborate with peers (product managers, engineering managers) in the organization to ensure the best experience is being put forward for the project or product they are accountable for.

Where Should This Person Be Hired From?

The strategist is typically someone who has built strong competency and collaborative skills as a practitioner and has been further groomed (in business thinking and outcomes) to be the orchestrator assigned to and accountable for designing and delivering the best experiences. (Read about the practitioner's game plan to evolve to a strategist in Chapter 47.)

Experience Collaborators

Given that the experience practice is part of a larger organizational ecosystem, understanding and engaging with collaborating partners is critical to its success. When there is no common organizational goal, the result is politics; when there is a common goal, the result is collaboration. A highly effective organizational system is one that is constantly collaborating and supporting a hyper-focus on user experience.

The collaborators are divided into two types, internal and external:

Internal Collaborators

Internal collaborators are colleagues, supporters, and influencers that are within the organization that the CXO and experience practitioners need to build strong working relationships with:

→ **Peer Practitioners:** These are peer practitioners from departments such as product, engineering, sales, marketing, customer success, professional services, and support. They are focused on day-to-day execution to achieve the larger organizational vision. Experience practitioners should actively involve these stakeholders in all aspects of experience design, which include design reviews, shared empathy activities, and ideation sessions, to name a few. On the other hand, peer practitioners should always reach out to the experience practitioners any time they see or identify a potential design problem or opportunity (Chapter 34: "Design Problems and Opportunities Play").

→ **Leaders:** The experience practitioners also need actively engage and collaborate with the following leadership.

    a. **Executive leadership** such as CFO, CMO, CPO, CIO, and CTO. They are focused on ensuring seamless execution for their areas of focus and driving toward the organizational vision.

    b. **CEO,** focused on shareholder value creation and seamless execution as a company as a whole. Owns and drive the organizational vision, goals, and objectives.

    c. **Board of directors,** focused on shareholder value creation and organizational sustainability. The experience practice needs to work closely with all of these partners to realize its outcomes. Because each one of them has different intentions and goals, practitioners should

> **When there is no common organizational goal, the result is politics; when there is a common goal, the result is collaboration.**

understand their intent and collaborate for mutual success. Traditionally, most experience practitioners spend the majority of their collaboration time with peer practitioners; instead, they should actively leverage their BIG DESIGN perspective to connect the dots with the other internal collaborators.

Collaboration Trinity

In organizations that are working on digitally transforming their users' experience, at the minimum, it is imperative for three internal partners to collaborate with each other. These three working collaboratively can effectively solve any business problem given to them using the bv.d process:

→ **Product Manager:** The person accountable for the go-to-market and business side of things.

→ **Experience Strategist:** The person accountable for user-centricity and designing the best experience for the user and the business.

→ **Engineering Lead:** The person accountable for the feasibility and product development of the user experience.

One big mistake is thinking that any one is greater than the others. The best collaboration model is when each one of them is pushing the other two: one as the advocate for the business, one as the advocate for the user, and one as the advocate for feasibility. Organizations should focus on aligning these three stakeholders to focus on the problems at hand for the user and the business. This will ensure deep collaboration, less churn, more problem-solving—and, more important, a fun working relationship.

These three also become the bridge to the rest of the organization by including peers from other groups or departments in times of collaborative decision-making. (For more on collaboration refer to (Chapter 36: "Cross-Functional Collaboration Play").

External Collaborators

Most organizations also need to consider external partners who deliver parts of the organization's user experience, including:

→ **Channel Partners/VARs (Value Added Resellers):** They market and sell the organization's products and services to a larger user group. They often control the experience layer as they are engaging with users, and this should be factored in by the experience practitioners to deliver the best user experience.

→ **Technology System Integrators/Solution Providers/Consulting Firms:** They help understand, build, deliver, and launch the product and services to customers of the organization. Experience practitioners also need to understand this role's impact on the user experience. Examples are organizations such as IBM, Deloitte, and PwC.

→ **Vendors:** They help extend the organization by providing essential services extending multiple touchpoints to its users and stakeholders. The experience practice should also build relationships with this group, given the "long tail" nature of their customer relationships. Often, users perceive the experience provided by this group as an extension of the overall business experience. Examples are organizations such as hiring partners, travel partners, conference partners, training partners, and media partners.

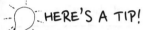

HERE'S A TIP!

[Thought for Practitioners] What impact have you created (in an attributable manner) for your users that you can share with internal leadership?

Ideal Organization Structure

I get often asked, "How do you structure an organization around a team of practitioners and collaborators?" While there are several variables to consider, it really hinges on the size and amount of investment an organization is willing to make to build the experience design practice. With that, I would recommend two models.

Enterprise Organization

For an enterprise organization that is large and can invest in building a robust experience design function, the organization should invest in a chief experience officer (CXO) who ideally reports to the CEO.

Multiple experience strategists then report to the CXO, with each strategist owning a specific user and/or product line. Their sole responsibility is to eat, sleep, and drink their designated user's design problems and opportunities. The strategist then leads a team of practitioners with all four relevant skills present.

Some organizations have also realized value by investing in a design operations (DesignOps) team that the CXO oversees. DesignOps's responsibility is to focus and optimize on all program level activities, such as mindsets, people, processes, and environment, within the practice. I will elaborate more later in the book (Chapter 23: "Experience Transformation Program Play").

Small Organization

For a smaller organization that does not have the same capacity for investment, I would recommend building a team of practitioners whom an experience strategist oversees.

One common pitfall I see and would strongly advise against is to hire an incomplete team with the hope that a very senior practitioner, such as the strategist, would perform all of the responsibilities required. This practice is akin to hiring a senior surgeon and expecting a person to be a substitute for the entire surgical team (e.g. anesthesiologist, nurse anesthetist, operating room nurse, surgical technician, and assistants).

As far as specific titles, do what is appropriate for your organization. We'll talk a bit more about this in Part 2 (Chapter 22: "Career Ladder Play").

THE TRANSFORMATION STARTS WITH YOU

Preparing yourself to lead the charge

Transforming an organization into being user experience–led isn't about creating technology that looks pretty and doesn't break. Those attributes are the cost of entry. Instead, it's about building products, systems, and tools that effortlessly meet users' needs—enveloped in a whole ecosystem that's dedicated to supporting them—so they work smarter and live better.

When the organization is able to bring this level of transformation by focusing on the right mindset, people, process and environment, everything changes for the better.

When the transformation is complete a user experience–led organization is characterized by the following:

→ Knows, at any given point of time, their users, their needs, and the design problems that matter to them.
→ Builds sticky products that their users find highly desirable.
→ Generates a larger, more loyal customer base.
→ Recruits top employees committed to the company's user-centric mission.
→ Keeps competitors at bay because they couldn't replicate what they're doing fast enough to catch up.
→ Attracts investment from private and public capital.
→ Above all, becomes highly profitable and grows by 2X to 5X in comparison to its peers and market.

We Need a Catalyst: YOU!

But the most important aspect of any organizational transformation depends on the critical actor who can help catalyze it.

This catalyst can be a business leader who is looking to enable their organization to become user-first. This can be the chief experience officer who aims to develop a practice around this charter. Or a practitioner who is looking to solve user problems and consistently add business value. It could also be a partner who is actively collaborating in the process of experience design. Or, in an enlightened organization, it can be all of them.

The intent of this Playbook is to equip and enable these catalysts of change to successfully help their organizations grow their business in a practical manner. In Part 2, you'll find a specific list of plays from UXReactor's PragmaticUX™ Playbook that will help set the stage for these catalysts. They are written with you in mind—and the transformation journey you plan to undertake.

Remember that if it were easy, everyone would have already done it. Transformation of this nature may take 18–24 months to get all aspects in a sustainable rhythm. It will entail changing beliefs, processes, people, measurements, incentives, culture—and above all, mindsets. So run it like a marathon, where every mile is a win, and every play is a path to the finish line.

> **Challenge yourself, it's the only path that leads to growth.**
> **– Morgan Freeman**

PART N°2

27 PLAYS

TO PRACTICE

"AMATEURS PRACTICE UNTIL THEY CAN GET IT RIGHT; PROFESSIONALS PRACTICE UNTIL THEY CAN'T GET IT WRONG."

- HAROLD CRAXTON

USING THE PLAYBOOK

"THE EYE SEES ONLY WHAT THE MIND
IS PREPARED TO COMPREHEND."
— ROBERTSON DAVIES

HOW TO NAVIGATE THE PLAYBOOK
Creating your own learning journey based on your intent

The most important part of this book is the Playbook, which is designed to help you drive business value. To navigate this part, understand its two components:

The first is the four pillars and the second are the plays that focus on different problems within each pillar.

Each play is created to help you mindfully navigate the solution to the problem of focus (framed as a "How do I ..." statement), by understanding all the key variables that you will need.

The playbook is structured around four pillars:

→ **Experience strategy:** building and sustaining your organization's focus on experience design;
→ **User research insights:** building and sustaining your organization's empathy for its users;
→ **Product thinking:** building and sustaining your organization's productization of great experiences;
→ **Design doing:** building and implementing high-quality experience design.

Each pillar ends with the **program play** aimed at leadership personas so your team can effectively build, structure, and govern that program for long-term sustainability.

This playbook is for everyone in the experience design ecosystem: **the apprentice, the practitioner, the design leader, the business leader, and the collaborator.** You'll recognize yourself in one or more of them.

The first play you'll read in the Playbook starts with the user empathy play in Chapter 14. This play sits outside of the four pillars because building user empathy is a foundational mindset and attitude one has to master before thinking about experience strategy, user research, product thinking, and design doing. Furthermore, it's everyone's job to develop and deepen empathy, whether you are a business leader, collaborator, or a designer. It's a core building block for all other plays. Once you have empathized with the user, you are ready to dive in.

If You're a Business Leader
looking to drive business value through design

How do I develop understanding to truly empathize with my user? → **Chapter 14: User Empathy Play**

How do I build a robust program around experience design? → **Chapter 23: Experience Transformation Program Play**

If You're a Design Leader
on the path to become a chief experience officer

How do I develop understanding to truly empathize with my user? → **Chapter 14: User Empathy Play**

How do I foster a user-first culture? → **Chapter 16: Culture Design Play**

How do I grow the collective empathy of my organization? → **Chapter 17: Shared Empathy Play**

How do I enable experience practitioners to grow professionally in their careers? → **Chapter 22: Career Ladder Play**

How do I hire experience practitioners? → **Chapter 21: Hiring Play**

How do I build a robust program around experience design? → **Chapter 23: Experience Transformation Program Play**

How do I run a research program? → **Chapter 30: User Research Program Play**

If You're a Practitioner
on the path to become a strategist...

How do I develop understanding to truly empathize with my user?	→ **Chapter 14: User Empathy Play**
How do I build a seamless experience for the user across the entire ecosystem?	→ **Chapter 18: Experience Ecosystem Play**
How do I create a roadmap around the experience of a user?	→ **Chapter 19: Experience Roadmap Play**
How do I convey an experience vision that activates my organization?	→ **Chapter 20: Experience Vision Play**
How do I ensure rigor in my research?	→ **Chapter 27: Research Quality Play**
How do I measure the success and quality of my user experience?	→ **Chapter 28: Experience Metrics Play**
How do I consolidate and leverage research insights organizationally?	→ **Chapter 29: Insights Curation Play**
How do I define "baseline" and "best-in-class" product experiences?	→ **Chapter 32: Experience Benchmarking Play**
How do I align for success at the beginning of the design phase?	→ **Chapter 33: Experience Design Brief Play**
How do I decide what the right problems to solve are?	→ **Chapter 34: Design Problems and Opportunities Play**
How do I ensure the delivery of a great product experience?	→ **Chapter 35: Product Experience Planning Play**
How do I collaborate across the organization to drive seamless and informed product experience design?	→ **Chapter 36: Cross-Functional Collaboration Play**
How do I catalyze great product experiences?	→ **Chapter 37: Product Thinking Program Play**
How do I run an effective Experience Design Doing Program?	→ **Chapter 44: Experience Design Doing Program Play**

If You're an Apprentice
on the path to become a practitioner

HERE'S A TIP!

If you would like to see how these plays come together, you can directly go to part 3 and pick the user's scenario you relate the most with

How do I develop understanding to truly empathize with my user?	→ **Chapter 14: User Empathy Play**
How do I know which method to use to gather insights?	→ **Chapter 25: Picking a Research Method Play**
How do I recruit the right participants for user research?	→ **Chapter 26: Research Recruitment Play**
How do I ensure rigor in my research?	→ **Chapter 27: Research Quality Play**
How do I decide what the right problems to solve are?	→ **Chapter 34: Design Problems and Opportunities Play**
How do I systematically optimize and build experiences?	→ **Chapter 39: Workflow Design Play**
How do I hone in on effective and quality design?	→ **Chapter 40: Detailed Design Play**
How should an experience design review be run?	→ **Chapter 41: Experience Design Review Play**
How do I build and scale experience designs with high consistency and quality?	→ **Chapter 42: Design System Play**
How do I test the quality of delivered vs. engineered experience designs?	→ **Chapter 43: Design QA Play**

If You're a collaborator like a Product Manager or Engineer
and are looking to work more effectively with your design peers

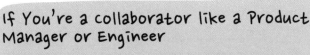

How do I develop understanding to truly empathize with my user?	→ **Chapter 14: User Empathy Play**
How do I collaborate across the organization to drive seamless and informed product experience design?	→ **Chapter 36: Cross-Functional Collaboration Play**
How should an experience design review be run?	→ **Chapter 33: Experience Design Brief Play**
How do I build and scale experience design with high consistency and quality?	→ **Chapter 42: Design System Play**

CHAPTER 13

HOW TO READ A PLAY

Understanding the mindful way of getting to your intent

The Anatomy of a Play

Each play has some common elements. The "How Do I …" and "Why Do You Need the … Play" sections help you understand if you're in the right spot to learn about what you're looking for. The mindful canvas is an effective guide for being mindful of various variables to successfully solve the problem. The rest of the play describes the variables to keep in mind in order to achieve your desired outcomes; it's sprinkled with examples, tips, and real-world stories.

Chapter #

Introduction

Why you need the play

Roles and responsibilities

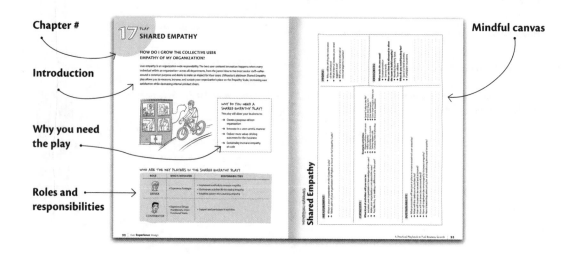

Mindful canvas

The how

Tips

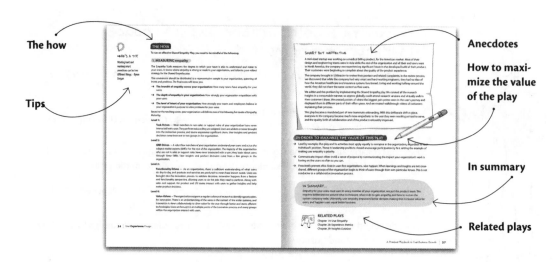

Anecdotes

How to maximize the value of the play

In summary

Related plays

→ **Introduction:** The context of why the play even exists, and what are its desired outcomes. This description is prompted by, "How do I...?" to define the problem space.

→ **Why you need the play:** This section describes the business impact of implementing the play.

→ **Roles and responsibilities:** This section calls out who is needed for successful implementation of the play, what their roles is (driver or contributor), and their responsibilities.

→ **Mindful canvas:** These are the variables, or the "ingredients," to consider when implementing the play. See "The Mindful Canvas" section below for more details. As you read the play, we have left some scribble space to write your own throughts and comments.

→ **Tip:** Any tips that are contextually in the "How" section are presented along the side with a lightbulb icon.

→ **The how:** The variables in the play canvas are described in further detail here. Each numbered section relates to the play canvas. Examples of what a data point could look like and questions to ask appear throughout.

→ **Example:** Examples help anchor the concept to a real-world scenario. They are in the "How" section; if they are long enough, they are visually called out, but otherwise they can be found contextually in the text.

→ **In summary:** A short recap of the thesis of the play.

→ **Anecdote:** Real-world experiences related to the play.

→ **How to maximize the value of the play:** You can think of this as a "tips" section for the overall play on how to drive maximum impact.

The Mindful Canvas

One artifact that is consistent for each play is the mindful canvas.

Every practitioner and every organization has different contexts, goals, and resources; therefore, it would be foolhardy to write a one-size-fits-all playbook for implementing the philosophy of user experience. Our solution is to approach it in a more mindful manner, helping you understand the system and its key variables so you can make the most effective decisions and plans for your own specific context.

 HERE'S AN EXAMPLE!

The Pizza canvas

For example, say you want to make a pizza. This book will not give you a follow-these-steps recipe; there are plenty of books that do that. Instead, it will give you a mindful canvas for making a good pizza, breaking down the process into the key variables you need to think through:

→ The base   → Toppings   → Utensils

→ A type of sauce   → A heat source   → Condiments

→ One or more types of cheese

Now, you have some grassroots decisions to make about these variables. Do you want a base made out of traditional dough, gluten-free dough, vegetables, or even no base? Do you want vegetable toppings, meat toppings, a combo, or no toppings? The objective is to deliberate on each variable before making a decision.

As you can see, the goal of the mindful canvas is not to solve each discrete problem for you. Instead, it's to create a deliberate process of decision-making so you can identify, understand, and experiment with the key variables that are at play. Once you've done that, you can make highly effective decisions that fit both you and your organization.

USER EMPATHY PLAY

How do I develop enough understanding to truly empathize with my user?

Creating a user-centric experience requires more than simply understanding your users' domain and what tasks they need to perform—it requires deep empathy. Empathy helps you avoid making erroneous assumptions about your users and instead uncover new opportunities based on what they actually want and need. This play is foundational to all subsequent plays because it will help you develop that deep understanding of who your users are, what their needs are, and which problems to solve for them. These insights will guide the decisions you make about your design and your product strategy in a way that puts the user first.

This play will allow your business to:

→ Develop deep empathy for your user;
→ Design and deliver products people actually want and need;
→ Create a culture of innovation built on user insights and uncovered design opportunities;
→ Be more confident in your product strategy and development decisions.

Who Are the Key Players in the User Empathy Play?

ROLE	WHO'S INVOLVED	RESPONSIBILITIES
DRIVER	Experience strategist	• Oversee research • Identify the best empathy-building method • Collect data through research • Synthesize data • Create and document artifacts • Drive greater empathy across organization
CONTRIBUTOR	User researcher; peer practitioner (e.g. product manager, engineering manager, other internal stakeholders)	• Conduct or contribute to research • Provide business or product insights

User Empathy

USER

→ Who are you looking to understand and empathize with?

CATALYSTS

→ How will you kick-start your organization's understanding of the user?
→ How will you immerse yourself in your user's context so you can truly empathize with them?

INSIGHTS

→ What information and insights do you need to extract in order to further understand and empathize?

ACTIVATION

→ How will you build opportunities to spread empathy, enabling others to share your level of empathy for the user?

THE HOW

To run an effective user empathy play, you need to be mindful of:

1. The USER You Want to Develop Empathy For

Your organization exists to add value to those who you serve. More likely than not, your organization or system contains a number of users, both internal (e.g. employees, partners, vendors) and external (e.g. customers, sales partners, consultants). Identify the specific user(s) you want to develop empathy for.

Ideally you should work on building empathy for each and every user in the context of your system. However, always try to prioritize the top users based on a business goal (e.g. exploring an untapped market), a product goal (e.g. enhancing the user experience), or a user goal (e.g. understanding user motivations and pain points). Knowing why you are looking to understand your users will anchor your research and ensure your original intent is met.

2. The CATALYSTS for Building Empathy

Building user empathy begins with suspending your own assumptions and instead striving to understand your user by stepping into their shoes or conducting research (Chapter 25: "Picking a Research Method Play"). Here are some techniques you can use to start the process:

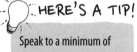

HERE'S A TIP!

Speak to a minimum of 10 users to collect enough insights to correlate and cross-reference. The smaller your sample size, the less reliable the data.

→ **In-depth interviews:** This technique involves speaking with the user directly, usually in a one-on-one setting. The goal is to listen and understand. Therefore, it's best to give the users the time and space to speak freely and openly. Ask probing questions to dig deeper. Refrain from judgment and avoid guiding them on how to answer the questions.

→ **Ethnographic studies:** This technique immerses researchers into the "field," the real-world living and working environment of the users you are studying. It is a tremendously valuable method for gaining contextual understanding of what people do, how they do it, and why they do it, especially if you have a very basic level of knowledge about your users and if your user's natural environments are vastly different than yours.

→ **User testing:** This technique involves watching real users interact with a product or design; it's typically implemented after a product or prototype has been built. The goal of this technique is to set aside your own assumptions and empathize with the user about what they see, know, can do, and can't do.

→ **Role play:** In this technique, the stakeholders who are engaged in strategizing, designing, and developing the products "become" the users themselves, adopting their physical, emotional, and psychological attributes.

Simulate their environments

Ford engineers wear suits that simulate the different types of body problems (e.g. backaches, joint problems) their customers might have in order to better understand how to design with end users in mind.

Trying things yourself elicits more visceral reactions, allowing you to resonate with the user and gain a deeper understanding of the people you are designing for. Keep in mind that this method should not replace or be classified as "user research," because you are not engaging with an actual user.

3. What INSIGHTS Are Necessary to Understand Your User

As you immerse yourself in the user's context, extract and collect valuable insights to deepen your empathy for the user. Dig deeper by trying to understand their role, responsibility, goal (intent), journey, larger ecosystem, success criteria, joys, and pain points to name a few areas to be mindful of.

→ **Your Users' Roles:** Learn how your users describe and perceive their roles and more specifically, how they describe the purpose of their roles.
Some helpful questions to inquire include:

   → What does your role entail?
   → What kind of outcomes are you responsible for?
   → What outcome are you looking to achieve in [context]?
   → Why do you use [certain products/services]?

In the ecosystem of a school, here are some roles and their purpose as perceived by a key user: elementary school teacher Ms. Smith:

HERE'S AN EXAMPLE!

ROLE	PERCEIVED ROLE	PERCEIVED PURPOSE
Teacher (Ms.Smith)	I deliver classroom instruction that helps students learn.	I nurture my students' interests in education and help groom the next generation.

→ **Your Users' Responsibilities:** "Responsibilities" describe what users do and the outcome they are aiming for. When building user empathy/running the user empathy play, look for details such as how your users break down their day, what tasks or activities they perform, and how they achieve their outcomes. Some illuminating questions to ask include:

   → What does a typical day look like for you? If it helps, let's take a look at what your day was like yesterday.
   → What goes into getting an outcome done?
   → What tasks do you perform regularly? Weekly? Monthly?
   → What do you spend the most time doing? Why?

HERE'S AN EXAMPLE!

After answering these questions, Ms. Smith might let you know that her responsibilities include:
→ Creating well-paced curricula that are engaging and enriching to students;
→ Establishing classroom rules that ensure students' physical and psychological safety;
→ Selecting assignments that allow students to apply their classroom learnings in a relatable manner;
→ Maintaining an online bulletin to keep a clear channel of communication between herself, her students, and their parents.

→ **Your User's Journeys:** Users rarely have just one touchpoint with your organization, product, or service. Rather, their experience is shaped by a multitude of interactions along a journey. A user journey illustrates this flow, providing a comprehensive, chronological recording of all the interactions, along with accompanying emotional states, that your users experience.

Insights from your user's journey are invaluable as you run the user empathy play.

To gather these insights, inquire about:

→ What outcome are you looking to achieve?

→ What are the major phases of the journey?

→ What is your intent during the journey? Or during the different parts of the journey?

→ What actions or activities are performed?

→ What level of frustration or delight do the users display or verbalize?

→ How efficient were they in completing the task? Where did they take too many steps?

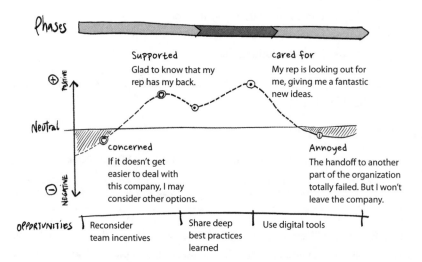

HERE'S A TIP!

Visually map out all the relationships within the system, using artifacts such as an ecosystem (Chapter 18: "Experience Ecosystem Play"). As you learn more about your users, this ecosystem map will serve as a living document showing how all of these roles interact with and depend on each other.

→ **Your User's Larger Ecosystems:** In order to understand your user's place in the larger ecosystem, find out what other people, tools, and resources they interact with. Not only will this help build your knowledge of and empathy for these particular users, but it may also help you discover other relevant users and objects.

Inquire about:

→ Whom do you interact with to get [an outcome] done?

→ Who else do you interact with, and why?

→ What kinds of tools do you use to get [a task] completed?

→ What is your reporting structure, and what is your working relationship with the people in these roles?

Your user's end-to-end experience is the summation of all their journeys and the interactions they've had with different people, tools, and technologies. Therefore, you have to take into consideration the ecosystem—the complex network of interconnected systems that your user inhabits—to get a fuller picture of why they may react or behave a certain way.

Within the ecosystem of a school, Ms. Smith's system might look like:

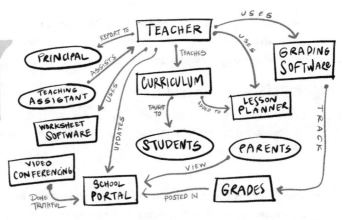

→ **Your User's Success Qualities:** Insights into how your users measure success and what they need to be successful will also help you understand how to design experiences in a way that drives value to your users.

Some helpful questions to understand include:

- → What makes someone successful in this role?
- → When hiring for this role, what qualities do you look for?
- → What are some things you struggle with when getting [outcome] done?
- → What kind of skills or knowledge do you think would be helpful in getting [outcome] done?
- → What does success look like and who measures it?

→ **Your User's Joys:** Understanding what your users like—what brings them joy—will help you get a sense of what their motivations are, uncover opportunities for delight, and discover unmet needs in their current experiences. These can be joys that users state or joys that you observe during research.

Some helpful questions to inquire include:

- → What are your top three favorite things about your job?
- → What was your best experience with getting [outcome] done?
- → If you had more free time, what would you want to spend that time doing?
- → What was your most memorable day at work? What set that day apart?

HERE'S AN EXAMPLE!

Some joys Ms. Smith might have are:
→ Seeing students evolve and succeed;
→ Finding new and creative ways to engage students;
→ Hearing that she has made an impact on students' lives.

→ **Your User's Pain Points :** Knowing and empathizing with your users' pain points sets a baseline for which problems to solve. These can be pain points that your users bring up themselves or pain points that you observe during research.

Some helpful questions to understand include:

- → What are the top three most frustrating things about your job?

→ What was your worst experience when trying to get [outcome] done?

→ What are the most time-consuming or mundane tasks you would like to remove from your routine?

→ What was your worst day at work? What set that day apart?

HERE'S AN EXAMPLE!

Some pain points Ms. Smith might have are:
→ The entire class is misbehaving;
→ Losing documents;
→ The time it takes to have a curriculum reviewed and approved.

HERE'S A TIP!

Build on the aha moments you've gathered to identify user problems, design problems, and opportunities (Chapter 34: "Design Problems and Opportunities Play").

→ **Your User Segments:** Are you looking to gain empathy for one particular population in a large and diverse group? Separate the group out into user segments—users with similar roles as the whole, but who operate in a specific context—and identify the segments you are looking to understand. What broad attributes do they share?

→ High school teachers vs. elementary school teachers;

→ Customer service agents in insurance vs. customer service agents in e-commerce;

→ Luxury ride-share user vs. budget ride-share user;

→ Experienced users vs. novice users.

Identify notable groupings of users based on demographic, psychographic, behavioral, and geographic attributes, or even levels of experience. Knowing these segments will provide guidance for follow-on user research recruitment, data synthesis, and even business decisions such as what kinds of offerings to provide for a particular segment.

→ **Aha Moments:** Aha moments are moments of sudden insight and clarity that have an oversized impact on the user. An aha moment could be the instant when a user understands the value they get from a product or when the researcher learns something completely new and wholly unexpected that leads to a product development breakthrough.

4. Ways to Build ACTIVATION and Spread Empathy

Data is only as valuable as the insights it informs and knowledge it builds in others. That's where artifacts and socialization kick in.

→ **Artifacts:** Distill what you've learned in user research and translate the insights into shareable artifacts such as **user personas, empathy maps, user journeys, and video reels**. Use these artifacts to foster empathy for your users even beyond those who were directly involved in the research. One word of caution: The mere development of artifacts does not automatically translate into deepened empathy for the user. The artifacts are useless unless they are filled with rich insights and achieve your original objective.

→ **Socialization:** Empathy is a core pillar of all user-first cultures; it isn't "mission accomplished" when you've completed your research and finalized your artifacts. Socialize your findings with anyone who plays a role in shaping the ultimate user experience. Share video reels and soundbites from actual users so the greater organization can have a heightened sense of empathy for the people you are designing for (Chapter 17: "Shared Empathy Play").

Empathy Is a Game-changer

"Empathy makes you a better innovator," declared Satya Nadella, the CEO of Microsoft—and he promptly launched the Xbox Adaptive Controller in 2018, giving gamers with a wide range of physical disabilities the ability to play. The controller's design was a perfect real-world application of user empathy. Every little decision, ranging from the placement of the buttons, the shape of the controller, the packaging, and even the product price, was designed based on user insights. For example:

Three threaded inserts: After discovering that some gamers place their gaming setup on a lap board and secure them with Velcro tape, the design team added inserts to give the gamers the freedom to mount their controllers onto their wheelchairs, lap boards, or desks.

Packaging: Designers learned that users with disabilities were forced to "use their teeth to open everything from cereal boxes to beer bottles" and that they had one deliberate design principle for packaging design: "No teeth." The developers took this request to heart and designed a controller package that was delightfully easy to unbox.

Price: The controller is priced at $99.99, which puts it in reach of gamers who might not be able to afford other pricey adaptive technologies. Microsoft made this decision after hearing from their users that the price point was important to them and they needed something affordable.

The Xbox Adaptive Controller embodied deep user empathy in action. Up until its introduction, gamers with disabilities were "[cobbling] together all sorts of things to get a similar effect." For them—and for Microsoft!—this controller literally has been a game-changer. And it all began with a deliberate culture of user empathy.

IN ORDER TO MAXIMIZE THE VALUE OF THIS PLAY

→ **Distinguish between assumptions and fact:** Clearly separate insights derived from users with those that were hypothesized by non-users. Assumptions need to be further validated by research.

→ **Empathy is not a one-and-done exercise:** It's an ongoing process. Continue to learn about your users with every interaction, and continue to add your learnings to your research repository.

→ **Call your users by an identifiable name:** "We need to solve this problem for the user" is not as personal as "We need to solve this problem for Sam." Humanize your users and increase your organization's empathy for them by talking about your users often and by name.

IN SUMMARY

Knowing your users on a surface level is not sufficient if you want to deliver great experiences. To solve your user's problems in a powerful way, you need to know what it is like to be them; you need a deep understanding of who they are, how they think, and what their surrounding system is like; and you need to feel the pain points they experience. Only with this level of deep empathy can you deliver experiences users will love. Therefore, the user empathy play is foundational for fueling business growth through user experience design.

RELATED PLAYS

Chapter 17: "Shared Empathy Play"
Chapter 18: "Experience Ecosystem Play"

Chapter 30: "User Research Program Play"
Chapter 34: "Design Problems and Opportunities Play"

EXPERIENCE STRATEGY

"STRATEGY WITHOUT TACTICS IS THE SLOWEST ROUTE TO VICTORY. TACTICS WITHOUT STRATEGY IS THE NOISE BEFORE DEFEAT."

- SUN TZU

CHAPTER 15

EXPERIENCE STRATEGY: INTRODUCTION
Building the right scaffolding for a user-centric organization

What Is Strategy?

The word "strategy" can mean different things to different people. So we turn to Michael E. Porter, the founder of modern business strategy and one of the world's most influential thinkers on management and competitiveness, to define the word.

In a *Harvard Business Review* article, Porter defines strategy as:

→ Creating a unique and valuable position through a set of business activities across the organization;

→ Making trade-offs as the company competes in the market—choosing what not to do;

→ Creating "fit" among a company's activities so that they interact and reinforce one another.

HERE'S AN EXAMPLE!

For example, Vanguard Group aligns all of its activities with a low-cost strategy; it distributes funds directly to consumers and minimizes portfolio turnover.

Strategy requires identifying and articulating a differentiated positioning. However, it also encompasses the choice and fit of the day-to-day activities that reinforce the strategy. That is the approach we take in this experience strategy section.

1. The Impact of Experience Strategy

As discussed in Part 1, the world we live in today is vastly different from the early 2000s and 2010s. People expect products, tools, and processes to be digitized—and that's the bare minimum. With a dizzying array of choices, customers will time and time again select the product or service featuring an experience that delights them and exceeds their expectations.

Organizations need to adopt a user-first and experience-centric strategy, because **a better user experience is the new and valuable edge** organizations need to compete and lead. If it comes with a well-executed experience strategy, users will not only choose your product, they'll be happy to pay more for it.

> **A satisfied customer is the best business strategy of all."**
>
> **– Michael LeBoeuf**

2. Experience Strategy Stands on Four Core Beliefs

→ **Leadership can't be replaced.** The core roles of a leader are identifying a strategy, being disciplined about making sound trade-offs, clearly communicating a vision of the future for the entire organization, and guiding experience transformation.

→ **Strategy includes execution.** A brilliant strategy or technology will get you on the competitive map, but you need solid (as opposed to flawless) execution to keep you ahead. It's not strategy or execution; it's both. And you need to plan for execution.

→ **There is a fit across activities.** Consistent, coordinated activities that reinforce the strategy give businesses a competitive advantage.

→ **Sustainability is achieved through (eco)systems.** The long-term sustainability of your market advantage comes from a system, not from individual parts. Experience strategy is the amalgamation of multiple systems: people, process, environment, and mindset.

3. Key Concepts

Here are a few key terms and concepts to understand before diving into the experience strategy plays:

→ **Have genuine care for your users.** Be motivated by a desire to positively affect someone's life, while simultaneously gaining monetary benefits from the product or service you provide. Start by building deep empathy and adopting an experience mindset.

→ A better user experience will allow you to command a price premium—**an experience premium**—for the same set of features and functionalities. By continuously investing in user experience, you'll incur less **experience debt.**

→ Defining, aligning, and transforming an organization to be user-first **will take time.** It's not a six- or eight-month project; it's a one- to two-plus-year endeavor. Build your people, process, mindsets, and environment systems over time to realize the **business value of design (bv.d)** and gain market competitiveness. Do it well and do it right, or risk your efforts being a time and resource drain for your organization.

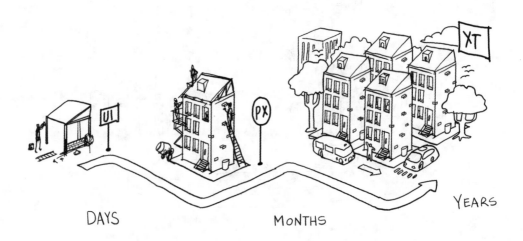

4. What to Expect in This Section

The experience strategy plays will allow you to answer the following questions:

→ How do I foster a user-first culture? (Culture design play)

→ How do I grow the collective empathy of my organization? (Shared empathy play)

→ How do I build a seamless experience for the user across the entire ecosystem? (Experience ecosystem play)

→ How do I create a roadmap around a user's experience? (Experience roadmap play)

→ How do I convey an experience vision that activates my organization? (Experience vision play)

→ How do I hire experience practitioners? (Hiring play)

→ How do I enable experience practitioners to grow professionally in their careers? (Career ladder play)

→ How do I build a robust program around experience design? (Experience transformation program play)

The plays in this section allow you to start differentiating your business from the lens of a superior user experience and sustain it through the creation of the people, process, and environment systems. They allow you to start building your experience strategy and give you the necessary tools to create a sustainable system.

CULTURE DESIGN PLAY
How do I foster a user-first organizational environment?

A user-first culture drives innovation by placing an emphasis on delivering great experiences for users. Peter Drucker famously said, "Culture eats strategy for breakfast." No matter how groundbreaking your strategy is, it will be held back if it is misaligned with your organizational culture, values, and mental attitudes. This play helps you create a culture that is aligned with your user-centric strategy.

Why Do You Need the Culture Design Play?

This play will allow your business to:

→ Enable an influx of novel ideas, experiments, and user-centric products;

→ Create products that your users love and value;

→ Adopt a multi-disciplinary approach to problem-solving;

→ Break down functional silos by increasing collaboration and knowledge-sharing across teams and departments.

Who Are the Key Players in the Culture Design Play?

ROLE	WHO'S INVOLVED	RESPONSIBILITIES
DRIVER	Chief experience officer	• Articulate what an experience culture entails; • Identify incremental activities for the organization to participate in; • Serve as the conduit for leadership and grassroots change efforts; • Obtain leadership support.
CONTRIBUTOR	Experience design team, individual teams across the organization	• Adopt new practices and activities; • Reinforce adherence to culture-building activities.

Culture Design

MINDSETS

→ How will you find individuals who exhibit the 5 mindsets?
→ How will you cultivate the 5 mindsets in each individual?

EMPATHY

→ How will you encourage greater empathy for your users across the organization?
→ How will you encourage greater empathy for one another across the organization?

COLLABORATION

→ How will you promote collaboration between teams and individuals?
→ How will you support collaboration between teams and individuals?

IDEATION

→ How will you encourage more people in the organization to contribute ideas?

ITERATION AND EXPERIMENTATION

→ How will you help your organization embrace and practice experimentation and iteration?

ACTIVATION AGENTS

→ Who are the teams, individuals, or groups that can serve as catalysts for change?

NURTURE AND SUSTAINABILITY

→ How will you assess your organization's user-first culture?
→ How will you celebrate your organization when the user-first culture is thriving?
→ How will you support your organization when the user-first culture is lacking?

THE HOW

To run an effective culture design play, you need to be mindful of:

💡 HERE'S A TIP!

When you're hiring experience practitioners, craft interview questions that will reveal their orientation toward the five mindsets.

1. Cultivating the Right MINDSETS in Individuals

A user-first culture, first and foremost requires its individual practitioners, whether they engage in design or any other specialty, to possess the five mindsets described in Chapter 8: an experience mindset, a design mindset, a systems mindset, a business mindset, and an outcome mindset.

These are the mindsets that will activate your organization's focus for its users, as well as kickstart an insatiable drive to continuously improve and develop a questioning spirit that challenges the status quo.

Cultivating and mastering these mindsets is a lifelong process. Find ways to incorporate them into all of your interactions, activities, and core processes, such as hiring (Chapter 21: "Hiring Play"), onboarding, cross-functional collaboration (Chapter 36: "Cross-Functional Collaboration Play"), and ideation.

Furthermore, they are the foundations for establishing the four cultural pillars all user-first organizations must exhibit:

→ High Empathy;
→ Seamless Collaboration;
→ Effective Ideation;
→ Consistent Experimentation and iteration.

2. Fostering EMPATHY for the User and for Each Other

💡 HERE'S A TIP!

Use the word "collaborate" instead of "help" when interacting with one another and external vendors. This removes hierarchical mindsets, rhetorically placing everyone on an equal footing to solve problems together.

Empathy is the ability to adopt another person's worldview and feel their pains and joys as if you were experiencing them yourself. Only when you deeply empathize with your user and understand their problems can you create solutions that drive real value. (Chapter 14: "User Empathy Play").

This is why empathy is a critical cultural pillar for everyone in your organization—regardless of role or seniority—to adopt. Organizations need a high level of shared-empathy maturity (Chapter 17: "Shared Empathy Play") in order to successfully solve their users' experience problems. Furthermore, it's important to build empathy not only for your paying users but also for the other users in your organizational ecosystem. This will allow teams to collaborate more effectively and overcome challenges with minimal angst.

Empathy must be promoted on an individual and an organizational level. In your day-to-day practices, encourage teammates to suspend their own assumptions and listen deeply to what their users and coworkers are experiencing. **Spread empathy by telling stories**. Stories resonate and inspire people to take action.

3. Promoting COLLABORATION

Building great user experiences is a team effort. Every person in the organization must embrace collaboration and work together toward the company's vision.

With the cultural pillar of collaboration, there's no "us" vs. "them." Departments are not siloed; instead, teams across the organization work together, exchange data, and meet on a regular basis to share knowledge about their users.

You should promote collaboration by bringing different departments together whenever possible, and encouraging participation in activities such as strategic planning, project kick-offs, design reviews, ideation workshops, design handoffs, user research readouts, and retrospectives. Create a space where everyone's multi-disciplinary perspectives are welcome, and leverage these perspectives to find novel ways to solve the user's problems.

You can share your user research findings with other departments, such as support, sales, or marketing. Learn from the data they have collected, as well, because their data might reveal a different perspective. As you continue to collaborate, you will have a substantial body of shared insights (Chapter 29: "Insights Curation Play") with which your organization can make business and product-related decisions.

> "Experimentation is the engine that drives innovation."
>
> – Stefan Thomke, Harvard Business School professor and author

4. Democratizing IDEATION

As Adam Grant found in his research on originality, "Being prolific actually increases originality because sheer volume improves your chances of finding novel solutions."

A user-first culture is constantly ideating.

The most important thing to remember about this third cultural pillar is that ideation is not exclusively reserved for designers. A company with high empathy and collaborative spirit means everyone in the organization deeply feels the user's problems and is given the agency to contribute solutions to solve these problems.

Create channels beyond ideation sessions through which anyone can share their ideas. Broadcast these ideas, and provide opportunities for others to weigh in on them. Some ideas to consider include:

→ Invite a new teammate, or a completely unrelated departmental teammate (that has built user empathy) to a design ideation as a guest attendee;

→ Have a bulletin board (virtual or physical) where all the top user problems are identified, and anyone can share an idea or solution from their perspective;

→ Have a company-wide "idea box" that any team member can share whatever thoughts they have.

You can crowdsource ideas by holding organization-wide hackathons or by creating an innovation lab where individuals can contribute and experiment on their ideas.

5. Supporting EXPERIMENTATION

Edison made 1,000 unsuccessful attempts—or, as we call them today, iterations—before he finally invented the working light bulb. Each unsuccessful attempt (or "failure") gave him input to inform his design for the next iteration.

Edison's approach offers an important takeaway many companies should internalize: failure needs to be a welcomed part of the journey to success. This is why the cultural pillar of experimentation and iteration is critical to building a user-first culture that delivers great experiences. Breakthroughs come from continuous experimentation and iteration.

The cost of not running experiments is huge. It's better to fail fast and learn from those failures early on than it is to fail after you've invested significant design and development resources into a product. Build cheap and fast prototypes, run experiments, get feedback from users, and embrace and learn from failures so you can improve on the final product.

6. Empowering the Necessary ACTIVATION AGENTS

To make a user-first culture a reality, you need the right activation agents—the teams, individuals, or groups that can serve as catalysts for change.

→ **Leadership:** A user-first culture requires leaders who set the tone and lead from the front by placing an emphasis on ensuring and improving the user experience. They monitor experience metrics and are not afraid to dive deep if the data shows a deviation. They lead by example, taking customer support calls to better empathize with users and advocating for users in business strategy and product development. Leaders also provide the necessary support for the organization to ideate, collaborate, experiment, and empathize with users.

→ **Grassroots agents:** Real cultural transformation happens when the new culture is anchored in the unspoken behaviors, mindsets, and norms of the individuals who make up the organization. Find catalysts who are passionate about the change to lead the cultural transformation and groom them to be agents of change who create a movement at the grassroots level.

7. The SUSTAINABILITY of Your User-First Culture

An organization cannot sustain its culture without constant nurturing. This means the mindsets and cultural pillars must be incorporated and practiced in all aspects of your organization, consistently and over time.

Leverage your activation agents to propagate the culture and put it into practice through all of your organization's activities. The culture should be reflected in how you hire and fire, how you ideate and develop, how you incentivize and reward teammates, and in how you make strategic decisions.

Use measurement methods such as the empathy scale (Chapter 17: "Shared Empathy Play") to assess the pervasiveness of the mindsets and cultural pillars on an ongoing basis. Use these measures to celebrate individuals and teams when they strongly exhibit the user-first culture, and provide more support and guidance to those who do not meet the mark.

Airbnb: A Case Study

Airbnb is a living example of a user-first culture, one that prioritizes user empathy, celebrates ideation and experimentation, and encourages collaboration through cross-organizational information-sharing.

→ **Empathy:** For the first year after Airbnb's founding, the team tried to "code [their] way through problems" behind computer screens. They quickly realized that code alone can't solve every problem, and found that meeting customers in the real world was the best way to come up with clever solutions. Even to this day, Airbnb continues to build an empathetic culture by providing a $2,000 stipend to all employees who are also Airbnb guests.

→ **Experimentation:** Airbnb encourages individual team members to make small bets on new features, and then measures if there's a meaningful return on the bet before investing more into it. This strategy has enabled Airbnb to move quickly, take productive risks, and continually explore new opportunities.

→ **Ideation:** As part of the onboarding process, Airbnb encourages employees to ship something new on their first day. This enforces their belief that "great ideas can come from anywhere," regardless of tenure or experience. The "heart" icon you click to add properties to a wish list was changed from a "star" by an Airbnb new hire!

→ **Collaboration:** At Airbnb, there's strong collaboration between functions. It is common for customer experience teammates to work on internal tools, and for engineers and designers to collaborate on how to make something work in real time. Furthermore, collaborating across non-overlapping pieces of the business is common and encouraged. In fact, the host and guests teams contribute to each other's roadmap share goals, and partner up on projects.

IN ORDER TO MAXIMIZE THE VALUE OF THIS PLAY

→ Keep in mind that it's everyone's job to build and reinforce an experience-first culture; it's not just the responsibility of one person (e.g. CEO) or department (e.g. human resources).

→ Make it an organizational mandate to fund and invest in experiments, a core activity in user-first culture.

→ Hire based on mindsets and an ability to demonstrate alignment to the cultural pillars.

→ Avoid a "big bang" cultural transformation. Focus on a few critical behavior changes, led by the people who are most passionate about the change.

→ Create an environment in which there is psychological safety for people to openly share dissenting and critical views and in which they are valued for doing so.

→ Build in appropriate incentives. A good experience-first culture empowers individuals and encourages behaviors that reinforce the cultural pillars.

IN SUMMARY

Having the right user-centered strategy is only half of the equation. Even the strongest strategy cannot be executed inside a misaligned culture. Your user-centered strategy requires a user-first culture. Build and foster this culture by prioritizing the five mindsets and enabling activation agents to support the four cultural pillars.

RELATED PLAYS

Chapter 14: "User Empathy Play"

Chapter 17: "Shared Empathy Play"

Chapter 21: "Hiring Play"

Chapter 28: "Experience Metrics Play"

Chapter 36: "Cross-Functional Collaboration Play"

SHARED EMPATHY PLAY

How do I grow the collective user empathy of my organization?

User empathy is an organization-wide responsibility. The best user-centered innovation happens when every individual within an organization—across all departments, from the junior hires to the most senior staff—rallies around a common purpose and desire to make an impact for their users. UXReactor's "Shared Empathy" play allows you to measure, increase, and sustain your organization's place on the empathy scale, increasing user satisfaction while decreasing internal product churn.

Why Do You Need a Shared Empathy Play?

This play will allow your business to:

→ Create a purpose-driven organization;

→ Innovate in a user-centric manner;

→ Deliver more value-driving outcomes for the business;

→ Sustainably increase empathy at scale.

who are the key players in the shared empathy play?

ROLE	WHO'S INVOLVED	RESPONSIBILITIES
DRIVER	Experience strategist	• Implement methods to measure empathy; • Orchestrate activities for increasing empathy; • Establish systems for sustaining empathy.
CONTRIBUTOR	Experience design practitioners, cross-functional teams	• Support and participate in activities.

Shared Empathy

MEASUREMENT

- → Where is your organization on the empathy scale?
- → Which parts of your organization fall higher or lower on the empathy scale?

CATALYSTS

What kind of activities will you use to:

- → Increase your organization's knowledge of the user?
- → Make your organization care about the user?
- → Feel like they are making a difference for the user?

Example activities:

- → Regular offsites to visit users
- → Video vignettes
- → Shadowing user research
- → Taking support calls
- → Company-wide dogfooding
- → Spend "a day in the life"
- → User story share outs
- → User testimonials
- → Cross-team insights share-outs
- → Scenario simulations

SUSTAINABILITY

- → What processes will you put in place to ensure sustained user empathy?
- → What will the cadence of activities be?
- → How will resources be curated and accessed?
- → How will outcomes be communicated?
- → How will employees be encouraged to increase empathy?
- → How is leadership advocating for and reinforcing increased empathy?

PEOPLE

- → Who will be driving the outcomes of the initiative?
- → What internal teams do you need support from?
- → Will you need any internal or external experts/coaches?

RESOURCES

What tools do you need?

- → Instrumentation
- → Survey tools

How can time be allocated to allow the team to build empathy?

- → Monthly/quarterly basis
- → Team offsites

What do you need funding for?

- → Space to hold activities
- → Participant incentives

THE HOW

To run an effective shared empathy play, you need to be mindful of:

1. MEASURING Empathy

The empathy scale measures the degree to which your team is able to understand and relate to your users. It shows where empathy is strong or weak in your organization and informs your rollout strategy for the shared empathy play.

This assessment should be distributed to a representative sample in your organization, spanning all levels and positions. The final score will show you:

→ The breadth of empathy across your organization: How many teams have empathy for your users;
→ The depth of empathy in your organization: How strongly your organization empathizes with your users;
→ The level of intent of your organization: How strongly your teams and employees believe in your organization's purpose to solve problems for your users.

Based on the resulting scores, your organization will fall into one of the following five levels of empathy maturity:

→ **Level 1: Task-Driven**—Most members in non-sales or support roles of your organization have never interacted with a user. They perform tasks as they are assigned. Users are seldom or never brought into the innovation process, and teams experience significant churn. User insights and product decisions come from one or two groups in the organization.
→ **Level 2: SME-Driven**—A select few members of your organization understand your users and act as the subject-matter experts (SMEs) for the rest of the organization. The majority of the organization who are not in sales or support roles have never interacted with a user; they learn about users through these SMEs. User insights and product decisions come from a few groups in the organization.
→ **Level 3: Functionality-Driven**—As an organization, there is sufficient understanding of what users do day-to-day, and products and services are produced to meet these known needs. Users are brought into the innovation process to validate decisions. Innovation happens from a feature and functionality perspective, allowing users to do the jobs they need to perform. Along with sales and support, the product and UX teams interact with users to gather insights and help make product decisions.
→ **Level 4: Value-Driven**—The organization supports a regular cadence of research to identify opportunities for innovation. There is an understanding of the users in the context of the wider systems, and innovation is done collaboratively to drive value for the user through better and more efficient technologies. Users are brought in at multiple points of the innovation process, and many groups within the organization interact with users.
→ **Level 5: Purpose-Driven**—The user is front and center at all times. There is high compassion for the user across the whole organization; everyone is driven by the desire to solve problems and

make a meaningful impact for them. Innovation is an organization-wide collaborative effort. Users are brought in not just for research but to interact and share their experiences with everyone in the organization.

Track your organization's score over time and re-assess on an ongoing basis. This will become one of the organizational KPIs you track when measuring experience impact. (Chapter 28: "Experience Metrics Play")

2. The Right CATALYSTS for Increasing Empathy

Institutionalize activities that will increase your organization's empathy for your users. These activities should:

→ Increase your organization's knowledge of its users;
→ Make your organization care about its users;
→ Feel like they are making a difference for its users.

These activities should be present at multiple touchpoints within your organization. Increasing empathy is an ongoing process, so all employees in your organization, regardless of position, should take part in these activities on an ongoing basis.

 HERE'S AN EXAMPLE!

Zappos.com is particularly known for promoting a highly customer-centric culture, and they have incorporated ways for all of their employees to interact with customers at various parts of their employee journey. Their four-week onboarding process is the same for everyone: In addition to learning about the company culture and participating in team activities, they are also required to take customer calls. Additionally, during the busy holiday season, every Zappos employee spends a mandatory two hours in the call center to observe the customer service team interact with customers.

Here are some empathy-increasing activities you can try with your organization:

→ Regular offsites to visit users;
→ Library of video vignettes of users;
→ Shadowing user research;
→ Taking support calls;
→ Company-wide dogfooding;
→ Spend "a day in the life";
→ User story share outs;
→ User testimonials;
→ Cross-team insights share outs;
→ Scenario simulations.

3. The SUSTAINABILITY of Your Empathy

Instilling empathy is not a set-it-and-forget-it endeavor; it is an ongoing effort. To ensure sustained and growing user empathy in your organization, institute processes around:

- → The cadence of your activities;
- → Keeping teams and individuals accountable for taking part in the activities;
- → Curating and sharing resources (Chapter 29: "Insights Curation Play");
- → Communicating outcomes;
- → Constant advocacy and example setting by leadership.

In many organizations, even if multiple groups are conducting research, the findings often stay in silos. An effectively run shared empathy play coordinates multiple activities at once, but just as importantly, it also puts systems in place to ensure collaboration and conversation are happening.

 HERE'S AN EXAMPLE!

Coursera is a highly purpose-driven company whose mission is "providing universal access to world-class learning." Coursera puts this mission at the center of their culture by sharing learner stories on a regular basis, hosting annual "Make-a-thons," and encouraging employees to use the platform to provide feedback.

4. The PEOPLE to Nurture Empathy

Facilitating shared empathy in your organization will require collaboration between many teams and a primary driver to take ownership of the final outcomes. To be successful in this role, the driver will need a strong understanding of the importance of empathy, how to establish measures of success, and how to orchestrate cross-functional efforts. Typically this should be led by the CXO or another designated driver for an organization.

 HERE'S AN EXAMPLE!

In 2005, Jennifer Liebermann became the founding director of the Garfield Innovation Center, a think tank for Kaiser Permanente team members to "explore care solutions through hands-on simulations, quick prototyping, and technology testing." The culture of design thinking and experimentation at the Garfield Center has led to hundreds of innovation projects produced each year; successful initiatives are then piloted at Kaiser Permanente facilities around the United States and the world.

5. The RESOURCES to Support the Initiative

Dedicate resources to this initiative to enable its launch and continued success. Based on the activities and processes you put into place, assess your need for:

- → Tooling, such as instrumentation and survey tools;
- → Time allocation for all team members to take part in the activities;
- → Funding for a space to hold the activities, participant incentives, ongoing maintenance, R&D, and more.

Smart but Ineffective

A mid-sized startup was working on a medical billing product for the American market. Most of their design and engineering teams were in Asia while the rest of the organization and all their end users were in North America, and the company was experiencing significant issues in the developed build of their product. Their customers were beginning to complain about the quality of the product experience.

The company brought in UXReactor to review their product and related complaints. In the review process, we discovered that while the company had very smart and hard-working engineers, they had no idea of how the American health care and insurance systems functioned. Living and working halfway around the world, they did not share the same context as their users.

We addressed this problem by implementing the shared empathy play. We curated all the research insights in a consumable manner, so anyone globally could attend research sessions and virtually walk in their customers' shoes. We created posters of where the biggest pain points were in the user's journey and displayed them in different parts of their office space. And we created walkthrough videos of customers explaining their process.

This play became a mandated part of new teammate onboarding. With this deliberate shift in place, everyone in the company became much more empathetic to the user they were working so hard to serve, and the quality of both collaboration and of the product noticeably improved.

IN ORDER TO MAXIMIZE THE VALUE OF THIS PLAY

→ Lead by example: This play and its activities must apply equally to everyone in the organization, regardless of each individual's position. Those in leadership positions should encourage participation by first setting the example of making user empathy a priority.

→ Communicate impact often: Instill a sense of purpose by communicating the impact your organization's work is having on the users as often as you can.

→ Proactively prevent silos: Even in user-first organizations, silos happen. When learnings and insights are not cross-shared, different groups of the organization begin to think of users through their own particular lenses. This is not conducive to a collaborative innovation process.

IN SUMMARY

Empathy for your users must exist in every member of your organization, not just the product team. This requires deliberateness around what to measure, what to do to gain empathy, and how to sustain the system company-wide. Ultimately, user empathy empowers better decision-making that increases value for users, and happier users equal better business.

RELATED PLAYS
Chapter 14: "User Empathy Play"
Chapter 28: "Experience Metrics Play"
Chapter 29: "Insights Curation Play"

EXPERIENCE ECOSYSTEM PLAY
How do I build a seamless experience for the user across the entire ecosystem?

Many companies make the mistake of focusing too much on one user or one product. They overlook the ecosystem—the complex network of interconnected systems that their product and company inhabits. The experience ecosystem play enables you to see the forest before focusing on the individual trees. Building an experience ecosystem is a powerful tool for unleashing tremendous business value. It allows you to identify M&A acquisition targets, reveals the new complementary services your users want, and streamlines the workflow and processes that will bring delight to your customers.

Why Do You Need an Experience Ecosystem Play?

This play will allow your business to:

→ Understand the discrete but interdependent components that make up the greater ecosystem;
→ See the big picture before diving straight into details;
→ Understand how users perceive and interact with the ecosystem;
→ Build a shared understanding of the ecosystem, allowing teams to deliver an intuitive experience for the user.

Who Are the Key Players in the Experience Ecosystem Play?

ROLE	WHO'S INVOLVED	RESPONSIBILITIES
DRIVER	Experience strategist	• Uncover how users see and use the system; • Visualize the greater ecosystem; • Share insights with other stakeholders that improve different aspects of the business, team, and processes.
CONTRIBUTOR	• Experience practitioners • Peer practitioners	• Provide perspective and gain alignment.

Experience Ecosystem

CONTEXT

→ **System:** What system are you looking to contextualize?
→ **Users:** Who are the most important users in the system?
→ **Intent:** What are your users looking to accomplish?

DATA EXTRACTION

→ **Research Planning:** How do you plan to extract the information from the users?
→ **Object:** What objects do the users interact with along their journey?
→ **Relationship:** What are the relationships that exist between users, objects, and/or users and objects?
→ **Interconnections:** How do the intent, goals, processes, objects, and tools intersect?
→ **Mental Model:** How does your users describe the system?

SYNTHESIS

→ What are the commonalities across the data that you can align and standardize?

VISUALIZATION

→ How will you visualize the ecosystem in an intuitive and easily digestible manner?

COLLABORATION

→ What opportunities can you see after analyzing the ecosystem?
→ Who are the key players that I need to share the insights with?

THE HOW

To build an effective experience ecosystem, you need to be mindful of the following:

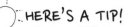
1. The CONTEXT of the User and the System

→ **System:** What system are you looking to contextualize? A system could be a product, platform, a business or organization, or a business unit.

PRODUCT	PLATFORM	BUSINESS OR ORGANIZATION	BUSINESS UNIT
Tesla Model X	Facebook Marketplace	Airbnb, local hospital	Intel customer Support division

→ **Users:** Who are the most important users in the system? Each system will likely have more than one user, and they will likely come from one of the following categories: revenue-generating customers, company employees, external vendors, or partners. List and then prioritize all the users who play a role in your ecosystem.

HERE'S AN EXAMPLE!

The users in a hospital ecosystem include: doctors, nurses, technicians, health care administrators, patients, patients' caretakers, pharmacists, government regulators.

A hospital looking to improve its patient care delivery experience would prioritize patients, doctors, and nurses.

→ **Intent:** Each of these users has a goal they want to accomplish in the system you have created. What is this goal? Identify your users' intent; this will serve as an anchor in creating the experience ecosystem.

HERE'S AN EXAMPLE!

If your user is a patient who was just invoiced for services provided by their physician, their intent could be avoiding a penalty by paying the bill on time.

If your user is an administrator who oversees five large hospitals in Maine, their intent could be ensuring the long-term profitability of the hospital system.

2. EXTRACTING DATA from User Research

Guided by your understanding of the system, users, and their intents, plan and conduct user research to extract the information necessary to visualize the ecosystem.

Research planning: There are multiple ways to extract information out of the ecosystem. You can either conduct user research (Chapter 30: "User Research Program Play") and/or speak with internal employees who interact with users on a regular basis.

Through these activities, try to understand the user and their journey navigating across the system to achieve an intended goal. Capture the following details:

→ **Objects:** Objects are artifacts that users encounter across the system while accomplishing certain tasks. Track the list of objects and organize them by user.

✎ HERE'S AN EXAMPLE!

An object could be a report, an email, a receipt, a statement, an article, a video.

→ **Devices and Channels:** How are your users receiving those objects? What devices (e.g. phone, desktop), channels (e.g. social media, phone, mail), and modalities (e.g. web, mobile) serve as the intermediary to transfer the objects? Make sure you group the devices and channels in conjunction with the corresponding object for easier mapping later on.

→ **Relationship:** Identify the relationships that exist between users, objects, and users and objects. Picture them as connected lines on a workflow or process map. Map the relationship between the elements, and denote flow by using arrowheads.

✎ HERE'S AN EXAMPLE!

A doctor [user] reads and updates [relationship] the patient's medical chart [object] through the patient portal [object].

→ **Users' Mental Model:** What users believe about the system at hand strongly influences how they use it. Mismatched mental models are common, especially with designs that are new or unfamiliar. That is why it's important to gather firsthand insights about the user's mental model. How does the user talk about the system in their own words? Don't assume—ask them to describe it. Anywhere there's a significant discrepancy, make a note; this may be an area where you should make the system conform to the user's mental models.

3. SYNTHESIZING Data to Find Patterns and Correlations

Synthesize and rationalize all of the data that you've extracted (e.g. objects, relationships, terminologies) across users. Individual users each have their own mental models, influenced by factors such as location, cultural background, technical knowledge, and functional silos. This may lead to different people using different terminologies to refer to the same objects or processes within the system. Thus, it's important to find commonalities, align, and standardize, employing further user research when necessary to bridge the gap.

HERE'S AN EXAMPLE!

What a billing specialist sees as distinct billing, sales, and support departments, a customer may just see as "customer support."

What one user calls a testing procedure specification (TPS) report, another calls a QA report.

4. VISUALIZING the Experience Ecosystem

Visualizing the full experience ecosystem, especially from a user's perspective, is a powerful tool: It presents an immense amount of data in an intuitive and easily digestible manner. Visualize the ecosystem by putting your user in the center. The other people or roles your user interacts with are denoted in circles, and the objects they receive or exchange are denoted in squares. The relationships and sequence of actions are illustrated using labeled arrows.

5. COLLABORATING Proactively across the Organization Based on Insights from the Ecosystem

Socialize the Experience Ecosystem

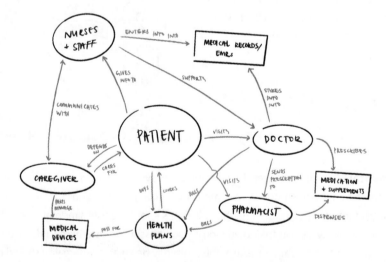

Share the ecosystem with the stakeholders who play a role in shaping your users' experience. Show them how their individual touchpoints with the customer contribute to the greater ecosystem. Establish a common understanding of the user and seek alignment across stakeholders.

Leverage the experience ecosystem's value for your team, business, or product experience as you:

→ Allow your team to focus (team);
→ Rationalize the design system to drive consistency across product and platforms (design);

- → Design and then build the best workflows based on the ecosystem (design);
- → Identify user experience gaps (design);
- → Identify and remove existing inefficiencies within cross-functional processes and departments (business);
- → Break down organizational silos that lead to a poor user experience (business);
- → Uncover gaps in business model, technology, or capability (business);
- → Pursue new markets that are complementary to your product and related experiences (business);
- → Forge new partnerships or identify mergers and acquisitions (M&A) opportunities (business).

Apple's Product Ecosystem

Apple has built a wildly successful user-centered ecosystem of devices (e.g. iPhone, iPad, Macintosh computers) and services (e.g. Apple Music, Apple Pay) that work seamlessly together. Users wear different "hats" on a daily and weekly basis (e.g. mom and spouse in the morning, manager during the day, friend on the weekend), and have different needs (e.g. on-the-go communication, mobile entertainment) corresponding to those roles. Along with designing products for these needs, Apple also has ensured that its users remain in the ecosystem "bubble" even while switching between devices (e.g. iPhone to desktop) and services (e.g. Apple News to Apple Music).

IN ORDER TO MAXIMIZE THE VALUE OF THIS PLAY

- → Just do it. You can build a first draft in a matter of hours and perfect it with dedication and commitment in less than one week. Immediately, the tool will allow you to see the broader context and get alignment across the organization.
- → Continually socialize the experience ecosystem to all the teams across the product.
- → Evolve and update the experience ecosystem on an ongoing basis. It's a living artifact that needs constant iterating, especially after changes in the organization or external forces have effected a material change to the user's experience.

IN SUMMARY

It's critical to think of the forest before the trees. The experience ecosystem play allows you to see the bigger picture and locate the deeply interwoven relationships that affect your user's experience. Use this play to keep your organization thinking, influencing, and collaborating at a higher system level and as a launch pad for follow-on business improvements or innovation.

RELATED PLAYS
Chapter 14: "User Empathy Play"
Chapter 28: "Experience Metrics Play"
Chapter 29: "Insights Curation Play"

EXPERIENCE ROADMAP PLAY
How do I create a roadmap centered around the experience of a user?

A clunky and frustrating end-user experience is the product of a siloed or inefficient organization. To mitigate that, an entire organization has to come together and collaborate cross-functionally by placing the user at the center of their world. An experience roadmap facilitates a clear and deliberate path that unites the entire organization. Grounded in insights, the experience roadmap play is a critical guide telling you what to focus on, when you should focus on it, and why.

Why Do You Need the Experience Roadmap play?

This play will allow your business to:

→ Gain clarity on which users and end-to-end experiences to focus on in a given time frame;

→ Get a clear picture of how to connect the user roadmap to the larger product and business plans;

→ Create a deliberate action plan that all internal teams and departments are aligned to and executing against;

→ Map scenarios or touchpoints across each user's specific journey in each system.

Who Are the Key players in the Experience Roadmap play?

ROLE	WHO'S INVOLVED	RESPONSIBILITIES
DRIVER	• Experience strategist	• Define experiences, scenarios; • Provide user insights.
CONTRIBUTOR	• Product lead • Engineering lead	• Support identification of scenarios; • Provide business insights; • Look for product aims.

MINDFUL CANVAS
Experience Roadmap

USERS

→ Which users have the greatest impact on the success of your business?

EXPERIENCES & SCENARIOS

→ What are all the experiences for one particular user?
→ What are all the scenarios for the identified experiences?

INSIGHTS

→ What are the key business insights for each of the experiences defined above?
→ What are the observed user insights?
→ What user and business metrics are impacted?

PRIORITIZATION

→ What are the most critical experiences to tackle in a defined time frame?
→ What is the Minimum Viable Experience (MVE) and prioritized scenario for each experience?

COLLABORATION

→ Which internal stakeholders should be brought together to deliver a loveable product experience?

THE HOW

To build an effective experience roadmap, you need to be mindful of:

1. Your USERS and Systems

Who are the users that matter most to the success of your business? Your users include your customers, of course, but they also include others involved in the entire experience ecosystem: suppliers, employees, and partners (see Chapter 18: "Experience Ecosystem Play").

HERE'S AN EXAMPLE!

In Amazon books' ecosystem, the users include readers, authors, publishers, copyeditors, and KPF formatters.

One of the biggest mistakes organizations make is focusing solely on paying customers and neglecting the employees who help troubleshoot, onboard, and interact with those customers and each other. A great user experience neither begins nor ends when customers buy your product. Instead, it is made up of the myriad interactions and touchpoints that customers experience with your larger organization—from the moment they first discover your product to the moment they are no longer a customer. These moments are made possible by your employees, partners, and suppliers. That's why it's critical to include these stakeholders as you define the users that matter most to your business.

2. Defining the EXPERIENCES and SCENARIOS Your Users Have within Your System

Prioritize the users that your organization wants to understand and for whom you want to orchestrate experiences. Once you've prioritized them, identify all the experiences and scenarios that matter.

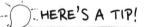
Experiences: An experience is an event or occurrence that leaves an impression throughout the user's life cycle with your organization. Experiences matter to your user or business, and when designed well, a great experience can have a magnified effect on your organization's success.

HERE'S AN EXAMPLE!

For example, the experiences for a product that focuses on cryptocurrency trading could include:

→ Crypto-currency learning experience   → Onboarding experience

→ Product awareness experience   → First trade experience

→ Account creation experience

If you have trouble identifying whether something is an experience, apply the test below. If it meets all three criteria, treat it as an experience.

→ Is this an important theme for your user or business?

→ Does it have a substantial scope?

→ Can you measure it?

Scenarios: Users move through many different individual scenarios in their overall experience of achieving (or not) their intended goal. Identify and record all of the possible scenarios in the experience you are evaluating.

HERE'S AN EXAMPLE!

For example, the scenarios for a product awareness experience could include:
→ Searching for key terms on Google on a desktop computer;
→ Viewing commercials on an iPad;
→ Seeing offline advertisements such as pamphlets and banners at a tradeshow;
→ Hearing from colleagues via word of mouth;
→ Discovering the product through print media such as a magazine.

Scenarios can be multi-medium, ranging from no-tech (e.g. friends, magazines) to higher-tech (e.g. computers, iPads, voice). To design a holistic and consistently superior user experience, all scenarios and accompanying modality need to be accounted for and designed.

3. Extracting Business and User INSIGHTS

Extract and map key business and user insights for each of the experiences defined above.

Key business insights across the customer life cycle typically fall into the following categories:

→ Adoption: conversion rates, customer acquisition cost (CAC), revenue per user (RPU);
→ Satisfaction: net promoter score (NPS), customer satisfaction score (CSS);
→ Engagement: drop-off rates;
→ Efficiency: cost/effort per experience;
→ Retention: renewal rates.

Key user insights are the actions, soundbites, observations, and research gathered directly from the user. These insights can include things that your user likes, dislikes, needs, feels, wants, clicks on, or does (Chapter 28: "Experience Metrics Play").

HERE'S AN EXAMPLE!

For example, here are some insights gained after conducting research on multiple users as they set up a new program on their computers:
→ Onboarding: Users want a guided setup process so they can learn from the process;
→ Efficiency: Users like to add multiple devices during setup so they can log in on their phone after work;
→ Engagement: Users need an easy and intuitive setup, as they lose motivation with the lengthy process and high volume of data that's currently being presented;
→ Troubleshooting: Users feel lost after starting the troubleshooting process, as there is no clear visibility into the status and resolution progress.

4. Planning for PRIORITIZATION of Experiences and Minimum Viable Experiences (MVEs)

In order to prioritize, consider your larger business goals. These could include:

→ Adoption (get new users);

→ Satisfaction (get more satisfied users who would recommend the product);

→ Retention (keep existing users);

→ Engagement (deepen engagement among current users);

→ Efficiency (help users accomplish the same task faster).

Triangulate your business and user insights you extracted with your business goals and objectives. This will help you surface the most user- and business-critical experiences to tackle in a defined time frame. Then, prioritize the experiences based on time frame, impact, and feasibility. The top experience(s) are the one all teams need to tackle together in a given time frame.

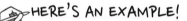

HERE'S AN EXAMPLE!

For example, if your business recently acquired an influx of new users and you've received numerous complaints about the cumbersome setup process, then onboarding is your top experience, and your teams should prioritize it.

Identify your minimum viable experiences (MVEs) and prioritized scenarios for each experience. An MVE takes into consideration the user's experiences across the entire journey and ensures that at least one deliberate scenario has been designed across all experiences in the users' journey.

HERE'S AN EXAMPLE!

Design for the "digital web ads" scenario for the awareness experience, the "guided tour" for onboarding, gamification for engagement, and "referral bonus" for advocacy.

The levels above MVE are more enhanced experience (MEE) and most transformed experience (MTE). Review Chapter 32: "Experience Benchmarking Play," which describes these levels in more detail.

5. Fostering COLLABORATION across Functional Silos

Bring the whole organization together when you are designing for the MVE and MTE. If you are working on perfecting your onboarding experience, involve the sales, implementation, and customer success teams to ideate, gather insights, seek feedback, and collaborate. A great user experience doesn't stop at one particular point. Your job is to orchestrate and bring together the needed parties to deliver a transformed product experience.

Who Is Handling Migration?

A multinational software company spent 18 months building and designing a product. When it finally launched, customers didn't want to buy it. They told the company that they had finally gotten the last deployment up and running, and they had no intention of ripping and replacing. "After all," they said, "who is going to help us migrate the data from that old system into this one?"

In this organization, migration was not the product team's responsibility; it was usually carried out by their professional services team or through a system integrator such us IBM or Deloitte. The company's professional service team wasn't ready or available to help migrate the data. It took 18 months to finally get everything up and running.

The company didn't think about the entire user journey and how it consists of interactions with many different parts of the organization (e.g. sales, product, professional services). If they had used an experience roadmap, it would have saved over a year's worth of time, resources, and lost revenue.

IN ORDER TO MAXIMIZE THE VALUE OF THIS PLAY

→ Create an experience roadmap for each user who matters to your business;

→ Make sure that each experience roadmap has an owner—either an experience strategist or another designated person;

→ Aim to finalize the experience roadmap in the first 90 days of defining the experience vision;

→ Expand the roadmap to account for variations in user contexts and technology modalities under each experience;

→ Document the experiences horizontally to identify any possible relationships, overlaps, or clashes;

→ Use the measuring experience metrics play to help define your experience metrics.

IN SUMMARY

Superior user experience doesn't happen by accident. It takes deliberate planning, strategy, and an experience-first mindset, and it requires the whole organization to come together to build a unifying experience for the user.

RELATED PLAYS
Chapter 14: "User Empathy Play"
Chapter 28: "Experience Metrics Play"
Chapter 29: "Insights Curation Play"

EXPERIENCE VISION PLAY

How do I create an experience vision that activates my organization?

Most of the organizations we interact with do not have a clear vision for their users' experience. An experience vision is the aspirational world-class experience you want your users to have and it's a north star for your team to understand, rally around, and align with on a consistent basis. The experience vision play will help you understand how to create and activate an effective vision in your organization.

Why Do You Need the Experience Vision Play?

This play will allow your business to:

→ Ensure that everyone in your organization is marching to the same goal;

→ Leapfrog your competitors by offering a differentiated and world-class experience;

→ Gain greater customer loyalty and satisfaction;

→ Help transform your organization into a purpose-driven organization.

Who Are the Key Players in the Experience Vision Play?

ROLE	WHO'S INVOLVED	RESPONSIBILITIES
DRIVER	• Experience strategist • Chief experience officer	• Identify and communicate the vision with their partners; • Govern the tracking of talent performance against the ladder.
CONTRIBUTOR	Peer practitioners, design collaborators (e.g. product manager, engineering manager)	• Collaborate closely with the driver to define and articulate the vision, using user insights; • Advocate for the vision, and share the vision with their respective organizations; • Operate on a day-to-day basis that aligns to the true intent of the vision.

MINDFUL CANVAS
Experience Vision

EXPERIENCE VISION

➔ What is the aspirational "new world" you want to create for your user?
➔ What is the aspirational world-class experience you want your product to deliver?

VISION-TYPE

➔ How will you articulate your vision in a way so that others can see, feel, and deeply understand?
➔ How will you "prototype" your vision?

ALIGNMENT

➔ Who needs to be involved to help you realize your vision?
➔ How, where, and when does the vision need to be communicated and reinforced?
➔ What are the ways to measure how well the organization has adopted the new vision?

PLANNING

➔ What are the different processes, artifacts, and documentation that need to be developed to reflect and support your vision?

GOVERNANCE

➔ How often will you measure the progress of your organization?
➔ What systems will you put in place to keep everyone aligned and accountable?

THE HOW

To run an effective experience vision play, you need to be mindful of :

1. Clearly Defining the EXPERIENCE VISION

To define a experience vision, identify all of the users who exist in the context of your system (Chapter 18: "Experience Ecosystem Play"). These could be external or internal users: a paying customer, a partner who helps deliver great customer experiences, an employee who orchestrates the behind-the-scenes.

For the key users that matter to the business, build the experience roadmap and prioritize the most critical experiences and the related needs and problems for the user (Chapter 19: "Experience Roadmap Play").

For the identified top experiences and problems through a market baselining play (Chapter 32: "Experience Benchmarking Play") further identify the most transformed experiences (MTE) by looking for inspirations and market analysis.

With the above understanding of the MTE's, answer this question:

What is the aspirational "new world" experience you want to create for your user as they navigate through your system?

Try to describe your answer in your words. Ideally you should be able to complete statements such as:

1. "We will create a world where [user]…"

2. "Imagine a world … where magically [describe experience] will happen in this [context]."

Statements such as these will help you articulate your experience vision.

→ We will create a world where merchants can interact with customers anywhere in the world.
→ Imagine a world where magically all the top candidates in the market will automagically be identified based on your previous interview notes, within seconds of you posting the role.

Collaboratively, ideate, and brainstorm the best experience that you would like to give the users of your system. An experience where all their identified pain points, inefficiencies as well as needs have been taken care of.

2. How Do You Prototype Your Vision, That is, How You VISION-TYPE It

Convert your vision from words into a format that allows others in your organization to see, hear, and feel the vision. Clickable screens are a classic "prototyping" option, but there are many other methods that can achieve the outcome in a more efficient and effective way. Storyboarding, enacting, and drawing a series of sketches are engaging and stimulating ways to communicate your vision. Or you can think even further out of the box and do a skit or make a short film. The goal is to show others the vision rather than telling them the vision. It'll be more effective and powerful when others can visualize the world that you see.

3. Socializing the Vision and Vision-Type for Organizational ALIGNMENT

Now it's time to start bringing your experience vision to life.

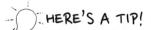 **HERE'S A TIP!**

Share your vision-type with new hires as a part of the onboarding process. The more you share the vision, the more likely it will happen.

→ **Stakeholder involvement:** First and foremost, identify the key individuals and departments within your organization that will bring this vision to life. Mobilize and rally them to align with the future-state experiences your company will offer. A great vision is contagious, and everyone should know the story and ask, "What will get us to the vision?"

→ **Communication plan:** Second, you need a robust communication plan. Think about the different platforms and media you can use to share, reinforce, and implement your vision. Build repetition and a regular cadence into your communication, sensitizing the broader team enough for the vision to take on a life of its own.

→ **Alignment:** Lastly, align your team on the plan and outcomes by identifying the target experience metrics (Chapter 28: "Experience Metrics Play") you are aiming for and the plan you will follow to get there (Chapter 35: "Product Experience Planning Play"). Remember that you will be working cross-functionally; therefore, your roadmaps should operate in sync and toward the same milestones.

4. Proper PLANNING to Set the Vision in Motion

The vision-type articulates the north star, while the experience roadmap (Chapter 19: "Experience Roadmap Play") provides you a roadmap to navigate toward the vision. Use the roadmap to obtain a holistic picture of the experience and what opportunities the team should prioritize.

Remember to mobilize every person and consider every artifact your organization produces, both internally and externally. They all play a role in creating a holistic and magical experience for the user.

Then, run micro-experiments that will help you refine and perfect the experience. Measure, iterate, and measure again.

5. Sustaining Progress through Ongoing GOVERNANCE

This play doesn't stop once you've created your vision. Keep going back to the vision. Has it evolved as a result of new technology or capabilities introduced in the market?

Use the experience and business metrics to benchmark how successful you are as you move closer to your vision.

Don't discard elements of the vision that were not prioritized early. Continue to curate your vision plan, as what may not be viable now may be viable in a few years' time.

The Knowledge Navigator

In 1987, Apple Computer's design team embarked on an ambitious project to envision what Apple's products and the user experience might look like in 2010, 23 years into the future. They vision-typed a few stories using short videos, one of which was called "The Knowledge Navigator." In the video, a UC Berkeley professor speaks to a digital assistant who helps him relocate and update his lecture notes, conduct a video call with a colleague (even Skype hadn't been invented yet), and pull an array of information from a large networked database (six years before the invention of the Internet).

In a time where people performed all computer actions with a keyboard and mouse, it was eye-opening to see sophisticated actions being performed using only voice and touch. It's also no coincidence that the iPads that shipped in 2010 had many of the capabilities and experience outlined in the 1987 video.

Apple built an experience vision, and it is clear that the organization used "The Knowledge Navigator" as the aspirational vision for "new world" for the next 23 years.

IN ORDER TO MAXIMIZE THE VALUE OF THIS PLAY

→ Define the vision before execution.
→ Communicate the outcome of the future experience. Refrain from specifying how the design would achieve that outcome.
→ Understand that "user" doesn't only refer to paying customers. Users can also include the individuals or organizations who contribute to a better end-user experience.
→ Have a vision for each of the users that matter in your organization.
→ Give your vision a name that everyone can easily anchor to and recall.
→ Enlist others for help. Build a community of advocates so that the words will travel further.
→ Practice curating your vision on a regular basis. What may not be feasible now may become possible as time progresses.

IN SUMMARY

Most organizations don't have a vision of what their user experience should be. If you want to compete meaningfully in the marketplace, you need a vision of experiences for each user you care about. Invest time in articulating one and mobilizing a plan around it; this will exponentially shift your company and product trajectory.

RELATED PLAYS

Chapter 14: "User Empathy Play"
Chapter 18: "Experience Ecosystem Play"
Chapter 19: "Experience Roadmap Play"
Chapter 28: "Experience Metrics Play"

Chapter 32: "Experience Benchmarking Play"
Chapter 34: "Design Problems and Opportunities Play"

HIRING PLAY
How do I hire Experience Practitioners?

Hiring experience practitioners is a critical step in transforming your organization. However, many companies focus too much on tools and technical proficiency rather than on the mindsets and problem-solving skills of their prospective employees. This play serves as a guide to help you hire the experience practitioners that you need to fuel business growth.

Why do you need the Hiring Play?

This play will allow your business to:

→ Recruit experience-centric practitioners with the relevant skills and mindsets;

→ Develop an effective hiring process based on industry standards and best practices;

→ Find the necessary talent to propel your business forward.

Who are the key players in the hiring play?

ROLE	WHO'S INVOLVED	RESPONSIBILITIES
DRIVER	• Chief experience officer	• Define the hiring criteria; • Facilitate the selection process; • Solicit and consolidate feedback from interviewer(s).
CONTRIBUTOR	• Experience practitioners (e.g. strategist, user researcher) • Peer practitioners (e.g. product manager, engineering lead) • Executive leadership (e.g. CPO)	• Conduct interviews; • Collaborate to define the hiring criteria; • Provide interview feedback; • Debrief on candidates with the hiring panel.

MINDFUL CANVAS

Hiring

ROLE

➔ What is the role you are looking to hire?
➔ How does this role fill or contribute to the needs of the larger team and organization?
➔ How do you source the role?

COLLABORATORS

➔ Who should be involved in the interview process?
➔ Do you have a diverse group to ensure a diversity of opinion to contribute to the final decision?

CRITERIA

➔ What are your organizational values? What would make the candidate a great cultural fit?
➔ Do they exhibit the necessary mindsets?
➔ Does the candidate have the relevant background and experiences to succeed in this role?
➔ Do they have the needed soft skills?

PROCESS

➔ What are the steps in the recruiting process? (i.e., resume review, phone interview, portfolio review, design exercise, data gathering and decision)

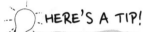
THE HOW

To run an effective hiring play, you need to be mindful of:

1. The ROLE

In addition to chief experience officer, there are five roles that make up the experience practice: experience strategist, user experience researcher, interaction experience designer, visual experience designer, and content experience designer.

Prioritize the roles based on the maturity of your organization, with the eventual goal of building the full practice with individuals who possess specialized skills.

ORGANIZATIONAL MATURITY	HIGHEST PRIORITY ROLE	TYPICAL PRACTICE SIZE	TYPICAL TENURE RANGE FOR EXPERIENCE PRACTITIONERS
Early-stage company	Interaction designer	1–3 practitioners	Between 3 and 5 years
Mid-sized company	Experience strategist	4–8 practitioners	Between 1 and 6 years
Large enterprise	CXO	9+ practitioners	Between 0 and 15 years

Remember that hiring good experience practitioners is not an easy job. As the organization matures, be more flexible with hiring on both extremes of the experience range to ensure sustainability.

Once you have defined the role, go to the places where great talent is most likely to reside. For junior practitioners, go to colleges with design and innovation programs or clubs. Get referrals from company employees, or look for individuals who are at or have worked for organizations known for experience-centricity.

2. Involving the Right Internal COLLABORATORS to Conduct Interviews and Evaluate Candidates

Given that the whole UX design practice is highly collaborative, involve the relevant internal collaborators to help you make the right hiring decisions. It's best to have a diverse group of interviewers across seniority, backgrounds, and expertise to be able to come to the decision table with different insights, observations, and perspectives. At a minimum, involve stakeholders from the products and engineering team because these are teams who will most closely collaborate with the experience designer (Chapter 10: "Getting the Right People Right").

3. Building a Multifaceted Hiring CRITERIA

Define the list of criteria that would make you want to extend an offer of employment. Depending on the specifics of the role, you may want to add a few more categories or choose to overweight certain categories over others. However, your standard list of hiring criteria for all experience practitioners and leaders should include the following:

→ **Cultural Fit:** The candidate will not thrive if their own values are misaligned with those of the organization. Each teammate in the organization plays a key role in building and reinforcing the organizational culture. Therefore, throughout the interview they must demonstrate a fit to the organization's value system and a proven ability to exhibit the cultural pillars of experience design: empathy, collaboration, ideation, experimentation, and iteration. (Chapter 16: "Culture Design Play"). For example, a candidate might demonstrate empathy by grounding their designs in user insights.

→ **Mindset Alignment:** Mindsets are indicators of how likely the candidate will thrive in the organization over the long term. There are five mindsets we recommend organizations look for during its interview process: design, experience, systems, business, and outcome. (Chapter 10: "Getting the Right People Right"). After the interview process, assess mindset alignment by asking the following questions: Can the candidate think about the bigger picture? Can they demonstrate problem-solving prowess? Can they think about the larger system and the interconnections around a particular problem? How interested are they in continuously growing and learning?
To evaluate an outcome mindset, ask the candidate, "Tell me about a time when you delivered an impact for your team." From their response, you can assess their understanding of impact and the tangible outcome they drove.

→ **Technical Fit:** Does the candidate have the relevant background and experiences to succeed in this role? Have they demonstrated their ability to execute quality design? If they are a lateral hire or a career switcher, what experiences are transferable that would indicate they will more likely succeed? At UXReactor, all experience designers interact and closely collaborate with the client on a daily basis. Therefore, we value candidates who have had prior client-facing roles (e.g. sales, business development, consulting) because we know they will be more likely to thrive at our company.

→ **Soft Skills:** An experience practitioner needs to be able to communicate their designs to non-designers, collaborate, and be proactive in reaching across the organization to bridge organizational silos. They need to care for the user, the larger business, and themselves to continuously learn in this growing profession. They also need to have an ownership mentality and take on responsibilities to deliver the best experience for the user.

Five Differentiators of an Awesome Practitioner vs. Mediocre Practitioner

MEDIOCRE PRACTITIONER	AWESOME PRACTITIONER
Describes the UI and screens by showing before and after designs.	Describes the user, their journey, and how they have solved the problems effectively.
Can only answer questions related to their skills and artifacts.	Can answer questions related to other areas such as product, business, and engineering. For example: Why did you build this feature? Why not build it for another user?
Only knows about the requirements given to them. For example: "I did this because the PM identified this on their backlog."	Has an opinion on what the top experience problems are for the system they are designing.
Is oblivious to the larger product and user ecosystem. For example, they would struggle answering: "If a design decision was made in one part of the flow, where would be the impact across the larger ecosystem?"	They can clearly describe the experience ecosystem, and how all the dots connect for the product and the user.
They "talk" about experience and participate in brainstorming.	They evangelize the experience mindset. They are also comfortable with rapid ideations, "own" the whiteboard, and can think on the go with the pen/pencil/marker.

4. Develop an Experience-Specific Recruiting PROCESS

Now that you know the criteria, develop a hiring process that is customized for experience practitioners, using the following components:

→ **Resume Review:** Resume review is an internal step designed to find technical fit by examining candidates' prior background and experiences. The key question to answer is: How likely will this candidate succeed in this role?

→ **Phone Interview:** The phone interview is your first real-time interaction with the candidate. The goal at this stage is to assess cultural fit and their level of motivation for joining your team. Treat the phone interview as a conversation you are having with the candidate. A good cultural fit is also one that adds diversity of thoughts, background, and perspective to enrich the team. Provide opportunities to learn more about the person beyond their professional background.

At UXReactor, this is the time we "scare" candidates by being candid about all the potential challenges they may face if they were to join the firm. Be upfront and make sure it's a mutual fit early on.

→ **Portfolio Review**: A portfolio review gives the candidate an opportunity to present their best work and an opportunity for the organization to evaluate the breadth and depth of the candidate's design experience. Though every portfolio is different, the portfolio review gives the organization insights into the candidate's design philosophy, their previous impact, and their communication skills. Assess their ability to articulate the following:
   → What was the problem? (Provide context.)
   → Why was it important? (Explain the relevance of this problem.)
   → How did they go about solving it? (Discuss process.)
   → How do they know they solved it? (Share results.)

→ **Design Exercise:** A design exercise allows the interviewer to assess the quality of the candidate's work, the soundness of their thought process, and how well they speak about and rationalize their design. Typically, a design exercise is provided after the portfolio review and is centered on a design problem. The design problems themselves can run the gamut from the fantastic ("How would you design a time machine?") to the very specific ("How would you design the checkout flow for ABC company?"). Furthermore, a few defined constraints, such as time and scope, typically accompany the design problem. The key qualities to assess are how well they understood the problem, stated their assumptions, navigated ambiguity, structured their thought process, communicated their design, and engaged the interviewers.

→ **Data Gathering and Decision**
The hiring process can span weeks and involves a number of different stakeholders across the organization. It's critical to have a process in place to collect and consolidate all of the inputs throughout the stages of the interview process in a timely manner. Furthermore, data should be collected on an individual basis and in confidence to avoid biasing other interviews and the hiring decision.

Zero to 12 in Three Months

We were tasked with building a design team from scratch for a Fortune 100 company. The team on the ground had never interviewed or hired a designer, so no processes had been built. The recruiter didn't know how to screen portfolios and could no longer filter candidates with keyword searches, which is what they were accustomed to when hiring for other roles.

We built a hiring process similar to the one described in this play. It took us a couple of months to develop the roles, design an interview process, coach the team, and define the scoring criteria used to evaluate the candidate. Once the entire system was established, the company successfully grew its team from 0 to 12 members in less than three months. Each teammate was able to immediately operate at a much higher level given their success and alignment throughout the rigorous hiring process.

You are only as strong as your team. Invest in the necessary time upfront to develop a rigorous process. You'll get quality talent, and rigor today will minimize potential headaches tomorrow that result from poor performance and a bad cultural fit.

IN ORDER TO MAXIMIZE THE VALUE OF THIS PLAY

→ The candidate is a user in your system. Give them a great candidate experience by treating the interview as a two-way dialogue, and make them feel valued and respected.

→ Don't place too much weight on technical background. Skills and knowledge can be taught, but attitude and mindsets cannot.

→ Have a diverse group of interviewers across backgrounds, experiences, and departments for a more well-rounded evaluation of the candidate.

→ Reflect on and continue to evolve your process. It'll only get better over time.

→ It takes approximately six to nine months for an experience practitioner to be fully effective after they've been hired. This timeline can be expedited if onboarding activities have been designed to get them familiarized with the context around the user, business, and product in the first two months.

IN SUMMARY

A great experience practice starts with hiring the right talent. Adapt your hiring processes by revisiting how you define and source the role, what the right evaluative steps (e.g. design exercise, portfolio review) and hiring criteria are, and which cross-functional decision makers should be involved. Your talent is your greatest asset. Therefore, invest in developing the best hiring process today to reap the benefits later.

RELATED PLAYS

Chapter 16: "Culture Design Play"

22

CAREER LADDER PLAY

How do I enable Experience Practitioners to grow professionally in their careers?

The experience practice is not a collection of skills; it is an emerging profession. This play will help your organization define a professional career ladder for experience practitioners that grooms them to be future strategic business leaders, all the way to the CXO.

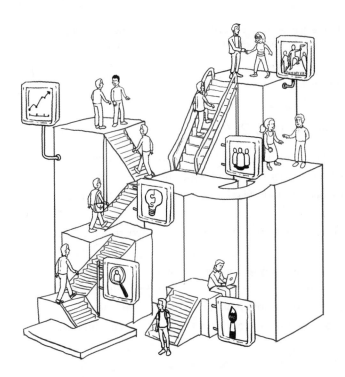

why do you need the career ladder play?

This play will allow your business to:

→ Develop a systematic way to evaluate and advance experience practitioners using proven techniques;

→ Quickly elevate experience maturity in your organization;

→ Start realizing business growth through user-experience design.

who Are the key players in the career Ladder play?

ROLE	WHO'S INVOLVED	RESPONSIBILITIES
DRIVER	• Chief experience officer	• Facilitate the development of the career ladder; • Govern the tracking of talent performance against the ladder.
CONTRIBUTOR	• Experience practitioners (e.g. user research, visual experience designer) • Peer practitioners (e.g. design operations, human resource manager)	• Influence the development of the career ladder.

Career Ladder

INDIVIDUAL RESPONSIBILITIES

Role
→ What is the experience practitioner role?
→ Where does it fall on the career ladder?

Mindsets
→ What mindsets are necessary for this role?
→ What level of mastery is required for each mindset?

Decision Making & Judgment
→ What decisions is this role responsible for?

ORGANIZATIONAL IMPACT

Org Experience Maturity
→ How will this role contribute to upleveling the organization's experience maturity?

People Management
→ What are the formal and informal people-management responsibilities?

INTERPERSONAL DYNAMICS

Influence
→ What level of influence does this role exhibit?

Collaboration & Communication
→ Who will this role closely collaborate with?
→ What level of communication, both written and verbal, is required to excel in this role?

Scope of Impact
→ What types of responsibility and accountability is expected of this role?

NURTURING ENVIRONMENT

→ How can you foster a nurturing environment?
→ What behaviors should you cultivate?

GOVERNANCE

→ How can you manage and govern the career ladder and talent management on an ongoing basis?

THE HOW

To build an effective hiring play, you need to be mindful of:

1. Accounting for INDIVIDUAL RESPONSIBILITIES

→ **Role:** Identify each rung on your organization's experience practice career ladder. The strategist is one of the hardest levels to climb before becoming a CXO. It requires the individual to understand the business and develop high levels of competency across five mindsets, in addition to having increased levels of responsibility and a heightened ability to influence and collaborate with teammates and internal collaborators.

LEVEL	ROLE	CURRENT INDUSTRY DESIGNATIONS
1	Apprentice	Entry-level designer
2	Practitioner	Designer (operating at an individual contributor level)
4	Strategist	Director / sr. manager / manager
6	Chief experience officer (CXO)	Executive, VP, general manager

→ **Mindsets:** Mindsets should be one of the criteria you use to evaluate candidates when you hire and promote them (Chapter 8: "Mindsets of a User-Centric Organization"). As individuals advance their career, certain mindsets will become more critical.

MINDSET	APPRENTICE	PRACTITIONER	STRATEGIST	CXO
Design	M	M	H	H
System	L	M	H	H
Experience	L	M	H	H
Business	L	L	M	H Profit and loss (P&L) responsibility
Outcome	L	M	H	H

(Key: L-Low; M-Medium; H-High)

→ **Decision-Making and Judgment Capabilities:** As individuals advance along the CXO track, their scope and responsibilities begin to increase. They will have more sources of information and more decisions to make that will have ripple effects on other departments, teams, and the overall business. Therefore, their ability to make sound judgments in a timely manner is key, a quality that will be more business-critical as the individual advances in the organization. Systematically evaluate their abilities in this category by taking a sample of their decisions over the past three or six months. What results did they drive from their decisions?

2. Factoring in Opportunities to Make an ORGANIZATIONAL IMPACT

→ **Scope of Impact:** Evaluate a talent based on the outcome they drive, not the output they create. What an individual can achieve increases in scope over time. For instance, an apprentice should be expected to affect deliverables. As they progress in their career, their scope of impact will increase to project, product, products, users, and finally, organizational and profit and loss (P&L) as a CXO. The CXO is responsible for overseeing and operationalizing the user experience across the entire organization. They also have P&L ownership responsibility, delivering top-line and bottom-line impact for the business. Regardless of seniority, all levels are held accountable to delivering results for the business and the user.

	APPRENTICE	PRACTITIONER	STRATEGIST	CXO
Impact	Deliverables	Project	User(s) experience	Organization + P&L

→ **Organizational Experience Maturity:** Many companies still only have a basic understanding of the importance of experience-centricity and the ways to integrate it across the organization. Therefore, one of the measures for each step along the career ladder is the individual's ability to identify and elevate the organization's level of experience maturity (Chapter 23: "Experience Transformation Program").

→ **People Management:** Early on, individuals are responsible for their individual actions and can serve as informal mentors to others. Later on, they will have formal people-management responsibilities, and will be accountable for the collective unit's ability to deliver outcomes. Below is a depiction of the formal and informal people-management expectations across levels.

CATEGORY	APPRENTICE	PRACTITIONER	STRATEGIST	CXO
Mentorship	Mentors new hires	Grooms lower rung	Educates cross-functional teams	Educates the market
Team management	N/A	Individual(s)	Product suite/ business unit	Organization

3. Developing INTERPERSONAL DYNAMICS Muscle

→ **Influence:** Influence is defined as "the capacity to have an effect," whether on another person, team, process, character, or behavior. Regardless of whether formal influence exists, each level still has the ability to have an effect. The individual's level of influence should increase as they progress up the ladder. Strategists and CXOs both are visionaries. Strategists are visionaries at the product level, and CXOs are visionaries at an organizational level, inspiring the whole organization to use user experience as an engine for innovation.

LEVEL	CHARACTERISTICS
Doer	They influence others to complete tasks or deliverables, following a predefined way of doing things.
Manager (Influencer)	They influence teams to experiment and go beyond the known knowns in achieving a certain goal. They are creative in managing teams to achieve outcomes.
Experience transformed	They are passionate and hold differentiated thoughts that inspire others to view the world through a new lens. They inspire behavior change and create movements.

→ **Collaboration and Communication**: Collaboration and communication are table-stake qualities at all levels. Experience practitioners are expected to seamlessly collaborate with stakeholders across the business. It's imperative that they are good teammates and have both the written and verbal communication skills to crisply convey an experience, design, or recommendation.

4. Fostering a NURTURING ENVIRONMENT

Practitioners need a nurturing organizational environment to grow, lead, and thrive. A nurturing environment is one where individuals are not afraid of making mistakes because they feel supported by their team, leaders, and organization. Such an environment provides ample opportunities to continuously challenge individuals to keep learning and growing. Below are some common behaviors of a nurturing environment:

→ The organization sponsors both internal and external training to develop critical and new skills and mindsets such as communication, business acumen, people management, or interpersonal dynamics at different stages of one's career;
→ Lunch-and-learns and cross-functional knowledge-sharing occur on a regular basis;
→ Teammates are constantly groomed to take on bigger challenges consisting of responsibilities that are "above their level," such as having the architect lead a workstream;
→ Teammates and leaders are not afraid to be vulnerable and share failure stories;
→ "Sandbox" environments are created to test and build new skills and qualities, such as a hackathon to practice design and innovation.

5. Ensuring Ongoing GOVERNANCE

The career ladder is not only a living document that can be adapted, it also is a talent management system that needs to be managed and governed on an ongoing basis. Develop processes for ongoing talent training, review, and grooming practices. In addition, plan for an annual salary and compensation review session to ensure your talent is properly compensated and incentivized.

A Leaky Talent Problem

After spending eight years as the only designer at a medium-sized technology company, Jake told his manager it was time. He wasn't growing professionally anymore. So he left the company to pursue new opportunities. Jake is not alone. Organizations are losing talent faster than they can groom and retain them.

There are three main reasons designers leave. First, they feel like they are stagnating. Second, they don't see a viable career path defined for them where they are continuously challenged and nurtured. Third, they don't have the necessary support of a full and specialized team to meet the growing requests from the organization. Most organizations treat design as a means to an end—design a couple of screens for the product launch, or improve the look and feel to have the visuals be on par with those of their closest competitors. They don't view design as a business-critical function where designers are strategic leaders who can have a powerful influence on the business.

Unfortunately, these underlying issues ultimately lead to employee turnover. Turnover is expensive and can cost up to 1.5 to 2 times an employee's annual salary, especially when you consider the resources spent recruiting, hiring, and training. To prevent this massive resource drain, invest in building a full team and a robust career ladder for the individuals on the team like Jake.

IN ORDER TO MAXIMIZE THE VALUE OF THIS PLAY

→ Advance and promote talent based on outcome and impact vs. timeline and tenure;

→ Complement your existing ladder with the qualities identified in this play;

→ Provide ample opportunities for experience practitioners to create greater organizational and cultural change.

IN SUMMARY

Experience design is an emerging profession, not a collection of skills. And if you don't treat it as a profession, you'll keep leaking talents. It's imperative to build a career ladder that allows you to manage, groom, and develop your design talent, so your organization can fuel its business growth through user experience design.

RELATED PLAYS

Chapter 17: "Shared Empathy Play"
Chapter 18: "Experience Ecosystem Play"

Chapter 23: "Experience Transformation Program Play"

CHAPTER 23

EXPERIENCE TRANSFORMATION PROGRAM PLAY

How do I build a robust program around Experience Transformation?

Many leaders believe that the secret to becoming a user-first company like Airbnb and Apple is investing in a team of designers. In reality, it takes much more—it requires an organizational system that supports a user-first strategy. A system that is geared to nurture and support the bv.d system that was discussed in Chapter 7.

The experience transformation program play deconstructs all the critical components to enable you to define, operationalize, and govern an organizational system around this strategy.

Why Do You Need the Experience Transformation Program Play?

This play will allow your business to:

→ Realize meaningful return on investment (ROI) on your investment in experience design;

→ Build a sustainable system with the proper tools and techniques for every facet of an experience design program;

→ Achieve market differentiation and long-term value by implementing an organizational focus on users and experiences;

→ Understand how to use experience design to drive growth and innovation.

Who Are the Key Players in the Experience Transformation Program Play?

ROLE	WHO'S INVOLVED	RESPONSIBILITIES
DRIVER	• Chief experience officer (CXO)	• Owns the vision and defines the strategy; • Builds the program; • Measures impact and results; • Drives organizational shifts.
CONTRIBUTOR	• Experience practitioners, internal partners, and stakeholders	• Support the vision through daily actions; • Collaborate with teams across the organization; • Report metrics and data.

MINDFUL CANVAS

Experience Transformation Program

EXPERIENCE VISION

→ What aspirational, world-class experiences do you want to deliver to your users?
→ What prioritized experiences and scenarios will create a superior user experience?

ENVIRONMENT

→ How can you foster an environment so people can do their best work?
→ What should your culture be?
→ What about the physical environment?
→ What tools should be in place to encourage greater collaboration?

OUTCOMES

→ Who are your users? What are their needs, values, motivations, and context?
→ What are your business needs, motivations and goals?

PROCESS

→ What processes do you need to support the experience design program and generate value to the business?

PEOPLE

→ Who is accountable for wow-ing users and winning their loyalty?
→ What are the "must-have" mindsets?
→ How will you manage your talent?

GOVERNANCE

→ How should you monitor and assess the program performance on a regular basis?
→ What metrics should you be measuring?

THE HOW

To run an effective experience transformation program, you need to be mindful of:

1. Articulating OUTCOMES for the User and Business

Distill a broad user-first strategy into tangible and measurable outcomes for your user and business. Compose well-defined outcome statements to provide a full, clear visualization of your desired end state. It should be both:

→ **Qualitative:** describe the impact the achievement of the future state would have on the user and business;

→ **Quantitative:** articulate the expected numerical units of improvement of the user-first strategy.

High-level approach + direction of improvement (i.e. increase, decrease) + unit of improvement (i.e. time) + measurement of improvement where possible (i.e. 5%)

2. Crafting an EXPERIENCE VISION to Reinforce Your Strategy

Drawing on your knowledge about the user, articulate experience visions for each key user that details an aspirational, world-class experience you want to deliver (Chapter 20: "Experience Vision Play").

An experience vision should consist of both a user vision and a product vision; it should reinforce the user-first strategy and outcomes you've articulated.

→ **User:** "We will create a world where [user]…"

→ **Product:** "In this new world, [your product] will enable…"

To put your vision into action, have a user-first strategic roadmap where decisions are made based on user journey, needs, and opportunities (Chapter 19: "Experience Roadmap Play") and an execution plan so that cross-functional teams are aligned and working toward the vision. (Chapter 35: "Product Experience Planning Play").

Build an organizational system to operationalize the strategy and the vision. An organizational system has four main components: mindsets, people, process, and environment. Start by investing the right talent and cultivating the critical mindsets.

3. Recruiting and Grooming the Right PEOPLE to Drive the Vision Forward

If you were to remodel your home, you'd recruit people with highly specialized skills (e.g. architect, carpenter, electrician, plumber) to make sure the project will be a success and that your money will not be wasted. In the same way, your organization needs the right people with the necessary skills and experience to bring the experience visions and the experience to life. Consider the following "must-haves" as you bring on people for your experience design program:

→ **Hiring for skills**—Effective experience design programs require practitioners to have five critical skills: experience strategy, user experience research, interaction experience design, visual experience design, and content experience design (Chapter 10: "Getting the Right People Right"). Based on the size and maturity of your organization, start building your experience practice by hiring individuals with one or more of these specialized skills. Your goal is developing the full practice with individuals who possess all five.

ORGANIZATIONAL MATURITY	HIGHEST PRIORITY ROLE	TYPICAL PRACTICE SIZE	TYPICAL TENURE RANGE FOR EXPERIENCE PRACTITIONERS
Early-stage company	Interaction designer	1–3 practitioners	Range between 3 and 5 years
Mid-sized company	Experience strategist	1–3 practitioners	Range between 1 and 6 years
Large enterprise	CXO	9+ practitioners	Range between 0 and 15 years

→ **Hiring for Mindsets**—As experience practitioners evolve to be multi-disciplinary and holistic problem solvers, they need to master five mindsets—design, experience, systems, business, and outcome—over the course of their professional career (Chapter 8: "Mindsets of a User-Centric Organization"). Continuously groom, challenge, and improve your talent by building a career ladder that supports mindset growth.

MINDSET	APPRENTICE	PRACTITIONER	STRATEGIST	CXO
Design	M	M	H	H
Experience	L	M	H	H
Systems	L	M	H	H
Business	L	L	M	H Profit and loss (P&L) responsibility
Outcome	L	M	H	H

(Key: H - High; M - Medium; L - Low)

→ **Driver or Experience Leadership**—Organizations need a single leader who is accountable for wow-ing users and winning their loyalty. This experience leader or chief experience officer (CXO) is responsible for overseeing all aspects of the experience design program. CXOs can come from a variety of backgrounds, but they must exhibit an experience mindset and be able to navigate the dynamics of a large organization to be effective in their role. See Chapter 10: "Getting the Right People Right."

→ **Partners**—The experience transformation play requires a significant amount of collaboration between the internal and external stakeholders who are supporting the vision of a superior user experience. These stakeholders include the CEO, the executive leadership team, practitioners from other internal departments and teams, channel partners, vendors, and systems integrators (Chapter 10: "Getting the Right People Right").

4. Developing the Right PROCESS to Achieve Your Desired Results Every Time

Too many high-potential organizations lack the robust and comprehensive processes needed to consistently deliver value to the business and its users at scale. To operationalize your user-first strategy and vision, invest in building a robust set of processes supporting these four pillars:

→ **Experience design strategy:** Honing an organizational focus on experience design;
→ **User research insights:** Developing an organization's empathy for its users;
→ **Product thinking:** Building an organization's productization of great experiences, by identifying and prioritizing the right problems to solve;
→ **Design doing:** Ensuring experience design solutions are designed and implemented correctly.

A well-defined process sets the foundation for creativity and innovation. These cornerstone processes give you the ability to scale your effort and teams quickly without compromising on the quality and consistency of the result.

5. Fostering the Right ENVIRONMENT

A great organizational environment enables people to do their best work. A highly effective environment has a clear strategic vision and is empathetic, collaborative, diverse, and trusting. A number of factors make up the environment:

→ **Culture:** Build and sustain an experience culture that is highly empathetic and collaborative. One that constantly ideates and fully embraces running experiments on new ideas. In this culture, it's okay if the experiment fails because the organization views failure as a learning opportunity (Chapter 16: "Culture Design Play").
→ **Incentives, recognition, and empowerment:** Develop the right incentives structure to foster an environment that rewards seeking long-term solutions versus solving for today's problem. In addition, given a majority of organizations have yet to undergo experience transformation, individuals need to be sufficiently empowered to drive change and be recognized for wins along the way.
→ **Design space:** A well-designed physical space creates the environment for teams to focus and do their best work. It allows for collision of ideas, constant brainstorming, chance meetings, and knowledge sharing across functional silos.
→ **Tools:** Specialized tools make the completion of tasks more efficient. The right tools also allow for greater collaboration across distributed teams.

Tools for specific purposes:

Research
UserTesting, UserZoom, Optimizely

Design
Figma, UXPin, Mural

Communication
Slack, Teams

Project management
Trello, Asana

Curation
Dovetail, UserTesting, AirTable

Document sharing
Google Suite, Dropbox

6. GOVERNANCE to Monitor, Track, and Evaluate

In order to thrive and consistently achieve business and user impact, the experience transformation program needs to be regularly reviewed, curated, tracked, and measured. Govern these four categories:

→ Business and user metrics;
→ Organizational maturity;
→ Curation;
→ Experience debt.

Business and User Metrics: Quantifying how each element of your experience transformation program is affecting your business and user will enable you to gauge what's working and how to improve the program.

Metrics to assess business impact include:

→ Financial: sales revenue, profit margin;
→ Customer: leads per month, customer acquisition cost, cost/effort per experience, churn rate, net promoter score, customer life time value;
→ Employee: satisfaction, engagement, turnover;
→ Process: product-market fit, time to market, cycle time.

Metrics to assess user impact include (Chapter 28: "Experience Metrics Play"):

→ Logical metrics: time to completion, number of errors per task, success rate, number of clicks;
→ Emotional metrics: user satisfaction, level of confidence, perceived value, user empowerment.

Organizational Maturity: Continue to assess your organization's level of experience maturity—since that is closely correlated with the type of user experience and outcome your organization can deliver. Proactively identify ways to increase your organization's experience maturity.

ORGANIZATION'S MATURITY LEVEL	CHARACTERISTICS
Experience apprentice	This is the lowest level of experience maturity. Roles in the experience practices are still undefined and undifferentiated (e.g. jack-of-all-trades). A great deal of focus is given to visual design, and research is used to validate existing designs. Organizations that have an experience-apprentice level of maturity delivers MVE experiences (Chapter 32: "Experience Benchmarking Play").
Experience enlightened	The organization is beginning to understand how user experience can help achieve market differentiation and is investing resources to help make itself more experience-aware and mature. These organizations deliver enhanced experiences.
Experience transformed	User-centered design is seen as an engine that drives innovation. Experience practitioners have specialized roles, and a dedicated research team extracts user insights using a portfolio of methodologies. Users and their needs are fully ingrained across all departments and serve as a North Star for decision-making. These organizations deliver transformed experiences.

Curation: Curation calls for unprioritized ideas and insights to be visited regularly and even repurposed. An idea or insight you may not use today may be the holy grail three years from now (Chapter 29: "Insights Curation Play"). A design problem or opportunity you did not prioritize to resolve yesterday may be the highest-severity user problem today (Chapter 34: "Design Problems and Opportunities Play"). Maintain a library system that allows you to revisit and repurpose.

Experience Debt: Like financial debt, experience debt are problems that have not yet been fully addressed. Govern the amount of experience debt your organization is accumulating to ensure the balance does not become so massive that it significantly detracts from the user experience.

IN ORDER TO MAXIMIZE THE VALUE OF THIS PLAY

→ Approach it as a change management effort. Start by changing people's mindsets and adopt user-first thinking.

→ Be patient, and solicit support from leaders, executives, and your board of directors (BOD). Change management takes time.

→ View the program as a holistic system. You need to build and maintain every single facet of the program to realize value.

→ Curate unused ideas and revisit at a later date.

IN SUMMARY

Serendipity is not a strategy. A multifaceted experience transformation program is your gateway to achieving an insurmountable market advantage for your organization, product, or services. It requires building, operationalizing, and governing a holistic system. Be deliberate in the details to maximize your ROI.

RELATED PLAYS

Chapter 14: "User Empathy Play"
Chapter 16: "Culture Design Play"
Chapter 19: "Experience Roadmap Play"
Chapter 20: "Experience Vision Play"

Chapter 21: "Hiring Play"
Chapter 29: "Insights Curation Play"
Chapter 34: "Design Problems and Opportunities Play"

USER RESEARCH INSIGHTS

*"SUPPOSING IS GOOD BUT FINDING
OUT IS BETTER."*

-MARK TWAIN

USER RESEARCH INSIGHTS: INTRODUCTION
Building and activating the portfolio of insights

What Is User Research?

User research is the discipline of gathering, curating, and tracking user insights. It allows you to develop a deep empathy for the user and guides all subsequent experience design activities. The discipline of user research requires a high degree of rigor, and when done correctly, it has far-reaching effects, not only on the experiences you create for your users but also on your capacity for finding opportunity and mitigating risk.

1. The Impact of Research

No matter the field, intelligence is the basis behind every significant decision. Different types of organizations—military, financial, consumer goods—all depend on their intelligence analysts to collect data to derive meaningful insights. Where might product companies find such insights? User research.

Not investing in user research (due to its nature of delayed gratification) is a mistake because competitors can easily replicate small design attributes (visual, interaction) but can't easily copy the research's insights and organizational focus.

User research lays the critical foundation for all aspects of experience design by generating intelligence on who, what, how, and why to build. When user insights inform business decisions, effective outcomes follow. In fact, user research can be the most significant value-driving investment a company makes.

2. The Research Mindset

People with a research mindset constantly seek to discover and have an objective curiosity about the "why" behind the "what." Those with a research mindset:

→ Approach each situation with the intent to discover and diagnose before moving toward a solution;
→ Believe all insights are out there waiting to be found;
→ Extract design problems and opportunities directly from users;
→ Stay free from biases;
→ Are driven by a sense of purpose for the user.

> **"I did then what I knew how to do. Now that I know better, I do better."**
>
> – *Maya Angelou*

The research mindset is not reserved just for user research practitioners. On an organization-wide level, it drives a culture of empathy, discovery, and experimentation—the foundation for all user-centered innovation. It manifests in people pursuing user insights to drive their decisions, collaborating and knowledge-sharing with cross-functional departments, experimenting frequently, and being willing to take the more difficult route to deliver the most value to the end user.

3. Key Concepts

Here are the critical concepts and key terms to understand before diving into the user research plays:

A portfolio of insights is a framework that helps an organization pursue the right mix of research activities. It allows business leaders and product teams to gather user insights that help them see how they are doing now and where they could be in the future. Three types of research make up the portfolio of insights: formative, summative, sensorial.

→ **Formative research** provides foundational insights that inform where businesses should focus its priorities. Formative research includes methods such as ethnographic studies.
   When to use it? At the beginning stages of product development.
   What does it tell you? What user problems to focus on.

→ **Summative research** provides insights that validate the PX or UI of a product or service. Summative research includes methods such as usability studies.
   When to use it? During the design or development stage, when you have design stimuli—sketches, wireframes, visuals, a first build, etc.—that users can react to.
   What does it tell you? If and how well your design solves the problem.

→ **Sensorial research** provides insights that give an indication, or a "sense," of how a product is doing over time. Sensorial research includes methods such as NPS (net promoter score), click analysis, and recurring baseline studies.
   When to use it? After a product launch, as it will give you data on how users are using and feeling about the product.
   What does it tell you? If the product is working the right way and how it is performing over time.
   What to Expect in This Section

We've curated a list of plays that will enable you to create a sustainable and powerful user research practice within your organization. The user research plays will help you answer these critical questions:

→ How do I know which method to use to gather insights? (Picking a research method play)
→ How do I recruit the right participants for user research? (Research recruitment play)
→ How do I ensure rigor in my research? (Research quality play)
→ How do I measure the success and quality of my user's experience? (Experience metrics play)
→ How do I curate all the insights in my organization? (Insights curation play)
→ How do I run an effective research program? (User research program play)

These handpicked plays will allow you to leverage research as a strategic value driver.

CHAPTER 25

PICKING A RESEARCH METHOD PLAY

How do I know which method to use to gather insights?

There are many different research methods to choose from. This play will help you identify the best method(s) for gathering the insights that you need and ensuring the salience of the insights you collect.

Why Do You Need the Picking A Research Method Play?

This play will allow your business to:

→ Identify the appropriate type of method(s) to gather your desired research insights;

→ Identify the method(s) that align with your resources;

→ Ensure research will drive the intended value.

Who Are the Key Players in the Picking a Research Method Play?

ROLE	WHO'S INVOLVED	RESPONSIBILITIES
DRIVER	• User researcher	• Define study timeline; • Define the method; • Conduct research.
CONTRIBUTOR	• Experience practitioners, cross-functional teams	• Contribute research questions and domain-specific insights; • Provide existing knowledge on users; • Provide stimuli for any studies; • Define budget.

Picking a Research Method

CONTEXT

→ What is the current phase of user experience design you are in?

→ What types of insights are best suited for that phase of user experience design?

RESEARCH QUESTIONS

→ What insights do you need?

→ What questions do you need to answer?

LOGISTICS

In how many weeks/months do you need your insights?

How much budget do you have for

→ Research efforts?

→ Incentives?

→ Tooling?

PURPOSE

→ How do you plan on using this data?

→ Who will be using this data?

METHOD

→ Which method aligns with your needs and constraints?

THE HOW

To effectively pick a method, you will need to be mindful of:

1. The CONTEXT of Your Research

Identify your user experience design phase to determine what types of insights (formative, summative, or sensorial) you need and the best research method to use to find them.

PRODUCT DEVELOPMENT PHASE	TYPE OF INSIGHT NEEDED
Strategy and planning: early stages with no stimuli	Formative or sensorial
Design: prototyped stimuli	Summative
Development: prototyped and coded stimuli	Summative
Launched: live product as stimuli	Sensorial

2. The PURPOSE of the Study

Different methods will produce different types of data and insights. Therefore, in addition to identifying the type of insights you need, it is also important to define your purpose—how you will be using these insights. Will you be using the research to define product requirements? To make improvements on an existing product? To decide which ideas and user problems to strategically invest in?

According to Chrisian Rohrer, user research methods can be placed along two spectrums: attitudinal vs. behavioral and quantitative vs. qualitative.

→ **Attitudinal** methods focus on what users say and share. These methods are ideal for quickly collecting insights from the users' points of view or for when you need an explanation of why users do or think something. The caveat is that attitudinal methods rely on self-reported data, which may not always be accurate.

→ **Behavioral** methods are based on observation and focus more on understanding what users do and how they do it. This can be ideal for discovering user needs and behaviors.

→ **Quantitative** methods focus on numbers and scores. These methods are ideal for finding trends or establishing standard measures with larger sample sizes.

→ **Qualitative** methods focus on gaining a more descriptive understanding of behaviors that are hard to measure. They are ideal for diving deeper into the surrounding context and discovering the "why" behind what users do.

PURPOSE	TYPE OF DATA/INSIGHTS
Roadmap planning	→ Qualitative insights on unmet needs and opportunities in the market; → Quantitative insights on how pervasive the needs are; → Behavioral insights on what is most commonly used; → Attitudinal insights on what users want.
Requirements gathering	→ Behavioral insights on how users perform their tasks; → Qualitative insights on what pain points and needs exist.
Measuring and tracking product performance	→ Quantitative data on where issues are trending; → Attitudinal data on what users like and dislike.

3. The RESEARCH QUESTIONS You Want Answered

The types of questions you want to ask will also affect which method you use to gather the insights. Take inventory of the research questions that you have gathered throughout the design phases, and see if they call for attitudinal, behavioral, quantitative, or qualitative data.

 HERE'S AN EXAMPLE!

→ "How do users make decisions when shopping for a product?" would best be answered through methods that involve observation or a direct conversation.

→ "What parts of the design help or hinder the user?" would best be answered through methods that involve interactive stimuli.

→ "How pervasive are these problems and where do they occur most?" would best be answered through methods that involve quantitative data and larger sample sizes.

4. The LOGISTICS That Affect Your Study

Two types of logistics have to be factored in during the selection of the method: timelines and budget.

Timelines

Different research methods require different timelines, depending on elements such as:

→ Experiment design;
→ Study complexity;
→ Recruitment;
→ Preparation of stimuli or resources;
→ The time required to conduct the studies.

Work with your peer practitioners to determine when they will need the insights. This will determine which methods are possible within that time frame.

Methods such as surveys or unmoderated usability studies are more suitable if you need results quickly; other methods, such as in-depth interviews or ethnographic studies, require more time to complete.

Budget

→ **Research effort,** research execution, participant recruitment, and incentives all will affect cost, so make sure you know your budget before selecting a method.
Research effort includes the time it takes for your researchers to prepare, conduct, synthesize, and create artifacts for a study. This will directly affect the people or teams that need to be involved and how much time each needs to invest.

→ **Research execution** includes the cost of using any research tools to conduct research, such as card-sorting platforms, eye-tracking software, and lab bookings/equipments. Some methods, such as unmoderated usability studies, may require the use of additional task-programming tools and metric-tracking instrumentation. Make sure you're taking into consideration what tools you have available and what you may need to bring in.

→ **Participant incentives** will vary depending on the type of participant you're recruiting, their role, the duration of the study, and the amount of effort required from the individual to participate. Recruitment services or platforms may have additional costs and fees that will need to be factored in.

5. The Right METHOD Based on Your Needs and Priorities

Narrow down the ideal method(s) based on the parameters you've identified in the previous points. In the case where there is no exact fit, rank the parameters in order of impact and feasibility to loosen the criteria and find the next best option.

HERE'S AN EXAMPLE!

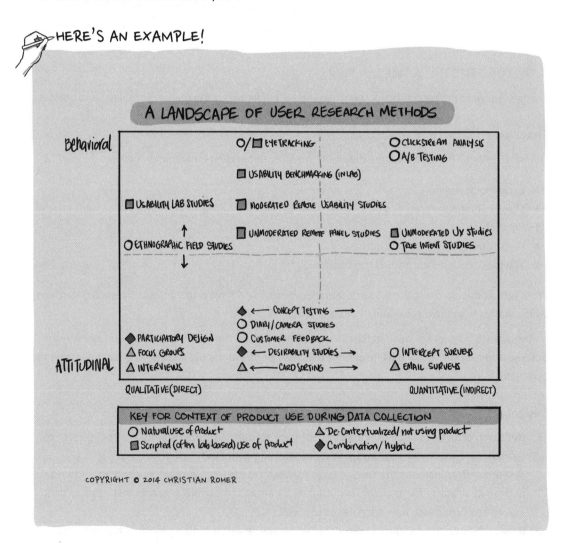

IN ORDER TO MAXIMIZE THE VALUE OF THIS PLAY

→ **Use more than one method in a single study.** Research methods are not mutually exclusive. Based on the goals of each research study, some questions can require a mix of methods, so use creative combinations of tools and methods to get the most accurate answers possible.

→ **Check the entire process.** Picking the right method will not guarantee the validity of your study. Make sure you are also identifying the right user, asking the right questions, synthesizing the data correctly, and communicating the insights effectively (Chapter 27: Research Quality Play).

IN SUMMARY

Make sure you evaluate your research method before conducting any study. Picking the right method(s) will improve the quality of your insights and increase the ROI of your research time and effort.

RELATED PLAYS

Chapter 26: "Research Recruitment Play"
Chapter 27: "Research Quality Play"

26

RESEARCH RECRUITMENT PLAY

How do I recruit the right participants for user research?

Identifying and recruiting the right participant for your study is the foundation for research success. Recruiting the wrong participant or selecting only a partial match will diminish the quality and breadth of insights that you gather. The research recruitment play will help you define participant screening criteria, plan recruitment logistics, and mitigate potential liabilities.

Why Do You Need the Research Recruitment Play?

This play will allow your business to:

→ Precisely define your ideal user;

→ Create a plan to find and recruit the right users to participate in your research study;

→ Avoid being prone to liability.

Who Are the Key Players in the Research Recruitment Play?

ROLE	WHO'S INVOLVED	RESPONSIBILITIES
DRIVER	• User researcher	• Establish recruitment criteria; • Execute recruitment efforts.
CONTRIBUTOR	• Research operations, design, cross-functional teams	• Support recruitment activities; • Contribute research questions and domain-specific insights; • Provide existing knowledge of users.

MINDFUL CANVAS

Research Recruitment

QUALIFYING CRITERIA

➔ What characteristics or traits does a user need to have in order to answer your research questions?
➔ What additional criteria have any of the contributors mentioned?

SCREENER QUESTIONS

➔ What questions do you need to ask to verify your participant's eligibility?

USER SEGMENTATION

➔ What are the known user segmentations that you will have to take into account?
➔ What specific type of user do you need to focus on?
➔ What specific demographic details do you want to know?

LOGISTICS

➔ How many participants do you need based on your selected research method?
➔ How and how much will you be compensating them?
➔ Who needs to be involved and/or informed?
➔ When is the study taking place?
➔ How will you schedule the participants?

CHANNELS

➔ Where will you be recruiting ideal participants?
➔ Where will you be able to find a sizable group of ideal participants?

BLACKLIST

➔ Are there any competitors from whom you should not recruit users?
➔ Are there any user types that you need to avoid?
➔ Are there any users that you can't recruit due to your organization's policies?

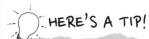
THE HOW

To run an effective research recruitment play, you need to be mindful of:

1. The QUALIFYING CRITERIA for Your Ideal Participant

Work with your peer practitioners to identify your research goals to determine the type of user you need to speak to and the qualities they need to have. Think through what the ideal user should know, be able to do, and what their context or environment should be like in order to answer your research questions.

Create a list of qualifying criteria to ensure that the right set of participants can be screened from a larger pool of candidates.

Typical criteria could include items such as (but not limited to):

→ Occupation;
→ Language spoken;
→ Familiarity to specifics tools or methods;

→ Type of tasks they handle;
→ What context should be exposed to;
→ What features and products do they use.

Note that the more criteria you have, the more difficult it will be to recruit, however, it would result in more accurate insight..

 HERE'S AN EXAMPLE!

Research question: How do customer service representatives manage tickets when serving multiple channels?

Qualifying Criteria: Screen for customer service agents, who use more than one channel, are involved in the intake and execution of tickets/cases, interact directly with customers

2. The Different USER SEGMENTS You Want to Assess

Unlike qualifying criteria, which either select or eliminate participants from the study, segmentation categories are nice-to-knows that can give you more context on your participants and help you eliminate selection bias.

One way to identify segmentation categories is to determine the different types of use cases your product supports. For example knowing the industry your participants represent can help produce a more distributed sample that represents more of these use cases.

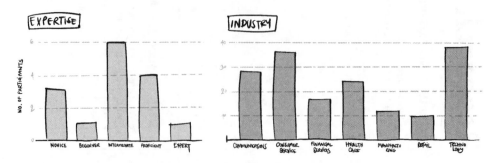

Segmentation categories are also useful for identifying category-specific trends during synthesis, further down the research process. You may find that certain segments have needs or pains that are not present in other segments.

> → Years of experience;   → Company size;   → Technical proficiency;
> → Level of expertise;   → Industry;   → Device used.

3. The SCREENER QUESTIONS You Use to Recruit Participants

Use the participant criteria and segmentation categories you identified as a foundation for creating your screener survey. Screener surveys will contain questions that are designed to help you find participants who meet your criteria and sufficiently determine whether their responses are honest.

Your screening questions should be specific enough for you to confidently define a match but also vague enough to prevent respondents from easily guessing exactly what you're looking for.

The screener should not be used as a way to answer your research questions. All insight gathering should take place during the actual research session.

4. The LOGISTICS of Recruitment

Once you know what research method you are recruiting for (Chapter 25: "Picking a Research Method Play") and have the participant screener prepared, start planning the logistics of screener distribution and internal and external communication.

- → **Sample size:** The number of participants you need will determine which channels you use to source your participants. Larger sample sizes may require the help of recruitment platforms or services.
- → **Recruitment complexity:** Niche user types, including specialized professionals, are more difficult to recruit than "gen pop" (general population) audiences and may also require you to use recruitment platforms and services.
- → **Participant compensation:** You should always compensate participants for their time. The minimum hourly participant compensation should be equal to or greater than the average hourly rate for their role. Disclose the compensation amount and method (example: PayPal, gift card, check, in kind) in your screener.
- → **Informed and involved stakeholders:** In addition to researchers, designers and product managers may want to be involved in the studies. Other departments, such as legal or finance, may need to manage compliance or payment-related tasks.
- → **Time frame:** Establish clear start and end dates for the study.
- → **Scheduling:** Most recruitment platforms already have scheduling capabilities. If you are not using one of these platforms, establish an alternative way to coordinate availability, such as an online calendar where participants can select available time slots.

5. The CHANNELS You Recruit Through

Depending on the number and type of participants you need, it may be necessary to choose more than one channel for recruitment.

HERE'S AN EXAMPLE!

channels you can consider include:

- → Research or recruitment platforms;
- → Recruitment agencies;
- → Internal user databases;
- → Marketplaces, such as Craigslist;
- → Intercept surveys;
- → Social media;
- → Paid ads;
- → Social networking platforms, such as Facebook or Reddit;
- → Referrals;
- → Professional networking; platforms and forums, such as LinkedIn.

Keep budgeting and operational constraints in mind, because the channel(s) you choose may affect:

- → How you launch your screener;
- → How you pay your participants;
- → How you schedule your participants;
- → The total spend for recruitment.

If you are reaching out to participants through community groups or forums, always make sure you are aware of their policies on recruiting before posting your screener.

6. The Recruitment BLACKLIST

Once you know what research method you are recruiting for (Chapter 25: "Picking a Research Method Play") and have the participant screener prepared, start planning the logistics of screener distribution and internal and external communication.

Before launching your recruitment, define your blacklist criteria: the types of participants you should not recruit. While this may seem counterintuitive, creating a blacklist can mitigate liability for your company.

Think about what kinds of roles, places of employment, or affiliations might expose your company to risk:

Employees or partners of direct competitors—they could gain access to your company's IP, and asking them for insights may be construed as unethical competitive intelligence.

Illegal lottery—this can affect how you communicate and distribute incentives.

Anti-bribery and corruption—this can affect the types of participants you recruit, as you can incentivize them to take part or pay more than a certain amount.

Unethical competitive intelligence—this can affect the types of participants you recruit.

Regional privacy regulations such as GDPR and LGPD—these will affect how you collect participant PII, among other things.

When in doubt consult with a legal team or cross-check your company policies to find out whether there are any other possible liabilities.

Once you've finished these steps, distribute your screeners and check your pipelines frequently.

IN ORDER TO MAXIMIZE THE VALUE OF THIS PLAY

→ Identify and eliminate potentially unmotivated participants.
Motivated participants are individuals who understand the use cases of the study, are eager and willing to share their insights, and are not driven by pressure from their superiors or by monetary compensation. Motivated participants feel that it is in their best interest to share their insights.
Unmotivated participants are individuals who may have been forced by another peer to participate, or who simply want the incentive. They are not driven to give you the best help they can.

→ Over-recruit so you have backups. It's good practice to recruit more qualified participants than you need. This provides a buffer if some respondents do not accept your invitation, or if others provide poor insights.

→ Invest in a panel of participants. Manage a ready-made panel of users who have given explicit consent to have their contact information stored to receive research opportunities. The panel should represent a wide range of users, and researchers can invite participants who meet each study's qualification criteria.

→ Start recruitment early: We recommend starting recruitment at least two weeks before you begin the study.

IN SUMMARY

Getting the right research outcomes begins with finding the right user. This requires you to define the type of participants you need and then find, vet, and coordinate with them.

RELATED PLAYS

Chapter 25: "Picking a Research Method Play"

RESEARCH QUALITY PLAY

How do I ensure rigor in my user research?

User research can significantly mitigate an organization's risk—but only when the studies are run correctly and insights are accurate. Unfortunately, user research is prone to error. Organizations need an effective system of governance to ensure research quality. This play lays out six attributes that will help you gain reliable insights and drive real value for your users and business.

Why Do You Need the Research Quality Play?

This play will allow your business to:

→ Be deliberate about all research activities;

→ Ensure the integrity of the execution and outcomes of research;

→ Collect the most reliable, unbiased, and value-driving insights possible;

→ Mitigate the risk of acting on false insights;

→ Generate value from the money, time, and effort put into research.

who Are the key Players in the Research Quality Play?

ROLE	WHO'S INVOLVED	RESPONSIBILITIES
DRIVER	• User researcher	• Design experiments; • Produce relevant, reliable, and unbiased insights.
CONTRIBUTOR	• Experience practitioners	• Provide research questions; • Create research stimuli; • Share accountability for relevant, reliable, and unbiased insights.

MINDFUL CANVAS
Research Quality

USER

➔ What characteristics or traits does a user need to have in order to answer your research questions?
➔ What additional criteria have any of the contributors mentioned?

QUESTIONS

➔ What research questions do you need to focus on to get the most value from your study?
➔ What questions are most relevant and important given your current phase of product development?

METHOD

➔ Which method is best suited for the phase of product development you currently are in?
➔ Which method is best suited for the insights you need?

EXECUTION

➔ What questions will you ask to get the insights you need?
➔ How will you maintain consistency in the execution of your study to keep the variance low?
➔ What kind of preparation will you do to avoid last minute changes?

SYNTHESIS

Is your data...
➔ Statistically significant?
➔ Factual instead of hypothetical?
➔ Showcasing the what, the why, and the so what?
➔ Free from biases?

PRESENTATION

➔ Who will be consuming the insights?
➔ What is the best way to deliver insights to these stakeholders?
➔ How will you present your key takeaways and next steps?

THE HOW

To run an effective research quality play, you need to be mindful of:

1. Talking to the Right USER

Insights must always come directly from the right users. These users can never be replaced by a proxy (an SME, support rep, sales rep, PM, or CEO), regardless of how well they may know them.

Recruit users (Chapter 26: "Research Recruitment Play") who most accurately represent the group of people for whom you are solving a problem. More specifically:

→ They have the specific needs that your product or service solves;

→ They are in the specific role/industry for which your product or service was made;

→ They have deep familiarity with the various contexts in which your product or service is most applicable.

2. Focusing on the Right QUESTIONS

While there's no such thing as "too much data" in user research, there are such things as relevant and irrelevant data. Think about the desired outcomes of your research, and define what insights you need in order to make decisions that will lead you to this outcome. In other words, identify which research questions (RQs) are most relevant. Be mindful of what phase of product development you are in when you identify your RQs.

If your desired outcome is to understand how to improve the next iteration of your network security product, some relevant research questions might be:

→ What parts of the design are helpful/hindering to the user?

→ What parts of the design are more/less intuitive to the user?

→ What parts of the design are most/least valuable to the user?

While some irrelevant research questions (in context of network security) might be:

→ What kind of social media platforms does the user use?

→ What are the user's retirement plans?

→ What is the user's marital status?

3. Choosing the Right METHOD

While there are many right methods you can use to get to the specific insight, you need to mitigate the risk of picking the wrong methods. Different research methods are best suited for answering certain types of questions or gathering certain types of data, so using the wrong research method can result in misleading insights and increased churn. For example if you are looking to understand what journey and problems a physician faces while using a surgical product, the right method could be leveraging the contextual inquiry or fly-on-the-wall methods, but a survey would not give you similar quality of insights.

Choose the method that best fits the needs of your study by evaluating key variables such as the current phase of the project, what you want to do with the insights, and the types of questions you want to ask (Chapter 25: "Picking a Research Method Play"). This will help achieve your research goals in the best way possible.

4. Carrying Out Your Method with the Right EXECUTION

Research is a rigorous craft. Any variance in the execution of your study can potentially skew your data and lead to false conclusions.

When you conduct your studies, maintain consistency and avoid making any last-minute changes.

→ Ask the same sets of question to all participants;
→ Present all participants with the same prompts;
→ Show the same stimulus to all participants;
→ Give all participants the same amount of time to complete tasks.

Conduct a pilot study at least two days prior to your first participant session to iron out any issues in the script or stimuli, and build in at least one hour between each session so you can have enough time to debrief and prepare for the next session.

Be mindful of how you frame your questions to your participants. How you ask your questions can affect what your participant says in response. In order to generate the most real and accurate responses, avoid asking:

Leading questions, which may influence users to answer in a way that confirms a preexisting assumption, opinion, or desired response.

→ Leading question: "Would you say this screen feels cluttered?"
→ Non-leading question: "Can you describe anything you may like or dislike about what you see on this screen?"

Dead-end questions, which expose the what, but not the so what or why. Try asking questions that start with "What," "Why," "How," or "Can you show me/tell me about a time…"

→ Dead-end question: "Is this feature valuable?" (Yes/No, or dead end)
→ Non-dead-end question: "How would you describe your experience with this feature?"

Dead-end questions that are not grounded in historical or behavioral data.

→ Hypothetical question: "What kind of features would you want to see listed when you evaluate a car?"
→ Non-hypothetical question: "Can you evaluate these two cars and walk me through your decision-making process?"

5. Finding Accurate Insights with the Right SYNTHESIS

Data interpreted correctly will lead to valuable, actionable insights. Misinterpreted data will lead to incorrect insights, which can lead to significant risk for your business.

Research findings can be misinterpreted in many ways:

→ A single or statistically insignificant data point may be over-amplified as an insight. Avoid this by objectively evaluating the statistical significance of the data.

→ Hypotheses are stated as facts when they are not backed by reliable sources. Avoid this by documenting and citing supporting data for each insight and by maintaining a running list of hypotheses and facts.

→ Observations, or what a user did or said, may be used to make knee-jerk product decisions. Avoid this by asking yourself, "Why did they say/do this, and why is this important to know?"

→ Biases may affect the direction of the synthesis, so the product designers should not be the ones running the tests. Avoid biases by looking at the data objectively and seeing where patterns naturally emerge, instead of searching for data points that specifically support predicted insights.

6. Socializing Your Insights with the Right PRESENTATION

The purpose of conducting research is to empower everyone in the organization to act on the findings. To do this effectively, insights must be presented in a way that is registered with different audiences; otherwise, all prior steps in the quality checklist will be in vain.

Most researchers will compile all the findings from a study in a comprehensive report, but the reality is that most stakeholders will not read the report. And if no one ever reads the report, does the research even drive any value?

What can you do to make sure your research insights are heard?

→ **Make the report relatable and consumable:** When most people hear "research report," they think "lots of pages of text, numbers, and graphs." There's no rule against using playful language, fun graphics, or even enticing animations in your artifacts! The takeaways of research should be memorable and attention-grabbing, and a big part of that is the actual presentation—the "skin," if you will—of the finding.

→ **Tailor your artifacts to the audience:** Different stakeholders have different perspectives, goals, and areas of interest, which is why the research insights you present need to be tailored to match these varying needs. Think of these stakeholders as your different "users," and design your communications and research artifacts so they are valuable and easy to comprehend for each of these users.

STAKEHOLDER	RESEARCH ARTIFACT
Leadership	Experience metrics scorecards or video highlight reels
Development	Trackable list of prioritized "to fix" issues
Product management	User journey maps or quick "cheat sheets" of insights
Designers	Screenshots with annotations of usability issues or detailed task flow diagrams

→ **Include user researchers in the design process:** The most important part of user research is making sure the insights are acted on in the right way. Ask your user researchers to contribute to ideation sessions and design reviews. This way, insights can be reiterated throughout the product development process, ensuring a higher likelihood of delivering a product that meets the user's needs.

The Cost of One Wrong Step

A user researcher was conducting a formative study to understand the needs of a certain niche-user segment. After weeks of active recruiting, she ensured that the right users were enrolled, and she crafted a detailed study protocol to extract all the necessary insights. On the study day, she asked the product owner to join the session as an observer to hear the user's perspective firsthand.

As the user researcher started the study, the product owner, with complete disregard to the planned protocol, jumped into the conversation and started sharing why the product he had in development would solve the users' needs. He asked leading questions, such as, "Wouldn't you say that solves the problem you just mentioned?" This went on for the first two interviews—and the researcher had to delay the synthesis and recruit additional users to reconduct the tainted study. Although all planning elements were conducted properly, the poor execution caused a 10-day project delay.

Now, she (the user researcher) makes sure to prepare for every execution eventuality, including setting expectations with observing collaborators.

IN ORDER TO MAXIMIZE THE VALUE OF THIS PLAY

→ Foster a shared vision. This will help the teams focus on common goals and work together to accomplish them.

→ Plan in advance. Avoid last-minute rushes, and always have a contingency plan.

→ Add buffers. Budget extra time for certain activities (i.e. research) to proactively protect the plan from being derailed by delays.

→ Develop checks and balances. Make sure the plan is reviewed regularly and is adapted to account for necessary changes that better reflect the current reality.

→ Take design hand-off and QA seriously. They are critical parts of the plan that will have significant downstream impact (e.g. product delays, engineering churn) if you don't spend the time to do it well.

IN SUMMARY

These are the six things (i.e., right user, question, method, execution, synthesis, and presentation) everyone MUST be mindful of when conducting research. Failure at any one of these points can compromise the entire research study.

RELATED PLAYS

Chapter 25: "Picking a Research Method Play"

Chapter 26: "Research Recruitment Play"

EXPERIENCE METRICS PLAY

How do I measure the success and quality of my user's experience?

Many businesses measure their success using financial or operational metrics, such as revenue or the number of sign-ups. However, when it comes to how valuable your product experience is to your user, these are indirect metrics. Businesses wanting to fuel their growth with a user-first philosophy should be measuring their success using experience metrics: metrics that quantify the quality of the experience, its value to the user, and its level of desirability.

The experience metrics play helps you identify and measure these metrics for each of your users. Consistently keeping them in sight will foster a user-first culture within your organization and will have a visible impact on your business metrics as a whole.

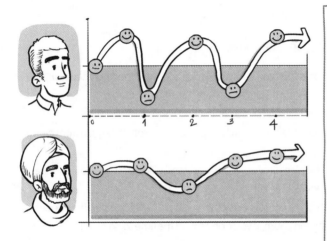

Why Do You Need the Experience Metrics Play?

This play will allow your business to:

→ Focus on metrics that matter most to each user;

→ Quantify the quality of an experience;

→ Assess an experience's improvement over time;

→ Deliver great experiences with tangible business outcomes.

Who Are the Key Players in the Experience Metrics?

ROLE	WHO'S INVOLVED	RESPONSIBILITIES
DRIVER	• Experience strategist	• Design experiments according to research goals; • Define experience metrics; • Conduct research; • Deliver insights; • Govern adherence to insights.
CONTRIBUTOR	• Experience practitioners, cross-functional teams	• Contribute research questions; • Provide existing user, product, and business insights; • Provide stimuli; • Convert research insights into deliverable outcomes; • Propagate awareness of insights.

Experience Metrics

USER

➔ Which user are you defining experience metrics for?
➔ What segment does your user belong to?

EXPERIENCES

➔ Which experiences are you defining metrics for?
➔ What experiences matter the most to the user?

EXPERIENCE METRICS

➔ What are the logical user metrics that you intend to measure?
➔ What are the emotional user metrics that you intend to measure?
➔ What are the product metrics that you intend to measure?

METHODOLOGY

➔ What stimuli do you need for this experiment?
➔ What research method(s) will you use to collect the metrics?
➔ What tasks will you prompt your participants with?
➔ What is the success criteria for each task?
➔ What questions do you want to ask your participant?

ACTIVATION

➔ How will you drive action in your organization to improve your user's experience metrics?
➔ What changes will you make to deliver a better experience?
➔ How will you track change over time?

CORRELATION

➔ What is the business impact of your experience metrics?
➔ What kind of changes should you see by improving your experience metrics?

THE HOW

To run an effective experience metrics play, you need to be mindful of:

1. The USER You Want to Focus On

Experience metrics are subjective to each user's unique needs, so they must be measured for each key user within your system. Clearly define the criteria for each user you want to focus on. Criteria to pick the key user could include how large this user segment is, the influence they have in their organization/context, and criticality to your business strategy.

For this play to be effective, you will need to recruit real users to help you measure experience metrics. Once you've identified your key users, create screeners and recruit people (we recommend between 10 and 15) to take part in this evaluation (Chapter 26: "Research Recruitment Play").

2. What EXPERIENCES Are Most Relevant to Your User

Identify the experiences that are most important to your user or most common in their line of work. List the relevant scenarios that help users achieve each of these experiences.

HERE'S AN EXAMPLE!

If your product is a point-of-sale (POS) system and your user is a cashier at a coffee shop, the key experiences (and the scenarios making them up) that you should test may include:

→ **Setup experience:** Setting up the POS for the first time;

→ **Transaction experience:** Entering an order and accepting payment;

→ **Transaction experience:** Issuing a return;

→ **Order management experience:** Voiding an order;

→ **Reconciliation experience:** Submitting a summary of all transactions.

As you define which experiences and scenarios to measure, keep in mind that this play is intended to be repeated over time. This means that every time you use this play, you will need to use the same experiences and scenarios so you can accurately compare the resulting metrics. This will eventually help you identify a clear trend for the direction in which the metrics are moving.

3. What EXPERIENCE METRICS You Want to Measure

Experience metrics focus specifically on aspects of the experience that are most important to the user—both **rational and emotional.** Many B2B products in the market today are built to serve the needs of the businesses (increasing productivity, reducing costs, streamlining processes), which is why products can have high sales yet have low user satisfaction scores—the person buying the product is not the person who ends up using the product. To truly be user-centric, we need to focus on who actually "experiences" the product and the things they care about most in an experience.

HOW DO YOU DO THIS?

Step 1: Understand your user insights.

All experience metrics must trace back to user insights. Leverage the key insights you know about your user (Chapter 14: "User Empathy Play") to identify what matters most to them.

User pains are the things that negatively affect users' experiences. Take note of what the users are struggling with and also what they wish for. These could surface hidden pain points or provide additional insight into what your users value.

User joys are the things that elevate a user's experience. Take note of details such as their stated delight factors, what they love most about their jobs, or their ideal experience.

User needs are the things that a user requires in an experience. Take note of what your users do and how they must be supported for them to reach their outcomes.

User successes reveal the goals and outcomes they want and need to achieve.

Step 2: Variablize these insights to find the possible root causes.

Identify all of the possible factors, aka variables, that contribute to each insight. For every insight, there can be any number of variables that make an experience a source of a pain, joy, need, or success to the user. By finding the variables, we can start to identify the root causes behind these insights and understand the user's mental model of a good or bad experience.

For each insight, ask, "What are all the things that make this a pain/joy/need/success to the user?

Step 3: Determine which variables are RATIONAL vs. EMOTIONAL, and assign quantifiable measures for each.

It is important to know both how well the product is helping users get their jobs done (rational) and how delighted and satisfied they feel while using the product (emotional).

→ **Rational variables** are quantitative variables, such as "transaction completion time" or "number of voided bills." They also can come from sensorial data that you regularly collect through telemetry, such as "number of clicks" or "load time." Rational variables can be used directly as experience metrics.

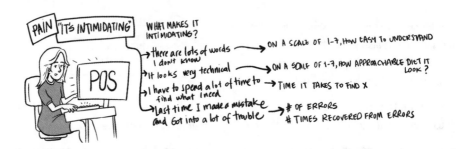

HERE'S A TIP!

Balance your tasks: Over the course of the evaluation, participants can become acclimated to your product, gradually improving their metrics and skewing the data to be more positive for later tasks. You can prevent this by balancing tasks—changing the order of the tasks for each participant—to generate a more accurate average.

→ **Emotional variable**s are qualitative variables such as "approachable" or "feeling empowered." Emotional variables cannot be measured concretely; they require other methods:

Applying a Likert scale (on a scale of 1–7) to the variable. Standard scores such as NPS or CSAT are great examples of how emotional variables are quantified in the market today.

Further variablizing the emotional variables to see if any rational metrics contribute to the emotion.

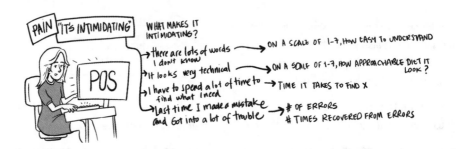

RATIONAL	EMOTIONAL
• Time to completion; • Number of clicks; • Load time; • Number of errors made; • Time it takes to find help; • Number of times help is needed;	• Satisfaction; • Confidence; • Empowerment; • Fun to use; • Helpfulness.

4. The METHODOLOGY You Use to Measure the Experience Metrics

There are many methods you can choose from (Chapter 25: "Picking a Research Method Play"), but whatever method you choose should provide the ability for:

→ Users to interact with your product;
→ Users to answer quantitative (rational) and qualitative (emotional) questions;
→ Users to provide candid feedback;
→ Researchers to accurately measure rational and emotional metrics.

You do not need to strictly adhere to only one method; instead use a combination of methods as you see fit. For example, you can combine elements of interviews (where user researchers can ask qualitative questions), usability tests (where users can interact with the product to test each experience and researchers can measure metrics such as "time to completion"), and surveys (where users can answer sets of standardized quantitative questions for research to later analyze).

As you plan your method, be meticulous about the **STIMULUS** and **PROTOCOL.**

The **STIMULUS** is the prototype participants will use during the evaluation. Stimuli can come in varying fidelities, but as a rule of thumb, the higher the fidelity of your stimuli, the more accurate your findings will be. Note that the fidelity of your prototype must be the same every time you run this study if you want to compare metrics over time.

The **PROTOCOL** is the script you will use to effectively capture all the data and insights you need. The protocol contains:

1. The tasks you will give to your participants: What are realistic scenarios your users might encounter during your selected experiences? When you write your tasks, include the context and the action you would like for them to perform. However, try not to be too prescriptive in your tasks; otherwise, the participants will spend more time remembering the task and less time showing you how they would go about it.

a. Do: "Your company just started using a new communication tool, and they shared the following email with you to help you get started. Create your account and set up your profile."

b. Don't: "Click on the link in the email. Select the 'create new account' option, then setup screen to add yourself as an employee, and when you are done, fill in your information and photo in the profile. Click 'Save' when you are done".

2. The success criteria for these tasks: The more specific your success criteria is, the more consistent your synthesis will be.

Success criteria: the participants must complete 80% of the following"

→ Select "Get Started" in the email;
→ Add all required fields in "setup";
→ Select "employee" as the user type;
→ Add all required fields in "profile";
→ Save profile and land in the main chat screen.

3. The questions you want to ask: Are there any qualitative or quantitative insights you want to know? As a best practice, try to standardize the questions you ask to make sure you are collecting the same information for each task from all of your participants. This is a great opportunity to gather more subjective and emotional metrics.

4. Questions to ask after each task:

→ What, if anything, did you like the most about what you just experienced?
→ What, if anything, did you dislike the most about what you just experienced?
→ How would you rate the intuitiveness of the tool during that task on a scale of 1–5 (1 being very unintuitive and 5 being very intuitive)?
→ How would you rate the usefulness of the tool during that task on a scale of 1–5 (1 being very not useful and 5 being very useful)?
→ On a scale of 1–7 how much do you agree with the following statement: I feel like I was recognized for my accomplishments (1 being strongly disagree and 5 being strongly agree).

Before starting your evaluations:

→ Run an initial evaluation in a controlled environment—for example, in a usability lab—to establish baseline experience metrics for the user's experience. This will allow you to compare subsequent results and single out the variables that are making your experience better or worse for the user.

→ Define thresholds for what defines a subpar, average, and excellent experience. This will keep everyone on the same page on what's good or poor when they receive the study results.

HERE'S A TIP!

Balance your tasks: Over the course of the evaluation, participants can become acclimated to your product, gradually improving their metrics and skewing the data to be more positive for later tasks. You can prevent this by balancing tasks—changing the order of the tasks for each participant—to generate a more accurate average.

→ A reliable and standardized method for evaluation is critical for measuring your experience metrics consistently over time. Consistency is absolutely necessary for comparing results.

5. ACTIVATING Your Findings

Experience metrics are meant to help all teams within your organization take action. So once you've measured and collated the results for each experience metric, socialize the results with the appropriate cross-functional team so you can collaboratively prioritize which design problems to solve for the user to improve the experience.

Ideate on the best solutions to solve these design problems, implement the solutions, and run the evaluation again. The results must be compared over regular time intervals—every quarter, every six months, or every year—in order to signal areas of improvement or continued opportunities for refinement.

6. CORRELATING Metrics with Business Outcomes

Delivering great experiences has a ripple effect across all aspects of the business. As you measure your users' experience metrics, map the downstream impact of these metrics to the business metrics you measure. You will see that all business goals can be traced back to the quality of your users' experiences:

→ **Financial:** User-centric experiences help companies have faster revenue growth. Products that deliver better user experience not only lead to greater adoption and retention, but they can also demand higher margins because customers are willing to pay more for a better experience.

→ **Customer:** Building more desirable, usable, and useful products improves the business performance across the customer life cycle. Specifically, you'll generate more interest among prospective customers, win more customers, keep more customers engaged and satisfied, see more repeat purchases, and generate more customer lifetime value.

→ **Process:** You will see positive changes in your internal innovation process and operations when you focus on delivering great experiences to your users.

    → Innovation process: Gathering user experience feedback jumpstarts the innovation process so organizations can build and sustain their competitive advantage.

    → Operations: Teams grounded in user feedback are more motivated to break down organizational silos and work collaboratively to revamp their products and give users a better experience (Chapter 36: "Cross-Functional Collaboration Play").

    → Employees: Focusing on delivering the best experience for users allows your employees to be more connected to a higher and more powerful purpose (Chapter 17: "Shared Empathy Play"). User-centric companies have higher overall employee satisfaction and a strong empathetic culture (Chapter 16: "Culture Design Play").

The types of metrics a company focuses on can speak volumes about what's important to them. Do they prioritize increasing profits and lowering costs? Or do they make their users' goals their own, and truly exhibit an empathetic, user-first culture?

A Race with No Finish Line

A leading tech company CEO often spoke about the importance of user experience. However, none of his company's tracked metrics focused on experience quality. Instead, they measured the output volume, evaluating practitioners on the number and frequency of the features they designed.

This was challenging for the design team. The company would release high-tech capabilities that users didn't want to use, launch entire products that were so complicated that they required user training, and added feature after feature that made navigation confusing. Output was extremely high, but the team had no idea whether they were improving or worsening their users' experience.

Eventually, the team began identifying basic experience metrics (such as time on task, completion rate, and satisfaction score), measured them release over release, and presented them to the receptive leadership. These metrics gave concrete answers to questions such as, "How do we know we're doing good work?" and "How well are we solving our users' problems?"

Soon, experience metrics became a clear gating factor for each release, allowing the organization to compare the quality of our experiences to other competitors' and plan product roadmaps more effectively. This was a pivotal moment: By introducing user-centric metrics to the larger organization, the focus shifted from quantity to quality and from feature to user.

IN ORDER TO MAXIMIZE THE VALUE OF THIS PLAY

→ Use experience metrics to drive cultural change. Socialize your experience metrics often, and use them to set clear goals for your teams. Create team success metrics that correlate with your experience metrics so you can keep the user as everyone's priority.

→ Keep the study design as consistent as possible. Standardize participant criteria, experience metrics, tasks, and methodology; otherwise, you will not be able to make apples-to-apples comparisons over time.

→ Know why you're measuring a metric. You could come up with a million variables that could generate a million experience metrics, but that won't help you accurately or effectively measure an experience. Anchor back to the core user problems that you are aiming to solve, and assess their impact on your user's experience.

IN SUMMARY

Every user-first business should be measuring the quality of their users' experience just as much as they measure their financial and operational metrics. Once you are able to identify the metrics that are most important to your user, you will be able to properly assess the entire experience and create solutions your users value—and you will nurture a user-first culture within your organization.

RELATED PLAYS

Chapter 16: "Culture Design Play"
Chapter 17: "Shared Empathy Play"

Chapter 25: "Picking a Research Method Play"
Chapter 26: "Research Recruitment Play"

INSIGHTS CURATION PLAY
How do I consolidate and leverage research insights?

Even when organizations conduct and prioritize user research, the insights and learnings are not always used to their full potential. The findings are not shared with a wide enough audience, stored in an accessible place, or presented in a meaningful manner—so other teams aren't aware that the resources even exist. This UXReactor play shows you how to centralize your resources, develop meaningful analysis, and use the data to find patterns and make predictions.

Why Do You Need the Insights Curation Play?

This play will allow your business to:

→ Make insights more visible to your organization;

→ Make insights a strategic resource for your organization;

→ Provide cross-functional teams a foundation for user-centricity.

Who Are the Key Players in the Insights Curation Play?

ROLE	WHO'S INVOLVED	RESPONSIBILITIES
DRIVER	• User researcher	• Inventory resources and artifacts; • Establish indexing process; • Index resources; • Maintain repository.
CONTRIBUTOR	• Experience practitioners, cross-functional teams	• Provide supporting artifacts; • Reference curated resources.

Insights Curation

SOURCES

→ What teams will your insights come from?
→ What static and dynamic sources will your insights come from?
→ Where will you store your research data?

STRUCTURING

→ How will the repository be organized?
→ Who will leverage the repository?
→ How will the repository be leveraged?

→ What is the naming convention that you will be following?
→ How will you structure your data intake?
→ How will the data be structured?

ANALYSIS

Level 1:
→ What are the POVs that matter to your organization?
→ What design problems and design opportunities can you extract in relation to all the POVs?

Level 2:
→ Are there any hidden patterns in the data?
→ Are there any trends in the data?
→ Are there any prediction models you can make for the users and business from this data?

SOCIALIZATION

→ Who will have access?
→ How will insights be shared throughout the organization?
→ How will you ensure that people leverage the insights?

MAINTENANCE

→ Who is responsible for maintaining the insights repository?
→ How will you keep the repository relevant?

THE HOW

To effectively establish insights curation, you need to be mindful of:

1. The SOURCES and Storage of Your Insights

User insights live in all departments of an organization, not just in user research. Departments such as marketing, support, sales, and even finance all generate and collect valuable user and business data; however, this data often remains siloed in those departments.

Key user insights are the actions, soundbites, and observations gathered about the user in the department. These insights can include things that the user likes, dislikes, needs, feels, wants, and does in the context of the ecosystem or the product.

Break the silos and create a collective repository of all of your organization's insights by:

→ Taking inventory of all the teams that are collecting data on the users and business;
→ Creating a single place for teams to store their data and insights.

The insights repository will need a designated digital storage space that is easily accessible for all parties in your organization but also secure enough for proprietary information. This allows for more transparency and collaboration across departments and ensures that data is not lost over time.

When building a robust repository, collect data of all shapes and sizes:

1. **Static data,** such as reports or analytics from instrumentation;
2. **Dynamic data,** such as social media chatter;
3. **Quantitative data,** such as satisfaction scores;
4. **Qualitative data,** such as videos or images from interviews.

2. What Systems You Put in Place for STRUCTURING Your Data

An insights repository is only helpful if its users can find the information they need. Once all of the data from across your organization is in a single place, structure the data to make it meaningful and easy to use.

Think about who will be leveraging the repository and what they will be leveraging it for.

Use this information to:

→ Establish structured naming conventions;
→ Create an intuitive information architecture;
→ Define meaningful indexing.

A new employee might leverage the repository to learn everything there is to know about a specific product. An experience practitioner might leverage the repository to find all of the pain points for a specific user.

3. The Maturity of Your ANALYSIS

With your data structured, you can now begin getting value out of your insights repository. At the very minimum, an insights repository should help the user find what they were looking for. Further enhancements to the insights repository could include helping the user discover additional related resources or even predicting what information they will need.

There are two levels of analysis your organization should be conducting as your repository grows. They represent different levels of value you can generate with your repository.

Level 1: Points of View (POVs)

A POV is a curation of data for a specific perspective. For example, if someone wants to analyze/study/research insights from the POV of a specific user, they should be able to access not only those user insights but all the related insights about products, teams, and experiences that pertain to that user.

> **Think about the different POVs that typically matter to your organization:**
> **User:** "I want to see all there is to learn about the agent."
> **Intent:** "I want to see all there is to learn about users who want to manage clients."
> **Product:** "I want to see all there is to learn about the 'Agent Portal.'"
> **Experience:** "I want to see all there is to learn about onboarding experiences."
> **Releases:** "I want to see all there is to learn about the Q2 2021 release."
> **Domain:** "I want to see all there is to learn about real estate."

Anyone in the organization should be able to pick any of the POVs above and get immediate value from the insights. Value comes in the form of increased knowledge, time saved, more informed decisions, and increased empathy.

This level of analysis should also provide enough information for you to extract design problems and opportunities for the user, product, and business.

Level 2: Trends and Correlations

The next level of data analysis maturity is connecting the dots between the insights to find correlations, identify trends, and eventually make predictions.

Look for trends between data points such as experience metrics user sentiment, different releases, or product performance. Understanding trends and correlations in your data can drive immense value to your business. It can shed light on the areas where your users' experience is doing well or not well, and it can highlight what kind of impact that might have on your business.

You may see an inverse correlation between user satisfaction and the amount of time it takes for them to complete a workflow. This tells you where opportunity lies. Or you may see that all users who have two or less years of experience complain the most about the intuitiveness of the product. This tells you that you need to make the experience friendlier to novice users.

As your repository grows, the volume of data you have access to also will grow. Eventually, your computation power will increase to the point where you can create models to predict future impact. This means you should be able to look at a set of insights around a certain topic and predict how it will affect something about the product later down the line.

Having this deeper level of knowledge will help your teams make more informed decisions, improving your users' experience and driving more short- and long-term value to your business.

4. Frequent SOCIALIZATION to Drive Utilization

When leveraged well, an insights repository can grow the tribal knowledge of your organization, increase overall empathy, and mitigate product churn. Everyone in the organization needs to be aware of and regularly leverage the repository.

→ Give everyone access;
→ Share insights often;
→ Encourage frequent usage.

5. Consistent MAINTENANCE

Just as a library needs a librarian to manage the curation of books, an insights repository needs an owner to manage and maintain it.

Assign an owner to maintain the data to ensure it can be easily accessed and findable. This owner will use standardized processes and guidelines to make the repository user-friendly, establish the cleanliness of metadata, and prevent churn for future owner(s) as the repository grows. They are responsible for keeping the repository up to date and relevant so that it will always drive value to your organization.

The Perils of Data Disorganization

A consultant was tasked with an initiative with a hefty goal: break the silos between products and think about health care horizontally across his client company's product suite. Over the previous five years, valuable data had been collected by several different teams: user research, sales, and marketing. But no one knew where this data existed—or even that it existed at all. It had never been cross-shared, and many of the individuals who had conducted the studies had since left. Finding and synthesizing the insights was nearly impossible. The consultant team spent over six months re-creating the data, which resulted in significant opportunity cost, frustration from the internal team, and a complete overhaul of the original project plan—problems that could have been avoided had there existed a strong system of insight curation.

IN ORDER TO MAXIMIZE THE VALUE OF THIS PLAY

→ Establish a single source of truth. Your repository should be a one-stop shop for your entire organization. Make sure that the repository does not contain multiple or varying versions of the same data.

→ Manage your permissions. To reduce the risk of accidental tampering, make sure your repository has sufficient levels of permissions.

IN SUMMARY

User research—or any form of data collection, for that matter—can only build user-centric mindsets across the organization if everyone is aware of and familiar with its findings. Having a strong insights repository will make these findings accessible organization-wide, promote insight-driven product decisions, and increase the value of research activities.

RELATED PLAYS

Chapter 17: "Shared Empathy Play"

USER RESEARCH PROGRAM PLAY
How do I run an effective research program?

Information is power, and the more specific the information, the lower the risk. The user research program play provides a framework for ensuring that the right mix of user insights is being collected to drive innovation, help your organization avoid risk, and deliver valuable products that consistently resonate with your users.

Why Do You Need a User Research Program?

This play allows your business to:

→ Solve today's users' needs while simultaneously discovering future opportunities;

→ Gather the intelligence to create products that resonate with your users;

→ Diversify data sources to bring visibility to user and business needs and priorities;

→ Empower teams to make informed business and design decisions;

→ Align teams on where to focus and prioritize their resources.

Who are the key players in the User Research Program play?

ROLE	WHO'S INVOLVED	RESPONSIBILITIES
DRIVER	• Experience strategist	• Catalyze a research mindset; • Orchestrate and govern research efforts; • Ensure insights are communicated across the organization.
CONTRIBUTOR	• User experience researcher	• Design experiments according to goals; • Conduct research; • Deliver insights; • Govern adherence to insights in company activities; • Ensure mix of insights are gathered.

MINDFUL CANVAS

User Research Program

PORTFOLIO OF INSIGHTS

Formative
- → What parts of your business require foundational insights?
- → Are there any insights that need to be "refreshed?"
- → For what users/experiences?
- → Through what kind of research activities?
- → How will the insights be reported?
- → What % of your effort and resources will be dedicated to gathering formative insights?

Summative
- → What experiences have stimuli that require validation?
- → What experience metrics are you measuring?
- → Through what kind of research activities?
- → How will the insights be reported?
- → What % of your effort and resources will be dedicated to gathering summative insights?

Sensorial
- → Which experiences are currently being used by users?
- → How is usage/sentiment data being collected?
- → What experience metrics are you measuring?
- → Through what kind of research activities?
- → How will the insights be reported?
- → What % of your effort and resources will be dedicated to gathering sensorial insights?

PEOPLE
- → Who will be responsible for the outcomes of your research program?
- → What skill mix do you need?
- → Which teams do you need to align roadmaps and collaborate with?

SOURCES
- → What are your sources of data?
- → What internal departments are you sourcing data from?
- → Where are you finding your participants?

TOOLS
- → What kind of tools do you need to make research operational?
- → What kind of tools will you need to collect your insights?

CURATION AND COLLABORATION
- → Where will insights be stored and tracked
- → How is visibility being brought to research findings?
- → How are insights being communicated?
- → How are others being encouraged to take interest in and get involved with research?

GOVERNANCE
- → At what frequency is research of all types being done?
- → How is the team being held accountable? Are decisions being driven by data?
- → Is there a Research Checklist to ensure the quality of research? How else is the quality of research being managed?

THE HOW

To run an effective user research program, you need to be mindful of:

1. Managing a PORTFOLIO OF INSIGHTS

A portfolio of insights is a collection of three different types of research insights: formative, summative, and sensorial (Chapter 24: "User Research Insights: Introduction"). These insights should be collected from various sources and methods (Chapter 25: "Picking a Research Method Play") on an ongoing basis to sustain a current and relevant portfolio that your teams can leverage.

A portfolio of insights is the cornerstone between user-centricity and business value for many reasons:

→ It ensures that the user is kept in the loop at all times;
→ It gives you multiple perspectives and data points on the user;
→ It gives you insight into what problems to solve today;
→ It measures how well you are solving the problems;
→ It directs you to the problems you should be solving tomorrow.

The proportions of investment you make across the portfolio of insights will change depending on what phase of maturity your organization or product is in—build, grow, or maintain.

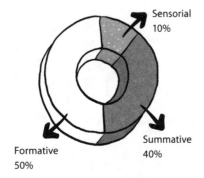

Organizations in the Build Phase

Formative research will help you gain a foundational understanding of your users, their needs, and the problems that need to be solved. Formative research informs requirements and business priorities and is performed before any designing takes place. It uses methods such as ethnographic studies and contextual inquiry.

Organizations in the Grow Phase

Usability testing is a popular summative method used by many companies to quickly validate their designs and identify any issues prior to launch. Usability testing can be done at any level of design fidelity, from sketches to coded UI, as long as the participants have a stimulus they can interact with. However, the quality of the resulting data will increase with the fidelity of your design.

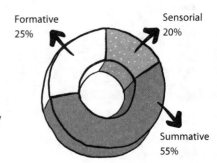

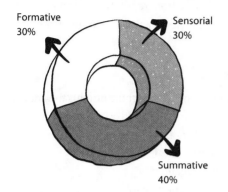

Formative
30%

Sensorial
30%

Summative
40%

Organizations in the Maintain Phase

Sensorial research can be used to inform upcoming roadmap for products you already have in the market. By collecting data on an ongoing basis—either through instrumentation or regular measurement (Chapter 28: "Experience Metrics Play")—you can easily identify where the experience has gone up or down over time and what to focus on next.

2. Investing in the Right PEOPLE to Drive the Program

Make sure you have the right mix of people needed to run an effective user research program:

→ **Program driver:** The experience strategist is responsible for modeling and nurturing a research mindset while orchestrating successful program outcomes.

→ **Skill diversity:** Ensure adequate head count with a balanced skill mix so you can gather your needed insights (Chapter 25: "Picking a Research Method Play").

  → Quantitative vs. qualitative;
  → Behavioral vs. attitudinal;
  → Formative vs. summative vs. sensorial.

→ **Cross-functional collaborators:** Design, product, engineering, and marketing together must support the user research program, share insights, and align roadmap. Only with the collective effort of all teams can the organization create truly user-centric experiences.

3. Extracting Data from Reliable SOURCES

Your sources of data will make or break the validity of your research. Sources can be categorized in two main ways:

Primary sources are the users themselves. Nothing can replace talking to real users! Be mindful of where and how you're recruiting to ensure you're engaging with people you can trust and fit the participant criteria (Chapter 26: "Research Recruitment Play").

Secondary sources may be subject matter experts from internal departments at your organization and sources from sales.

Engineering, customer support, marketing, and the CTO office can offer insights on how users engage with a product/organization. Tap into these individuals for technical knowledge and primers before talking to real users. Talking to SMEs should supplement, not replace, talking to real users.

Understanding the market context of a particular product and/or experience is often secondary research, unless your organization is conducting the research themselves. Be wary of sourcing information from opinions in blog posts. Instead, look toward research done from reputable market research organizations: annual reports, earnings calls, collective app store reviews, and other industry reports.

4. Providing the Right TOOLS for the Team to Be Effective

User researchers need the right tools to make research operational and to collect the insights they need.

From an operational perspective, user research requires tools for:

- → Recruitment;
- → Scheduling;
- → Incentive payment and processing;
- → Video editing;
- → Analysis;
- → Artifact creation;
- → Insights management.

From a data collection perspective, user research requires tools for:

- → Unmoderated and moderated research;
- → Survey;
- → Video recording;
- → Transcription;
- → Instrumentation (telemetry).

Tools can help you with documentation, accuracy, and efficiency. Prioritize the ones that help you become more accurate and efficient.

5. Establishing a Cadence of CURATION AND COLLABORATION

Frequently communicate insights and outcomes to the rest of the organization to sensitize everyone to research developments and to increase shared empathy (Chapter 17: "Shared Empathy Play"). To make user research meaningful and actionable, aggregate, track, and make insights accessible (Chapter 29: "Insights Curation Play").

Having proper systems of curation in place will allow insights to be shared and tribal knowledge to grow, making cross-functional collaboration more efficient and effective. In addition, the UX, product, and engineering roadmaps will operate in sync with one another, reducing product churn.

HERE'S A TIP!

Make research visible to the rest of the organization by placing visual artifacts such as posters, infographics, or user quotes in high-traffic areas of your office (or virtual workspaces!). Share highlights in cross-functional and all-hands meetings.

6. Having Proper Systems of GOVERNANCE

Work with your leadership and cross-functional teams to implement proper systems of governance that help your organization prioritize a research mindset, keep teams accountable for producing honest and accurate insights, and increase the overall value and sustainability of your user research program.

- → Monthly/quarterly/annual cadence of all three types of research activities;
- → Regular socialization of research findings;
- → Institutionalization of researcher participation in design reviews;
- → Onboarding processes that sensitize teammates to research.

Unleashing the Power of User Research

In the 2000s, while everyone else was doing research to validate the usability of their screens and keyboards, Apple was investing in formative research to discover consumer needs. This led to the development of the iPhone. Today, Apple consistently invests in a robust portfolio of insights. This generates their regular releases of novel products such as the iPad, their frequent updates and improvements to existing products, and even the deprecation of older product lines such as iTunes.

IN ORDER TO MAXIMIZE THE VALUE OF THIS PLAY

→ Get data only from real users: No one can replace the end user. Talking to proxies or SMEs who are not actual end users will increase your organization's risk of acting on false insights.

→ Encourage and reward involvement: All teams inside an organization, from the product team to the finance team, should feel accountable for driving user outcomes. Encourage others to get involved in insight-gathering activities to instill a sense of ownership of and pride in the end result.

→ Cross-verify your insights: Employing a strong portfolio of insights and collecting data through various methods and sources will allow you to triangulate data, extract insights with a higher level of confidence, and increase their reliability.

IN SUMMARY

Good intelligence is the key to competitive advantage. This is why user research has the potential to be the most value-driving investment a company can make. To maximize the ROI of research, you need to invest in the right systems to manage and govern these investments.

RELATED PLAYS

Chapter 17: "Shared Empathy Play"
Chapter 25: "Picking a Research Method Play"
Chapter 26: "Research Recruitment Play"

Chapter 27: "Research Quality Play"
Chapter 28: "Experience Metrics Play"
Chapter 29: "Insights Curation Play"

PRODUCT THINKING

"IF I WERE GIVEN ONE HOUR TO SAVE THE PLANET, I WOULD SPEND 59 MINUTES DEFINING THE PROBLEM AND ONE MINUTE RESOLVING IT."

– ALBERT EINSTEIN

PRODUCT THINKING: INTRODUCTION
Building a system to identify, prioritize and coordinate the right problems

What Is Product Thinking?

Product thinking is the discipline of **understanding, curating, prioritizing, and coordinating** the myriad experience and design problems within an organization. In simple terms it helps identify the right problems to solve in order to create the maximum value for both the user and the business.

The Impact of Product Thinking

According to recent research published in Harvard Business Review, 75 to 95% of product launches fail every year. This is because most of these organizations do not focus on solving the real problems that matter. Product thinking will help you holistically understand and ensure delivery of the best product experience and the interdependencies across experiences by:

→ Identifying the relevant users and problems before jumping to a solution;
→ Evaluating how your user experience stacks up against other products in the market, to ensure that you identify the most significant, relevant problems;
→ Aligning innovation with the vision and the goals for the product experience;
→ Encouraging collaborative ideation, planning, and execution based on understanding the why.

Key Concepts

Here are a few key terms and concepts to understand before diving into the product thinking plays:

→ Productization is the process of taking a design solution for an (or a set of) identified need or problem and developing it into a fully tested, packaged, and marketed product. A product in the context of this book is any digital screen, suite, platform, and/or service that is offered to the market to satisfy the needs of a user.

→ The experience ecosystem incorporates the various users and their experiential journey in the context of the product. An ecosystem might include the users, objects, relationships, and interlocking technologies.

→ The portfolio of problems is the spectrum of design problems you must solve in order to achieve your short-, mid-, and long-term business goals in the pursuit of creating an effective product experience.

What to Expect in This Section

These plays will help you think about a broader product experience before the finer details. The product thinking plays will help you answer these questions:

→ How do I define baseline and best-in-class product experiences? (Experience benchmarking play)
→ How do I align for success at the beginning of the design phase? (Experience design brief play)
→ How do I decide which problems to solve? (Design problem and opportunities play)
→ How do I ensure the delivery of a great product experience? (Product experience planning play)
→ How do I collaborate across the organization to drive seamless and informed product experience design? (Cross-functional collaboration play)
→ How do I catalyze great product experiences? (Product thinking program)

Users care more about experiences than features. These plays allow you to start differentiating designing experiences from the craft of detailed design.

EXPERIENCE BENCHMARKING PLAY

CHAPTER

32

How do I define baseline and best-in-class product experiences?

Competitive analysis is commonly used to discover what competitors are doing and if any of their practices should be followed. However, in most cases, analysis is only conducted on direct competitors who may not actually be creating the best experiences. You can generate significant value by borrowing learnings from different domains and businesses. The experience benchmarking play will help you find these learnings to create a clear set of benchmarks for your product experience.

Why Do You Need an Experience Benchmarking Play?

This play will allow your business to:

→ Identify the market baseline and gold standards for an experience;

→ Evaluate where your experience stands against others in the market;

→ Anticipate shifts in the market and spot new trends;

→ Avoid blindly following others, and instead assess the best possible experience for your users.

Who Are the Key Players in the Experience Benchmarking Play?

ROLE	WHO'S INVOLVED	RESPONSIBILITIES
DRIVER	• User researcher	• Conduct analysis; • Document findings.
CONTRIBUTOR	• Experience practitioners	• Provide insights on users and their mindsets; • Prioritize design scope based on findings.

MINDFUL CANVAS

Experience Benchmarking

USER AND EXPERIENCE

- Who is your user?
- Which experience will you be focusing on?

RESEARCH QUESTIONS

- What do you want to learn about in a [experience name] experience?
- What do you want to assess in various [experience name] experiences?
- What do you want to compare across various [experience name] experiences?

COMPETITORS AND INSPIRATIONS

- Who are your main direct competitors who have a [experience name] experience that you will assess?
- What other domains have a [experience name] experience that you will assess?

ASSESSMENT

Minimum viable experience (MVE)
- What are the most common attributes of a [experience name] experience?
- What is the bare minimum that needs to be done for a [experience name] experience?
- What outcomes do these MVEs achieve for the user?

Enhanced
- What are some ways this experience helps users be more efficient and more accurate?
- What are some ways this experience is tailored to the specific user?
- What outcomes do these enhanced experiences achieve for the user?

Transformed
- What are some ways users are delighted by a [experience name] experience?
- What are the attributes of a highly differentiated [experience name] experience?
- What outcomes do these transformed experiences achieve for the user?

BASELINE

- What MVE outcomes have you already achieved and not yet achieved?
- What Enhanced outcomes have you already achieved and not yet achieved?
- What Transformed outcomes have you already achieved and not yet achieved?
- Which of these outcomes should you focus on first?

COLLABORATION

- How will you share the findings of your analysis for your peer practitioners to take action on?
- How will you use these findings to achieve your vision?

THE HOW

To run an effective experience benchmarking play, you need to be mindful of:

1. Which USER and EXPERIENCE You Are Evaluating

Because the intent of this play is to clarify what makes a table-stakes vs. best-in-class experience, you should identify only one user and one experience from the experience roadmap to analyze in detail (Chapter 19: "Experience Roadmap Play"). This will help you gather in-depth data from the experience while mitigating against scope creep.

Choose the experience that you think you have the most opportunity to disrupt, or the experience that you feel lacks sufficient insight.

2. What RESEARCH QUESTIONS You Are Trying to Answer

Research questions act as guardrails for analysis. They provide a clear starting point, showing you what to look for and allowing you to assess the experience more efficiently. Ask questions like:

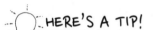

HERE'S A TIP!

As an experience practitioner, be firm on the issues that will positively affect the users' experiences.

What do you want to learn about this experience?

→   What attributes define a good or bad trial experience?
→   What are the different ways users are educated in a trial experience?
→   What makes content easy to consume in a trial experience?

Is there anything in particular you want to compare?

→   How are businesses helping users educate themselves in a trial experience?
→   How are businesses compelling users to start a trial?
→   How are businesses converting trial users to paying users?
→   Why are most trial experiences not doing well?

3. Your Direct and Indirect COMPETITORS AND INSPIRATIONS

Assessing your direct competitors is a given, so start by documenting which of them you will include in the assessment. Keep in mind that the trends within your own domain may not necessarily be best-in-class. Of course, this does not mean you cannot find examples of best-in-class experiences, but the main intent of assessing direct competitors is to establish a baseline industry standard and general user expectations.

Next, think about companies from other industries and domains that are well known for delivering the same experience. Evaluating the same experience across multiple domains will uncover disruptive ideas and approaches that you can incorporate into your own product experience.

4. How You Conduct and Document ASSESSMENT

Using your research questions and list of competitors as a starting point, begin assessment by going through each experience as a user would and documenting your learnings. Pay close attention to what these companies are doing, and try to reverse-engineer why they are doing it. In other words, what outcomes are being achieved in the experience, and what are the different ways these outcomes are achieved on a UI, PX, and XT level? (Chapter 4: "Experience Value Chain")

Once all of the data points have been collected, synthesize the data and categorize your findings in the following buckets:

→ **Minimum viable experience (MVE):** Attributes that are non-negotiable; these are the attributes that most competitors exhibit and are the bare minimum that the experience must have in order to be delivered to the user.

→ **More enhanced experience (MEE):** Attributes that make the experience faster and easier; these attributes are less common than the MVE attributes because they help make the experience more tailored to the user to make the end results more efficient and accurate.

→ **Most transformed experience (MTE):** Attributes that differentiate the experience, create delight, and deliver exponential value to the user; these attributes truly differentiate the experience and wow the user. Experiences with these attributes act as a value multiplier for the user.

Anatomy of a best-in-class trial experience

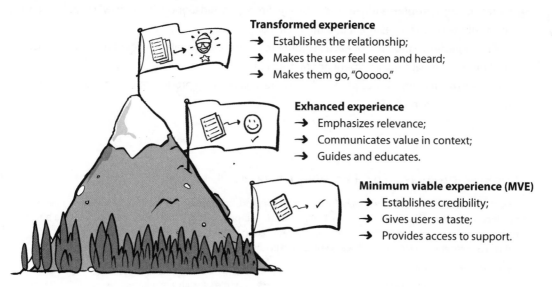

Transformed experience
→ Establishes the relationship;
→ Makes the user feel seen and heard;
→ Makes them go, "Ooooo."

Exhanced experience
→ Emphasizes relevance;
→ Communicates value in context;
→ Guides and educates.

Minimum viable experience (MVE)
→ Establishes credibility;
→ Gives users a taste;
→ Provides access to support.

5. Establishing a BASELINE for Your Own Product

Now that you know where the world is going and what the benchmarks are for minimum viable, enhanced, and transformed experiences, run the same assessment on your own product to baseline how many of the attributes your product's current experience meets. This will show you where your product is doing well where it needs improvement.

Once you have conducted your assessment, prioritize which findings to take action on. Give each unmet criteria a 1–5 ranking (1 being least relevant/feasible and 5 being most relevant/feasible) based on:

→ **User impact:** How much will this affect the user's experience?
→ **Business feasibility:** Given your businesses' current resources, how likely are you to be able to complete this for the next release?

Add the two rankings together to get a final score for each criteria.

Criteria that score high on user impact and business feasibility (8–10) should be put into the roadmap for the next product release and socialized to the rest of the product team. Other lower-scoring (1–7) criteria may need to be placed further down the mid- and long-term roadmaps to give the business enough time to plan and prepare.

HERE'S A TIP!

Include other departments in the prioritization process. They will advise on how well equipped their teams are to take on the work (business feasibility) and share their professional perspective on user impact. Getting cross-functional buy-in early on will help mitigate risk down the road.

6. How You Take Action through COLLABORATION

With the insights of the assessment and audit in hand, mobilize your peer practitioners by communicating the results of the assessment and audit, and collaborate with them to create outcomes that will move you closer to your company's experience vision (Chapter 36: "Cross-Functional Collaboration Play," Chapter 20: "Experience Vision Play").

You and your peer practitioners can use the experience benchmarks to:

→ Extract **design problems** (Chapter 34: "Design Problems and Opportunities Play") by leveraging the attributes of the assessment and the results of the audit.
→ Define **experience metrics** for each attribute to measure the quality of your and your competitors' products (Chapter 28: "Experience Metrics Play").
→ Create a **product experience plan** to deliver the best possible product experience (Ch 35: "Product Experience Planning Play").

Looking Outward for the Way Upward

One of our partners came to us with a hefty goal: increase product adoption and create a best-in-class trial experience for their data warehouse solution. Before running this play, we asked ourselves: Who delivers the best trial experiences in the world? We did not limit our research to industry peers but looked across products and industries. Here are a few trial experiences we included in our assessment:

→ Tesla's test-drive experience;
→ Costco's food sampling experience;
→ Kickstarter's pitching experience;
→ Airtable's table simulation experience;
→ Google's search experience.

The learnings we gathered from other industries gave us clear benchmarks on what our client's MVE, MEE, and MTE should look like. For example, we learned that a most transformed trial experience should "create a relationship with the user," which was not something we could have extrapolated from direct competitors. This attribute later became one of the key principles that guided future design decisions.

IN ORDER TO MAXIMIZE THE VALUE OF THIS PLAY

→ Think as far outside the box as possible. To truly understand how to deliver the best experience, look at industries and business models that are the furthest from your own. If you work at a tech company, look at experience-focused industries, such as entertainment, health care, and tourism/hospitality. You will discover more this way than if you only look at other tech companies.

→ Run the experience benchmarking play regularly. The market is evolving at a much more rapid pace than it did before. This means that benchmarks are also evolving rapidly. Run this exercise every 1–2 years to identify any shifting or emerging trends and to keep your experience at the forefront of the evolving industry.

IN SUMMARY

In order to deliver experiences that will disrupt the industry, organizations must avoid blindly following what their direct competitors are doing. Instead, they must borrow learnings from organizations that have disrupted other industries. This play will give you clear direction as to where your starting point should be (the MVE benchmark) and where you need to go (the transformed experience).

RELATED PLAYS

Chapter 19: "Experience Roadmap Play"
Chapter 20: "Experience Vision Play"
Chapter 28: "Experience Metrics Play"
Chapter 34: "Design Problems and Opportunities Play"

Chapter 35: "Product Experience Planning Play"

Chapter 36: "Cross-Functional Collaboration Play"

33

EXPERIENCE DESIGN BRIEF PLAY
How do I align for success at the beginning of the design phase?

A design brief is an internal "contract" between key stakeholders that clearly states the agreed-upon terms (e.g. timeline, scope, artifacts) an upcoming project will follow. Create a design brief at the very beginning of every project and as a first step in the product experience plan. It'll anchor all the stakeholders and minimize points of confusion that may derail the project later on.

Why Do You Need the Experience Design Brief Play?

This play will allow your business to:

→ Define the design context;

→ Align on the intended user and business outcomes;

→ Create clear expectations for stakeholders;

→ Identify gaps right at the beginning.

Who Are the Key Players in the Experience Design Brief Play?

ROLE	WHO'S INVOLVED	RESPONSIBILITIES
DRIVER	• Experience strategist	• Define the brief; • Secure approval from the stakeholders; • Monitor adherence with the brief at all times.
CONTRIBUTOR	• Experience practitioners • Peer practitioners	• Provide perspective and gain alignment; • Check for timeline feasibility.

MINDFUL CANVAS
Experience Design Brief

CONTEXT
→ What background information do you need to know?

PROBLEM
→ What user, business, or product problem are you solving?
→ What is the pain point?
→ What is the root cause of the pain?
→ What is the impact?

STAKEHOLDERS
→ Who are your key stakeholders?
→ What are their roles and levels of involvement, following the DACI decision-making framework?

SCOPE
→ What is the defined project scope?

OUTCOMES
→ What are the user, business, and/or product outcomes you are looking to achieve?
→ What do you want the world to look like for your business and your user?

TIMELINE
→ What are the key milestones?

ARTIFACTS
→ What are all the artifacts that will be delivered?

LESSONS
→ What are the major lessons learned that you can apply to the next project?

THE HOW

To build an effective design brief play, you need to be mindful of:

1. Ensuring Universal Alignment on CONTEXT

Ensure each stakeholder, especially new hires/team members, has all the contextual information about the business, customer segment, or product necessary to be successful in the design phase. At the highest level, key elements to gather include the business, its product lines, unique selling propositions, product history, and target customer profiles.

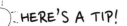

HERE'S A TIP!

If you realize that your team is not in agreement, bring in the key stakeholders and have a discussion to clarify and align before proceeding further. The earlier you resolve this, the better.

2. Defining and Communicating the Insights and the PROBLEM Space

Identify and align on the problem you need to solve. Three sources of insights guide the definition of the problem space, the users, the business, and the product, so start by answering these questions:

What is the (user/business/product) pain point? + What is the root cause of the pain? + What is the impact?

HERE'S AN EXAMPLE!

It takes five extra minutes **(impact)** for patients to stand in the queue to find the appropriate doctor **(pain point)** to treat their health problem at this hospital because there is no other way **(root cause).**

It's crucial to involve all of the key cross-functional stakeholders to align and agree on the problem space. If not everyone is in agreement, then the team will be solving different problems—and time and resources will be wasted.

Once you have identified the insights and honed in on the problem space, leverage the design problem and opportunities play to correctly frame the questions before starting to design.

3. Clearly Stating a Set of Desired OUTCOMES

For the identified problems identify and align on: What are the user, business, and/or product outcomes you are looking to achieve? Compose a well-defined outcome statement providing a full, clear visualization of your desired end state. It should be both:

→ Qualitative, describing what the world looks like for the business and the user;
→ Quantitative, articulating the expected numerical unit of improvement.

When documenting the outcome use the following syntax to add specificity and decrease ambiguity.

High-level approach + direction of improvement (i.e. increase, decrease) + unit of improvement (i.e. time) + measurement of improvement where possible (i.e. 5%)

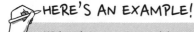

HERE'S AN EXAMPLE!

With real-time services and doctors' information provided in the digital platform (**high-level approach**), the time (**unit**) to find doctors is reduced (**direction**) by approximately 70% (**measurement**).

Make sure you get alignment across all key stakeholders. At the end of the project, revisit the outcome you've defined and ask yourself, "Have we achieved our goal?"

4. Identifying the Relevant and Necessary STAKEHOLDERS for the Project

Identify the relevant stakeholders you'll involve throughout the process. Otherwise, there'll be confusion around "Who is owning what," "Who is the final approver," "Whose feedback should I prioritize," and so forth. Applying the DACI model, assign roles based on expertise and expected level of project involvement.

→ **Driver:** the individual who has the highest level of accountability for the whole project, typically the experience strategist.
→ **Approver:** The individual who is the final approver and has decision rights, typically the head of product or a general manager.
→ **Contributors:** The individual or group of individuals who contribute to the project, typically consisting of the experience design practice and team members from the product and engineering teams.
→ **Informed:** The individuals who should be kept in the loop about the status of the project, typically consisting of subject matter experts (SMEs), individuals from other business units such as marketing and customer support, and department heads.

5. Agreeing on SCOPE

Coming to an agreement on scope with all of the stakeholders is key to setting expectations and smooth execution. Scope comes from prioritization and alignment conversations between the key stakeholders, conversations that are typically held during initial project kickoff meetings.

Consider the following to help you define the scope against which your team will deliver:

→ **User**—who are the user(s)?
→ **System**—what is the system?
→ **Product**—what product(s) are involved?
→ **Experiences and scenarios**—what experiences and scenarios will you enhance?

Try to be as specific as possible when writing the scope. Make sure to clarify what is out of scope, as well; it's a proactive way to mitigate potential scope creep.

6. Defining the TIMELINE and Major Milestones

Product experience plans contain detailed dates and deliverables. In contrast, design brief timelines only include major milestones, such as:

→ Project start and end dates;
→ Key meeting or review dates;
→ Other major milestones.

7. Identifying the ARTIFACTS That Will be Delivered

Right from the beginning, set clear expectations about what deliverables will be handed off during the course of the project. The following major artifacts should be delivered:

Research:

→ Research plan (with recruitment screener); interview discussion guide; final research report.

Design Cycle:

 HERE'S A TIP!

→ Discovery: design brief;
→ Ideation: list of prioritized design problems (DPs) and design opportunities (DOs) and design concept explorations;
→ Design doing: workflows, wireframes, visual designs, clickable prototype;
→ Hand-off: design specs and QA results.

Collaboration:

→ Meeting minutes;
→ Documented list of key decisions and actions.

8. Reflecting on LESSONS Learned during the Project

At the end of the project, revisit the design brief to reflect on and document any learnings. Bring back your original group of stakeholders, and discuss what worked, what didn't work, and how to better work together so you can apply the learnings next time. This is an important step because it fuels constant growth and improvement.

Could Have, Should Have, Would Have

Our firm was brought in to redesign a device-monitoring experience over a five-week sprint. The project manager was our primary contact, and he gave us a number of insights that drove our design for the first 3.5 weeks. Then, it was time for us to meet with the VP of product to present our design. Ten minutes into the meeting, the VP of product stopped us and said, "This is not what I was thinking …" It was a classic "oh-crap" moment. We didn't know who the final approver was, and we didn't have the right set of insights. The VP had a drastically different set of business insights that she thought we were using for our work, and consequently, over the previous 3.5 weeks, we had been solving the wrong problem.

The project went downhill from there. We had to sprint hard toward the finish line, effectively condensing a 5-week design into 1.5 weeks. We worked nights and weekends to catch up for lost time. It was miserable. The team's motivation dropped and angst built up, and the business wasted a ton of time and resources.

This could have been prevented by having an upfront design brief that identified all of the necessary stakeholders and that clearly aligned with the scope upfront and before doing any design.

IN ORDER TO MAXIMIZE THE VALUE OF THIS PLAY

→   Make sure all key stakeholders review and sign off on the document before starting any design work;

→   Keep referring back to it in later meetings, when confusion arises about the problem being solved and the desired outcomes to be achieved;

→   Keep the design brief up to date. Monitor the timelines regularly, and escalate any deviations immediately.

IN SUMMARY

Do not underestimate the value of a design brief. It is a critical decision document that will maximize your team's success by setting clear expectations, removing ambiguities, and aligning with key stakeholders upfront. One hour invested here will save 10 hours of headache and frustration down the road.

RELATED PLAYS

Chapter 34: "Design Problems and Opportunities Play"

DESIGN PROBLEMS AND OPPORTUNITIES PLAY

How do I decide what are the right problems to solve?

Too often, practitioners dive straight into solution-ing before clearly defining the problem and determining whether it's important to solve. Rooted in a deep understanding of user and business needs, design problems (DPs) and design opportunities (DOs) are reframed questions that catalyze breakthrough ideas and design. The DP and DO play will instill focus, propel teams and organizations from paralyzed inertia to excitement and progress, and ultimately lead to user delight and high business impact.

Why Do You Need the Design Problems and Opportunities Play?

This play will allow your business to:

→ Extract the right problem to tackle;

→ Generate more ideas by exploring the problem from multiple perspectives;

→ Increase your team's focus and overall productivity;

→ Deliver greater impact by focusing on the problems that matter most to your organization.

Who Are the Key Players in the Design Problems and Opportunities Play?

ROLE	WHO'S INVOLVED	RESPONSIBILITIES
DRIVER	• Experience strategist	• Own the insights gathering from multiple sources; • Deconstruct and correctly frame the problem; • Prioritize the design problems and opportunities.
CONTRIBUTOR	• Design practitioners • Peer practitioners.	• Contribute to the problem identification; • Trace the design solutions back to the original insight and identified problem; • Collaborate with partners.

MINDFUL CANVAS

Design Problems and Opportunities

SOURCE

➔ What are the key user, business, or product insights?

FRAMING

➔ What is the reframed design problem and design opportunity?

DECONSTRUCTION

➔ What is the unit level of the larger problem that you and your team are equipped to solve?

PRIORITIZATION

➔ What are all the DPs and DOs that will solve the user, business, or product problem?
➔ What is the ranked-order list of DPs and DOs that you'll solve?

COLLABORATION

➔ Who are the key players that you need to collaborate and share the DPs or DOs with?
➔ Who needs to be involved in validating the DPs have been solved?

THE HOW

To build an effective design problem and opportunities play, you need to be mindful of:

1. Identifying the SOURCES of Insights That lead to DPs and DOs

All DPs and DOs can typically be sourced from three primary types of insights:

→ **User insights** are collected from interviews and observations conducted by the user research team. They are a record of the pain points and/or joys that your users experience.

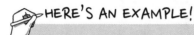HERE'S AN EXAMPLE!

Users enjoy collaborating with their peers to ideate on project plans.

→ **Business insights** are unique to one organization and come from intelligence gathered on the industry, business, or competitors (Chapter 28: "Experience Metrics Play").

HERE'S AN EXAMPLE!

Subscription renewals have decreased by 15% in the last quarter.

→ **Product insights** are centered around a product or platform. They originate from product metrics and usage details or direct user feedback on the product.

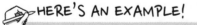HERE'S AN EXAMPLE!

It took users 20% longer to complete the task compared to the previous product releases.

2. DECONSTRUCTING the Larger Problem

When you arrive at a user, business, or product insight, further break down the identified challenges into sub-components (Chapter 28: "Experience Metrics Play"). The goal is to understand all of the different variables that, when considered together, help answer the question of why the problem occurred in the first place. Break the larger problem down to its unit-level problems, and focus on the ones you or your team are equipped to solve.

Now that you have a clear idea of what problem variables you will solve, it's important to shape the problem statement. This will serve as your anchor moving forward. How you frame the problem will determine whether you are going after the right problem and consequently, how well the solution will solve the user, business, or product problem.

There are two ways to frame the problem:

> **"People don't want to buy a quarter-inch drill. They want a quarter-inch hole!"**
>
> *– Professor Theodore Levitt*

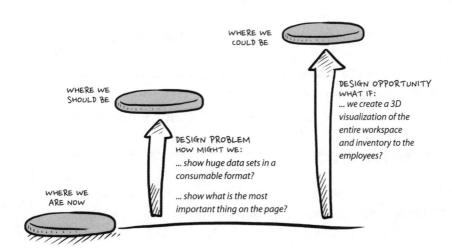

→ **Design problems** start with "How might we" (HMW) questions. A well-framed "HMW" question turns your problem and insights into questions that beg ideation and participation from others. One mistake we often see is a tendency to include solutions in the framing of design problems. Good design problems don't mention specific ways in which the problem will be solved, but rather ask how to achieve an end goal.

HERE'S AN EXAMPLE!

Wrong: Solution oriented: HMW create a purchasing experience for young mothers using voice command?

Right: Goal oriented: HMW create a purchasing experience for young mothers that eases the chaos of shopping with children?

In the first example, "voice command" prescribes a solution rather than opening up a space to brainstorm all of the different ways the problem can be solved. The second DP avoids including any solutions in the problem statement and focuses instead on stating the goal—i.e. easing the chaos of shopping with children.

→ **Design opportunities** start with "What if we" (WIW) questions. Design opportunities differ from design problems in that they transform challenges into problem statements that spur out-of-the-box thinking, ultimately leading to solutions that question the status quo and bring tremendous delight to the user.

HERE'S AN EXAMPLE!

Observation: While you're conducting research on a sign-up experience, multiple users give you feedback that the process feels cumbersome and has too many steps.

DO Framing: What if we could magically avoid the sign-up process altogether?

In this example, customers don't expect the company to provide a sign-up experience through a single interaction, because they are used to the industry norm of a long sign-up process. However, the company is fully equipped to deliver that experience by bringing multiple departments together. A well-framed design opportunity truly delights the user.

DPs and DOs can sit across multiple levels: UI, PX, and XT (Chapter 4: Experience Value Chain).

HERE'S AN EXAMPLE!

UI DP: How might we make the call to action (CTA) more evident on the screen?

PX, XT, DP: How might we increase the engagement of the migration experience?

HERE'S A TIP!

Typically for 10 design problems that you identify, try to identify one design opportunity to focus on.

Design problems and design opportunities both respond to the same problem and challenge identified in the user, business, or product. However, design problems prompt solutions that answer "What the experience should be"; users expect them—they are table stakes. Design opportunities go beyond to build solutions that answer, "What the experience could be"; even though users don't expect them, the solutions are within the team or organization's current capabilities and will oftentime push their capabilities further.

4. Properly PRIORITIZING of all DPs and DOs Before Solving for Them

A large volume of ideas spurs originality. Brainstorm and ideate as many DPs and DOs as possible.

Prioritize your wealth of DPs and DOs. This way, you can surface the problems you should start solving and designing solutions for them. There are many ways to do so, including using a 2x2 prioritization matrix with an impact x-axis and a frequency y-axis, or an impact x-axis and a feasibility y-axis.

After prioritization, you'll have a focused and ranked-order list of DPs and DOs to tackle that will ultimately solve the user, business, or product problem.

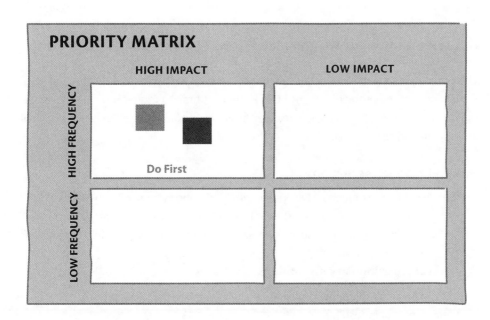

5. Ongoing COLLABORATION and Hand-Off

The next step for DPs and DOs will vary depending on the level (i.e. UI, PX, XT), scope (e.g. how big is the problem or opportunity), intent or overarching objective, and existing organizational capabilities.

Achieve traceability for each DP and DO (Chapter 40: "Detailed Design Play"); this helps govern and hold the team accountable for solving them. Document the source of the solution, the variation of solutions, the final solution, and the efficacy of the solution.

Typically, the prioritized DPs and DOs are given to the design team, which triggers the design doing process and collaboration with the product and engineering teams.

Here are some other hand-off scenarios:

→ **White-space brainstorming:** If the DO reimagines how the product will evolve (e.g. what if the system didn't exist?), then the next step is putting together a vision of your reimagined future state (Chapter 20: "Experience Vision Play").

→ **Ecosystem mapping:** If the DP or DO requires multiple departments to come together, visualize the entire ecosystem across departments (Chapter 18: "Experience Ecosystem Play").

→ **Workflow improvements:** If poor user experience is caused by gaps within existing workflows, then figure out how you can optimize the workflow (Chapter 39: "Workflow Design Play").

→ **Design doing:** If prioritized DPs and DOs are ready for the next stages of the design cycle, then pass them over to the design team to start ideating and building design solutions.

→ **Validation research:** Once a DP has been designed for, validate its impact. The research team closes the loop on whether the DP was solved in real life with real users.

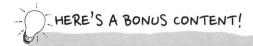
HERE'S A BONUS CONTENT!

Triggering Mindful Inspiration from DPs and DOs

When practitioners eat, sleep, and drink the DPs and DOs, they have a heightened sense of awareness of the problem at hand. This is the best time to trigger mindful ideation, as inspiration can emerge from anywhere. Specifically, incorporate these three levels of inspiration-gathering so you can build an effective solution:

→ **Level 1: Direct Inspirations**

Ideas inspired by solutions developed in similar situations from industry peers.
An e-commerce product team asking, "How might we establish trust with our user?" can look to industry leaders, such as Amazon, Etsy, and Shopify, for level 1 inspirations.

→ **Level 2: Cross-Industry Inspirations**

Ideas inspired by solutions employed by similar teams in organizations that are outside your domain or industry.
The e-commerce product team can research how fintech and health tech systems build trust with their users.

→ **Level 3: Conceptual Inspirations**

These are ideas that surface from unlikely or non-traditional sources. Conceptual-level inspirations can come from anywhere—pictures, actions, human behaviors, and nature. It's critical to maintain the highest level of awareness of the problem at hand, but conceptual inspirations can lead to disruption and yield transformative outcomes.

The e-commerce product team can contemplate how doctors establish trust with their patients or how hostage negotiators establish trust with hostage-takers.

DPs and DOs That Launched the Mobile Revolution

It was the early 2000s. Research In Motion (RIM) was focusing on improving its QWERTY keyboard, asking, "How might we make the keyboard more efficient to type on?" Sony was focusing on improving the lens of their cameras while maintaining competitive pricing, asking, "How might we help our customer capture stunning photos?" Both RIM and Sony were prioritizing design problems that focused on refining technologies that had already been released.

However, Steve Jobs, at Apple, looked at a new set of emerging trends and discovered a whole new design opportunity. He witnessed the iPod's tremendous success; people loved taking music on the go. He also noticed that people were looking to do more with their mobile devices beyond merely making phone calls—browsing the web, checking emails, exchanging instant messages, and taking photos; however, they were juggling multiple devices to do so.

In contrast with his CEO peers, who were trying to tweak their existing technology, Jobs focused on solving the user problem. Asking, "What if the user can do everything on one device?" opened up a groundbreaking design opportunity for Apple. In 2007, the iPhone launched the mobile revolution. It all began with user insights and a reframed question that challenged the status quo.

IN ORDER TO MAXIMIZE THE VALUE OF THIS PLAY

→ Always trace the DP and DO back to the original business or user insight.

→ Maintain a practice of insights curation (Chapter 29: "Insights Curation Play") for all unprioritized DPs and DOs. This prevents knowledge drain, especially when key team members leave.

→ Designers should always anchor back to the right problem whenever they are presenting their designs. Identify the problem first, and then show the design. This will ensure the team focuses on the problem rather than getting distracted by the design and will enable the designer to guide the conversation toward deriving a magical solution.

→ Be vigilant. User problems and insights can be surfaced throughout the product journey, beyond the most obvious phases such as research and stakeholder interview.

IN SUMMARY

Breakthrough innovation and design start with asking the right question. These come from insights and correctly framed DPs and DOs that spur collaboration, out-of-the-box thinking, and collective action. Don't underestimate the power of asking the right question and correctly framing the problem—these are more important than the solution itself.

RELATED PLAYS

Chapter 29: "Insights Curation Play"

CHAPTER 35

PRODUCT EXPERIENCE PLANNING PLAY

How do I ensure the delivery of a great product experience?

Product experience planning is an essential navigational tool that guides experience practitioners from a robust understanding of the product, business, and user intent, to a finished design that is ready to be handed off to the engineering team.

Time invested developing and aligning with stakeholders on the plan will pay off handsomely down the road. The resulting product experience plan is a powerful risk mitigation tool for your business, ensuring your product will launch on time and on budget.

Why Do You Need Product Experience Planning?

This play will allow your business to:

→ Promote cross-functional alignment and collaboration by having a single plan of action that everyone is tracking;

→ Remove ambiguity about why certain activities are being done and what outcome is being achieved;

→ Deliver products on time and on budget by not overlooking important steps along the research and design cycles;

→ Increase team productivity by lowering churn and process confusion.

Who Are the Key Players in the Product Experience Planning Play?

ROLE	WHO'S INVOLVED	RESPONSIBILITIES
DRIVER	• Experience strategist	• Uncover the product experiences and UX activities across research and design teams; • Ensure alignment on the plan across the organization; • Take up the ownership for delivery of experiences.
CONTRIBUTOR	• Experience practitioners • Experience partners	• Provide individual plans and experiments; • Provide perspective and gain alignment.

Product Experience Planning

OUTCOME

↑ What are you looking to accomplish? Why?
↑ Who is your user? What prioritized experiences will the design efforts focus on?
↑ What user, business, or product problems are you trying to solve?

EXPERIENCE DESIGN ACTIVITIES

Research

↑ What are the research questions you are trying to answer?
↑ What research method will you employ?
↑ What are the research activities that you will plan for?

Design

↑ What problems are you solving?
↑ What design experiments will you be conducting?
↑ What design activities you will plan for?

Collaboration

↑ Who will you collaborate with?
↑ How will you collaborate with other teams to deliver the best experience?
↑ What are the collaboration activities?

GOVERNANCE

↑ How will you govern the execution of the plan?

PLANNING

↑ What is the duration of the plan?
↑ What is the sequencing of all these activities?
↑ What are the key milestones and timeline?

THE HOW

To build an effective product experience plan, you need to be mindful of:

1. Aligning to the End OUTCOME

A product experience plan is a project management play that the experience strategist develops, manages, and governs during the product thinking phase and before any design activities start. Before spending any time building the plan, it's critical to have a crystal clear picture of your destination and answer the following questions:

→ Who is the user? What prioritized product experiences will the design efforts focus on?
→ What does the design aim at accomplishing? And why?
→ What user, business, or product problems am I trying to solve?

Visualize the end outcome. More often than not, the goal is to achieve a vision, solve a pain point the user is currently experiencing, or deliver an enhanced experience through your product. Clearly articulate and align on what it is you are looking to achieve.

2. The EXPERIENCE DESIGN ACTIVITIES

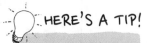

HERE'S A TIP!

Don't overlook collaboration activities. It's just as important to get alignment, sign-off, and feedback as it is to do research and design.

User research activities need to be effectively factored into the plan, both to ensure that the relevant user problems are being addressed, and to mitigate the risk of designing ineffective solutions for those problems. There are a number of different research methodologies (Chapter 25: "Picking a Research Method Play"); pick the methods that are most appropriate for the outcome you are looking to achieve. Based on the chosen method include the related research activities into your product experience plan:

→ **Study plan:** a summary of the research plan, logistical requirements, timeline, and team members involved;
→ **User recruitment:** identifying suitable research participants and creating screener questions;
→ **Research study:** the actual user research designed to achieve your research objective;
→ **Synthesis:** an analysis of all types of user data consolidated into actionable insights;
→ **Presentation:** a summary that highlights research insights and recommendations.

In a highly efficient research organization, user research typically takes three to five weeks of active research activities. However, there are two unique scenarios that you may want to plan for by budgeting in additional time:

→ Recruitment for formative research often takes much longer than expected, so plan for an additional three to four weeks to recruit and screen research participants.
→ If you are conducting research that involves stimuli (i.e. artifacts that will be shown to the participants), then plan for an additional three to four days to prepare and package the stimuli.

Design activities typically consist of problem identification and framing, concept generation, ideation, prototyping, validation, hand-off, and QA.

Consider the following sample of design activities for inclusion in your product experience plan:

→ **Discovery:** Outline the problem space, outcomes, scope, timeline, and key learnings, providing enough evidence for what to do next. Include this activity in your plan if you don't understand the product, business, or the problem space.

→ **Ideation:** Gather inspirations and generate ideas through collaborative sessions to address the design problem or design opportunity statements. This is a critical activity because it forces you to frame the problem, allowing you to start your design process with alignment and focus (Chapter 34: "Design Problem and Opportunities Play").

→ **Workflow, Wireframe, and Iteration:** Begin the iterative design process by outlining the paths of a potential user, creating a visual guide that represents the skeletal framework of a website or application, and iterating the design based on feedback. Make sure you budget for at least three rounds of iterations—one for the first draft, one for after user research and validation, and one with the final approver.

→ **Content and Visual Design:** Specify the details of the visual style and copy that will go in the product experience.

→ **Prototyping:** Transform the proposed solution into an interactive model for testing the designs.

→ **Validation:** Review the final prototypes with stakeholders to ensure that the proposed solution achieves the overall business objective and meets user requirements.

→ **Hand-offs:** Transfer the designs to the responsible team with detailed documentation and interaction notes.

→ **Quality Assurance (QA):** Assess the usability of the implemented design with users in order to identify potential challenges before releasing it to the market.

Your timeline will vary based on the scope of the project and your team's resource availability. So plan your roadmap accordingly.

Generally, the end-to-end design cycle takes 18 weeks (22 weeks if you plan to conduct summative testing).

HERE'S AN EXAMPLE!

Below is a breakdown of how long each activity typically takes for:

→ **Discovery and Ideation:** 1 to 3 weeks;

→ **Workflow, Wireframe, Iteration:** 8 weeks;

→ **Visual and Copy:** 3 weeks;

→ **Prototype:** 3 week;

→ **Validation:** 4 weeks to test with a sample of five to eight users;

→ **Hand-off and QA:** 1 week.

Finally, **collaboration** is key to experience design. Planning collaborative activities is often overlooked, causing significant churn in the planned process. The following collaboration activities bring

> "Design is not just what it looks like and feels like. Design is how it works."
>
> – Steve Jobs

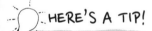
together different sets of stakeholders from business, design, product, and engineering teams across different types of activities.

→ **Problem definition and alignment:** Define the right problem to solve by considering varied perspectives from across the organization. Align on the final problem statement, outcome, and approach.

→ **Ideation:** Generate ideas throughout the design cycle. Bring together diverse and relevant stakeholders to generate ideas from multiple perspectives.

→ **Validation:** Sign off on key decisions or artifacts such as the research and business objectives, user insights, and requirements.

→ **Reviews:** Provide feedback and ensure the design outcome has been aligned with the original user, business, or product intent.

→ **Hand-offs:** Hand over key deliverables, insights, and clear documentation to the next team.

Collaboration activities typically take about two weeks to complete. However, you need to make sure that they are interspersed across the product experience plan.

3. PLANNING and Documenting Your Activities

After identifying the different activities that need to be considered for the product experience plan, build a three-month forward-looking plan, adapted if necessary for agile software development or another approach.

Include these key elements:

→ **Sequencing:** Arrange the activities in a particular way that takes into account the relationships that exist between activities. Every activity and its sub-activities should be staggered such that outcomes inform the next activity. This will help you avoid major roadblocks.

→ **Timelines:** Define the durations for each activity, grouping them to make the forward-looking plan manageable and realistic. Make sure these durations are acknowledged by all involved parties, or else the plan will inevitably fail and the project will be delayed.

→ **Milestones:** Call out the specific intermediate milestones and checkpoints, such as reviews, ideations, hand-offs, accountability checks, and validations, that will enable a smooth and seamless product experience process.

4. Building Proper GOVERNANCE during the Execution

Governance provides the necessary oversight to ensure activities are being executed according to plan. The experience strategist owns the responsibility of maintaining a healthy plan and conducts regular syncs with key stakeholders through activities like weekly stand-ups and monthly planning. This ensures that everyone has clear visibility into the progress of the plan and proactively communicates potential roadblocks so there's ample time for risk mitigation.

Where the Rubber Meets the Road

A CEO of one of our clients shared a bold new vision with her leadership team: "We will invest in being a customer-obsessed organization." Everyone in the company was energized by this vision, including the product team that started working on redesigning the incumbent product in earnest.

Unfortunately, no one truly defined the roadmap or proactively populated it with all of the research, design, and collaboration activities. So when user research began, they ran into unplanned four-week delays caused by difficulties in recruiting relevant participants.

Furthermore, no one proactively brought product or engineering into the initial problem definition and alignment conversations. So when design started, the product and engineering leads were surprised—they had different views about which prioritized problems ought to be solved.

These surprises snowballed and led to unnecessary churn. Ultimately, they resulted in a six-month delay to the original product release date and cost approximately $250,000 in design and development loss. Having an effective product experience plan that factored in the various steps would have prevented this churn.

IN ORDER TO MAXIMIZE THE VALUE OF THIS PLAY

→ Foster a shared vision. This will help the teams focus on common goals and work together to accomplish them.

→ Plan in advance. Avoid last-minute rushes, and always have a contingency plan.

→ Add buffers. Budget extra time for certain activities (i.e. research) to proactively protect the plan from being derailed by delays.

→ Develop checks and balances. Make sure the plan is reviewed regularly and is adapted to account for necessary changes that better reflect the current reality.

→ Take design hand-off and QA seriously. They are critical parts of the plan that will have significant downstream impact (e.g. product delays, engineering churn) if you don't spend the time to do it well.

IN SUMMARY

The product experience plan is a project management play that grounds you in the big picture while helping you account for all the minute details that go into achieving your intended goal. Operating without a plan is like throwing darts in the dark and crossing your fingers that they'll somehow hit the target.

RELATED PLAYS

Chapter 25: "Picking a Research Method Play"
Chapter 34: "Design Problems and Opportunities Play"

36 CROSS-FUNCTIONAL COLLABORATION PLAY

How do I collaborate across the organization to drive seamless and informed product experience design?

As management guru Ken Blanchard notes, "None of us is as smart as all of us." Unfortunately, many teams operate in silos, where multidisciplinary collaboration and problem solving do not inform experience design. The cross-functional collaboration play helps you dismantle these silos and ensure that the right internal partners share the right knowledge, processes, deliverables, and visibility at the right time. Breaking down these silos will reduce churn and increase productivity and ultimately ensure that sound decisions are made to achieve experience design goals.

Why Do You Need the Cross-Functional Collaboration Play?

This play will allow your business to:

→ Dismantle communication and information silos;

→ Reduce ambiguity about the roles and outputs of the different teams that participate in the product experience design process;

→ Better manage expectations around dependencies;

→ Reduce frustration among cross-functional teams;

→ Increase alignment and productivity to deliver quicker business outcomes.

Who Are the Key Players in the Cross-Functional Collaboration Play?

ROLE	WHO'S INVOLVED	RESPONSIBILITIES
DRIVER	• Experience strategist	• Orchestrate collaboration across the organization
CONTRIBUTOR	• Product manager, experience practitioners, engineering lead, and peer practitioners from other parts of the business (sales, marketing, customer support, etc.)	• Provide necessary inputs, expertise, and perspectives for problem-solving; • Participate in cross-functional discussions and workshops; • Bring the necessary artifacts to the table.

MINDFUL CANVAS

Cross-functional Collaboration

EXPERIENCE VISION

➔ What is your vision of your users' future-state experiences, that you need to collaborate on in order to achieve?

SHARED UNDERSTANDING

➔ Who are the users?
➔ What is the vision?
➔ What are the user and business outcomes all teams should be striving for?
➔ What are the experience metrics that need to be achieved?

SHARED PROCESSES

➔ What processes are interdependent with different teams?

PARTNERS

➔ Who are the experience practitioners and partners that need to be aligned and at the table?
➔ At what cadence do they need to be involved or informed?

SHARED ACTIVITIES

➔ What activities require the inputs of multiple teams?

SHARED REPOSITORY

➔ Where can all shared artifacts be found?
➔ How can they be shared?

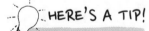
THE HOW

To run an effective cross-functional collaboration play, you need to be mindful of:

1. The EXPERIENCE VISION

The experience vision is always the north star for experience design. It encompasses an understanding of who your users are, knowledge of your business goals, and an understanding of your competition (Chapter 20: "Experience Vision Play").

2. Relevant PARTNERS

Recent research has demonstrated that horizontal relationships actually are more important. This is why user experience design encompasses more than just product touchpoints: peer practitioners parallel to the design team need to be involved.

Identify peers from various departments who need to be aligned on the product and user goals, and who will have inputs into the processes and activities to achieve those goals.

At minimum, the collaboration trifecta of product manager, engineering lead, and experience practitioners must partner with one another. This core team should have a regular cadence to share knowledge and feedback.

However, true value will be driven when more representation is included from a wider team: other collaborators, influencers, and supporters such as peer practitioners (sales, marketing, customer support), CEO, executive leadership, and the board of directors. Establish a regular cadence with this wider team, as well.

3. A SHARED UNDERSTANDING of the User and Business Context

To achieve product innovation that is rooted in driving value for both your users and your business, ensure that your collaborators have a shared understanding of the following:

→ Who your users are (Chapter 14: "User Empathy Play");
→ What the vision for the experience is (Chapter 20: "Experience Vision Play");
→ What your experience metrics are (Chapter 28: "Experience Metrics Play");
→ What the user and business goals are (Chapter 33: "Experience Design Brief Play").

In a user-first approach, organizations curate and disseminate a deep understanding of and empathy for their users and their experiences—before authorizing internal groups to make any product decisions. For example, shift the line of thinking from "I'm in finance; how does the user affect me?" to "I'm in finance; what can be done on my side that is part of creating a meaningful experience for the user?" Partners should be able to answer this question, as well as propagate information on the user, the vision, goals, and metrics within their own teams.

4. SHARED PROCESSES

To design and develop great end-to-end product experiences, identify the processes that partners need to be part of to ensure visibility and accuracy of information.

These processes include:

→ **Collaboration Planning:** Create a product experience plan to bring the experience vision to life (Chapter 35: "Product Experience Planning Play"). Ensure collaboration is happening between product, user experience design, and engineering. Identify a driver that is accountable for the activity taking place and the outcomes being achieved.
Take a cue from agile software development: It calls for multi disciplinary teams ("scrums") to take an iterative approach and collaborate in the construct of "sprints"—a timeboxed duration given to complete a set amount of work.

→ **Communication at Large:** Establish a communication channel or channels by which to engage and inform core and wider team members. For example, the core team may have a dedicated chat channel for day-to-day questions and updates, while the wider team may be best communicated to as a group through email.

→ **Feedback:** Determine how to capture feedback from multiple disciplines during various stages of the product development process. For example, feedback can be given in live design reviews, as comments on artifacts, and/or as tickets on JIRA.

→ **Approvals:** Determine how sign-off from approvers is conveyed, how it can be traced, and how it moves from one team to another. For example, tracking approvals can be done by moving an item on a Kanban board or changing the status of a ticket.

5. SHARED ACTIVITIES

In the design and development process, define and plan the activities where it is vital to have multidisciplinary representation and inputs at the table. The intent of this is to break through information silos and get expertise input at the right time. These activities can include:

→ Kick-offs to launch new projects/sprints/phases of a project;
→ Design reviews to elicit feedback from product management, engineering, SMEs, and other wider team members;
→ Ideation workshops to effectively extract ideas and ward off tunnel vision;
→ Design hand-offs to the development team (Chapter 42: "Design System Play");
→ User research readouts to socialize research insights to the wider organization to build user empathy and keep others informed;
→ Cross-functional retrospectives to allow the multidisciplinary team to check in and course-correct;
→ Design QA to check the engineered build against the designs delivered (Chapter 43: "Design Quality Assurance (QA) Play").

Track all shared activities in a deliberate manner by having an identified driver. This should be done with the help of a product experience plan (Chapter 35: "Product Experience Planning Play").

True collaboration happens when relevant teams are given a stake in the product experience design

Print out artifacts such as user personas, experience visions, and roadmaps and poster them around the office. Make the artifacts highly visible, to prevent them from falling out of sight—and therefore out of mind.

Pick a tool that allows for collaboration within the repository, i.e. one that has commenting functions.

process. Core team members should be involved, not just informed, and should hold each other accountable. Information should be registered, not just read. True collaboration becomes evident when:

→ A common language starts being spoken;
→ Everyone can rally for the vision and end goals;
→ Multidisciplinary inputs are baked into deliverables/artifacts;
→ The end result catches no one by surprise.

6. A SHARED REPOSITORY of Curated Artifacts

Finally, it is imperative that all partners have access to shared artifacts, whether they be research insights, requirements, roadmaps, design artifacts, meeting minutes, or documentation of processes.

Establish a repository of this information and communicate how it can be accessed. Set aside a few minutes each week to ensure it is updated.

Reengineering collaboration

We worked with a historically engineering-first firm to map their engineering activities and agile development process onto their wider design process. Sensitizing to the various collaboration activities listed in this play helped provide product management and engineering visibility into when and how much of their inputs were needed from the design perspective, something which had been lacking. In simple terms this allowed everyone to play in the game of created world class experiences.

A noteworthy outcome of this exercise was that different disciplines collaborated on creating an experience vision. It wasn't just experience practitioners who recommended ideas; engineering and sales team members also started pitched in. This created a deeply collaborative environment where everyone felt invested in the design process, regardless of their job title.

In addition, every quarter, we hosted a meeting with internal partners and any new staff to refresh the collaboration model and discuss any improvements.

IN ORDER TO MAXIMIZE THE VALUE OF THIS PLAY

→ Find collaborators within each department to be your point of contact for scheduling and for rallying their troops;
→ Hold each other accountable. Don't cut corners on having the right people involved in the shared processes and activities for the sake of time; this will only cause churn in the long term.

IN SUMMARY

Cross-functional collaboration means more than having once-in-a while meetings to inform multidisciplinary yet passive stakeholders in a room. It means having teams actively engage with one another—rallying around common goals; sharing knowledge, artifacts, and ideas; eliciting feedback; fine-tuning processes across teams; and maintaining a level of visibility into the moving parts of the product experience design process. Cross-functional collaboration is not just a nice-to-have; it is vital to reducing churn and frustration and ultimately, to ensuring that an experience is designed effectively with informed decisions throughout the way. As the saying goes, "If you want to go fast, go alone; but if you want to go far, go together."

RELATED PLAYS

Chapter 14: "User Empathy Play"
Chapter 19: "Experience Roadmap Play"
Chapter 20: "Experience Vision Play"

Chapter 35: "Product Experience Planning Play"
Chapter 42: "Design System Play"
Chapter 43: "Design Quality Assurance (QA) Play"

PRODUCT THINKING PROGRAM PLAY
How do I catalyze great product experiences?

The product thinking program play provides a framework for creating transformative experiences by identifying, prioritizing, and catalyzing all the moving parts of the organization together. It helps the organization work toward a larger experience vision while being mindful of the details, adjacent experiences, constraints, and tangible measures of success.

Why Do You Need a Product Thinking Program?

This play will allow your business to:

→ Drive business value through user-centricity;

→ Shift the focus away from features and UI level problems;

→ Orchestrate multiple moving parts into a unified experience;

→ Solve a broad range of problems and opportunities while staying anchored to a single vision.

Who Are the Key Players in the Product Thinking Program Play?

ROLE	WHO'S INVOLVED	RESPONSIBILITIES
DRIVER	• Experience strategist	• Catalyze an experience mindset; • Orchestrate and govern products vision and experience; • Ensure problems and opportunities are resolved across the product experience; • Ensure alignment across the organization.
CONTRIBUTOR	• Experience practitioner • Experience design partners	• Support the vision; • Collaborate with teams across the organization; • Report metrics and data.

MINDFUL CANVAS
Product Thinking Program

PORTFOLIO OF PROBLEMS
➜ What users will you solve problems for?
➜ What user/business problems will you solve? (DP/DO?)
➜ What short-, mid-, and long-term problems will you solve?

PEOPLE
➜ Who will lead the product thinking program?
➜ What skills do you need on your team?
➜ What other teams do you need support from?

EXPERIENCE ECOSYSTEM
➜ How are all the dots connecting for the product experience to work?
➜ What other users does the user interact with in the system?
➜ What technologies support the experience?
➜ What departments support the experience?
➜ What external partnerships will you invest in?

PRODUCT PLANNING
➜ How will you manage your roadmaps?
➜ How will you address your requirements?

CURATION AND COLLABORATION
➜ How will you collaborate with other teams to deliver the best experience?
➜ What and how will you communicate?
➜ How frequently will you communicate?

GOVERNANCE
➜ How will you measure the business impact of design?
➜ What process will you use to keep the team aligned?
➜ How will you foster continuous innovation?

THE HOW

To build an effective product thinking program, you need to be mindful of:

1. Curating a PORTFOLIO OF PROBLEMS

HERE'S A TIP!

How you frame your problems will affect how you solve the problem (Chapter 34: "Design Problems and Opportunities Play").

To be a catalyst for great experiences that drive value to your users and to your business, you need to solve a broad spectrum of design problems (DPs) to achieve the short-, mid-, and long-term goals for your experience vision (Chapter 20: "Experience Vision Play"). Along with this you would also need to focus on identifying a set of key design opportunities (DOs) to achieve the intended vision.

This mix of DPs and DOs prioritized across various time horizons is called the **portfolio of problems.** Like any healthy portfolio, the proportions of investment you make across the portfolio of problems should constantly be monitored and tracked on an ongoing basis.

2. Investing in the Right PEOPLE

Consider the following must-haves as you bring on people for your product thinking program:

→ **Program driver**: Organizations need a single owner who is accountable for the program, ideally the experience strategist. This will enable consistent oversight and collaboration on the portfolio of problems.

→ **Program partners:** Ensure that you have dedicated time available to invest in strategic collaboration between design leaders, design practitioners, and design partners (especially product management and engineering lead) as there will be constant prioritization, trade-off, planning, and constraint management related dialogue.

3. Factoring in the Larger EXPERIENCE ECOSYSTEM

Be mindful of the larger system in which the product experience is built. Never lose focus on the various elements that can directly or indirectly affect the product experience.

These could include influencers such as:

→ Adjacent experiences and users that might impact your user;

→ Which internal teams need to be involved;

→ Which external partnerships to invest in;

→ The different technologies that need to work together to drive functionality.

Think about how they might all come together in a single experience.

Make sure that experience roadmaps (Chapter 19: "Experience Roadmap Play"), experience ecosystem (Chapter 18: "Experience Ecosystem Play"), and experience benchmarks (Chapter 32: "Experience Benchmarking Play") are actively curated and tracked across the product organization so you can help broaden the understanding of the system that is needed to connect all of the dots that enable a great product experience to work.

4. Effective PRODUCT PLANNING

Ensure that clear and effective plans are put in place that constantly identify the key priorities and activities around the product experience and always have up-to-date plans.

→ **Roadmaps:** Use the portfolio of problems to understand problems and outcomes you need to solve, achieve, and coordinate cross-functionally to sequence the efforts of the various teams that are helping you solve them (Chapter 35: "Product Experience Planning Play" and Chapter 36: "Cross-Functional Collaboration Play").

→ **Requirements:** Make sure you actively collaborate with the product manager to manage your product backlog: the kind of documentation needed to keep everyone aligned on what to build and what outcomes to go for.

Use this documentation to anchor yourself and your team to the big picture as well as the smaller details. Cross-reference them frequently to check that the two remain in sync to work toward the same vision.

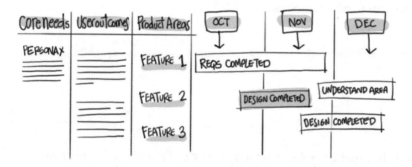

5. Have Frequent CURATION and COLLABORATION

Make sure all documentation and resources are accessible to other contributing teams for effective cross-functional collaboration (Chapter 36: "Cross-Functional Collaboration Play"). Work with your counterparts in the other contributing teams to establish the frequency and method of sharing work and giving feedback to ensure all efforts stay aligned to the vision.

HERE'S A TIP!

Host monthly "demo" events where each contributing team can showcase what they have been working on, and use this as an opportunity for others to ask questions and provide feedback.

6. Establish Systems of GOVERNANCE

To ensure the continued success of the product thinking program there are several key aspects of the program that need to be tracked on an ongoing basis:

→ **Impact of experience:** Establish experience metrics and business metrics (Chapter 28: "Experience Metrics Play") you need to track overall and for each contributing team, and measure them often. This will allow the teams to track the success of their individual contributions and have visibility into the larger impact on the overall vision.

→ **Team accountability and alignment:** Standardize systems such as DACI to establish roles and responsibilities for each facet of collaboration. Not only will this assign clear accountability, but it will also streamline the decision-making process.

→ **Continuous innovation:** Revisit your portfolio of problems regularly and evaluate if you have been successfully solving a broad range of problems and if you are adding new problems on an ongoing basis. Collaborate with your counterparts who are driving the research program (Chapter 30: "User Research Program Play") to make sure you are solving problems for today as well as exploring what to solve tomorrow.

Breaking Monotony through Product Thinking Program

We keep frequently coming across organizations that have invested in a lone designer to help them in the pursuit of making better product experiences. In one such company the designer was very unhappy as he felt he was in a "monotonous job" (his words) of creating designs for incremental feature enhancements. He was starting to lose motivation in continuing his journey at the organization.

As part of our engagement with this organization, we introduced the larger team to the product thinking program that included plays related to the portfolio of problems and product experience planning. This shift was profound for this designer as he now had a view of the variety of design problems to go after, and subsequently he volunteered to go after a specific long-term problem (onboarding experience) in addition to his existing workload. Having an agreed-upon product experience plan also allowed him to plan his discovery activities and collaboration activities around the short-term problems.

In a matter of a few months his time invested to understand and solve the design problem of reducing friction in the onboarding experience paid huge dividends. Not only did this enable a better experience for the user and he decreased the churn of new users by 30%, but it also helped him make the business leadership more aware of the impact design can make, and over the next 18 months helped grow the team to over five practitioners with him being promoted into the experience strategist role.

IN ORDER TO MAXIMIZE THE VALUE OF THIS PLAY

→ **Develop an increased empathy for the other contributing teams:** Having a deeper understanding of the craft that goes into other disciplines will help you collaborate and plan more effectively.

IN SUMMARY

Product thinking means you are always thinking of ways to solve problems for the user, and this can only be done through a deep understanding of the breadth of problems the user has and effective orchestration of many moving parts.

RELATED PLAYS

Chapter 18: "Experience Ecosystem Play"
Chapter 28: "Experience Metrics Play"
Chapter 30: "User Research Program Play"
Chapter 32: "Experience Benchmarking Play"
Chapter 34: "Design Problems and Opportunities Play"
Chapter 35: "Product Experience Planning Play"
Chapter 36: "Cross-Functional Collaboration Play"

EXPERIENCE DESIGN DOING

"MAKE IT SIMPLE, BUT SIGNIFICANT."
– DON DRAPER

CHAPTER 38

EXPERIENCE DESIGN DOING: INTRODUCTION

Building an effective "solutioning" rhythm in your organization

What Is Experience Design Doing?

Experience design doing is the discipline that allows experience designers to consistently create effective solutions for relevant design problems. In this section, you'll learn how to leverage people and processes to create powerful experience design solutions as an organization.

The Impact of Experience Design Doing

Good design is good for business. The most evident outcomes are tangible design solutions that your users can engage with. This is where the user-first strategy manifests into actual experience design.

When done well, design doing goes beyond just designing a specific solution; rather, it results in creating a new "solutioning" rhythm within the business. Your team will become a well-oiled machine whose members routinely think through **problems** systematically, **ideate** broadly, **collaborate** strategically, and **execute** effectively.

Key Concepts

Here are a few key terms and concepts to understand before diving into the experience design doing plays:

→ **Product thinking** will help you establish what your product is and identify the key design problems you want to solve. From there you can create experience design that addresses the right problems and the right users.

→ **BIG DESIGN and small design** both have a role in designing effective solutions. While this section is primarily about the craft of design (small design), you can't miss the forest for the trees. Think holistically about experiences and the systems that support them. You need both types of design (Chapter 5: "Business Insanity").

What to Expect in This Section

We've curated a collection of plays that give practical methods for designing powerful, user-centered experiences.

The experience design doing plays will help you answer these questions:

→ How do I systematically optimize and build experiences? (Workflow design play)
→ How do I hone in on effective and quality designs? (Detailed design play)
→ How should an experience design review be run? (Experience design review play)
→ How do I build and scale experience designs with high consistency and quality? (Design system play)
→ How do I test the quality of the delivered vs. engineered experience designs? (Design quality assurance [QA] play)
→ How do I run an effective experience design doing program? (Experience design doing program play)

The experience design doing plays will enable you and your team to utilize your process as a way to solve design problems and drive value. Use this section to make the design process effective, pragmatic, and easy to govern.

> **"The best kind of design isn't necessarily an object, a space, or a structure: it's a process—dynamic and adaptable."**
>
> *– Don Norman*

WORKFLOW DESIGN PLAY

CHAPTER 39

How do I systematically optimize and design experiences?

When it comes to designing a user's experience, most practitioners and businesses overlook the value of workflows. They dive right into the design, only to run into problems with the overall systemic connections, interdependencies, and redundancies. The workflow design play will help you think through, optimize, and build experiences systematically, and establish scope by documenting the entire system of steps (touchpoints).

Why Do You Need a Workflow Design Play?

This play will allow your business to:

→ Focus on the system before the specific design details.

→ Visualize the entire system of touchpoints;

→ Convey the scope of work to your engineering team.

who Are the key Players in the Workflow Design Play?

ROLE	WHO'S INVOLVED	RESPONSIBILITIES
DRIVER	• Interaction experience designer (experience practitioner)	• Systematically think, optimize, and build the experiences; • Identify experiences, problems, and outcomes and defines scenarios; • Identify activities, challenges, systemic relationships, and dependencies; • Frame goals, design problems, design opportunities; • Think through optimization, come up with flow variations to reach the outcome; • Illustrate the flows and add goals and descriptions for each screen.
CONTRIBUTOR	• Product manager	• State intent; • Review scenarios, outcomes; • Review design problems and design opportunities; • Review the activities, goals flow, and descriptions; • Sign off.
	• Engineering team	• Look for intent; • Look for development effort and integrations needed.

MINDFUL CANVAS
Workflow Design

CONTEXT

- What is the experience vision of the product?
- What are the user, business, and product problems that you are trying to solve?
- What are the user and business outcomes that you are trying to achieve?
- What experiences make these outcomes happen?
- What scenarios are part of these experiences?
- What are the highest level relationships in the ecosystem?

FRAMING

- For each step: what is the goal and what are the design problems and design opportunities to consider?

MAPPING

- What are the activities that users need to do to achieve the outcomes of the scenarios?
- What challenges/pain points do you think users will have while doing these activities?
- What systemic relationships need to be established and maintained on a user, system and data level?

OPTIMIZATION

- What are the areas/activities that can be optimized?

CONSOLIDATION

- What does the full system look like?
- How many total unique screens are there?
- What are the goals, design problems, design opportunities that need to be addressed in the detailed design phase?

THE HOW

To build an effective workflow design play, you need to be mindful of:

1. The CONTEXT

Before starting the workflow design, you need to deeply understand the context. This includes the **experience vision, user journey**, and **design problems**, as well as the larger **interconnected ecosystem.**

With the context in mind, identify the experiences that solve the problems and effect the desired outcomes. Then pinpoint which experiences and scenarios the design team should address out of all those identified during the discovery phase.

 HERE'S AN EXAMPLE!

While designing a student portal for a university, the first key experience that was identified is payment experience: where students can pay their tuition. A couple of scenarios as part of this experience: Sam wants to pay his third-trimester tuition fee through the university portal before the deadline. John wants to set up a monthly payment plan using his credit card, instead of a lump-sum payment.

Once you identify all the scenarios, define their outcomes. Ask yourself, "As an experience practitioner, what do I want the user and business to achieve from this scenario?"

 HERE'S AN EXAMPLE!

User outcome: Sam and John are able to pay the tuition fee seamlessly and with no more than three steps.

Business outcome: The university is able to better collect tuition fees on schedule.

2. MAPPING Interactions, Potential Challenges, Dependencies, and Systemic Relationships

Once you have identified the activities, list all the challenges that users might face while trying to complete the tasks. For example, Sam might not remember his student ID number. Or he might not know where to find the required student loan information.

 HERE'S AN EXAMPLE!

For example, Sam must:
→ Fill in his student information;
→ Fill in his payment information;
→ Authorize and complete his tuition payment;
→ Collect his receipt.

Next, identify the user-, system-, and data-level systemic relationships that need to be established and maintained.

HERE'S AN EXAMPLE!

Once Sam provides his information, it should be validated in the university records. A systemic relationship exists between university records and information provided by the student.

"Working hard and working smart sometimes can be two different things."

– Byron Dorgan

After you define the systemic relationships, visualize the workflows by defining the scenario's start and end points. These are the points where your user begins their digital experience and where they end their experience after successfully achieving the scenario. Map the activities in the linear order that the user needs to complete to achieve the outcomes. Every step will act as a screen when you are designing the workflow for the digital experience.

3. Identifying Ways to Build OPTIMIZATION

Now that you have workflows, brainstorm with your peer practitioners about where you can optimize. Identify those areas where technologies can reduce the number of steps, time, and effort, and make the magic happen. Remove activities and steps that cause friction in the user's journey, and update the workflow accordingly. Benchmarking with competitors' products and understanding your users' behavior also can help you think through optimization.

HERE'S AN EXAMPLE!

Brainstorm activities that can be automated, such as generating email notifications after the tuition fee has been submitted, or pre-populating the loan information by interacting with the internal financial aid system.

4. FRAMING Goals, Design Problems, and Design Opportunities

Now that you have created an optimized workflow, establish and frame the goals that need to be achieved, design problems (DPs) that need to be solved, and design opportunities (DOs) that you need to pursue (Chapter 34: "Design Problems and Opportunities Play") at every step in the workflow. This will help you achieve the outcomes of the overall scenario.

HERE'S AN EXAMPLE!

For a screen capturing payment information:

Goal: Capture all relevant payment information from the user.

Design problem (DP): How might we instill trust that the payment information captured will be secure?

Design opportunity (DO): What if we showed students campus jobs that could offset tuition costs?

5. CONSOLIDATING All Scenarios That Will Be Solved in the Detailed Design

Once individual workflows are completed for all scenarios, juxtapose all the workflows together to create a consolidated workflow from the POV of the user and/or the product.

While you consolidate the workflows, also consolidate the goals, design problems, and design opportunities. Finally, tally the number of unique screens. Note the total number of screens, and break the number down by types (i.e. screens, pop-ups, error states, etc.).

This clarifies the product's big picture and reveals the interdependencies and connectivity of all the pieces of the workflow. It also helps to scope the effort.

Share both individual and consolidated workflows with your collaborators, and ensure alignment.

Workflow level agreement typically marks the start of the detailed design process (Chapter 40: "Detailed Design Play").

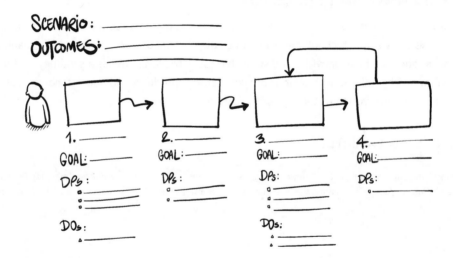

A Workflow in Time Saves Dollars

A client recently launched a payment product into the market. After their end users started complaining that they didn't understand the value of certain screens or how to use them to complete their tasks, UXReactor was brought in to collaborate.

When we evaluated the design, we noticed that the user interface quality was very good but there was no clear cohesion between the various screens and how they connected to each other. For example, the product dashboard screen displayed a negative account balance, but the user could not immediately navigate from the balance to the transaction that caused it to go negative or dispute the transaction. In other words, there were no comprehensive interconnected workflows.

We re-architected the whole product experience based on the user's need for ease and simplicity of navigation. While this work was valued and necessary, it also represented an opportunity cost for our client. If they had spent the time thinking through the system design by leveraging workflows before designing the various product screens, they would not have lost the past year.

IN ORDER TO MAXIMIZE THE VALUE OF THIS PLAY

→ Create multiple workflow variations for each scenario.

→ Do not think of screen design when creating a workflow; focus more on the intent, outcome, and actions. Otherwise, you will limit your potential for creativity.

→ Print out a hard copy of your consolidated workflow; use it as a visual reference for discussions about the scope of work and the overall system that is being designed.

IN SUMMARY

Always think of the system before the screens. Creating workflows will help you systematically think through, optimize, and build rich and seamless experiences for your users. It will also help you determine the scope and effort required of your design and engineering teams before they do the detailed design. Investing in creating thorough workflows ultimately saves a lot of time and effort over the entire product cycle.

RELATED PLAYS

Chapter 18: "Experience Ecosystem Play"
Chapter 20: "Experience Vision Play"
Chapter 33: "Experience Design Brief Play"
Chapter 34: "Design Problems and Opportunities Play"
Chapter 40: "Detailed Design Play"

DETAILED DESIGN PLAY

How do I hone in on effective and quality designs?

Most marathon runners say that the last mile is the hardest. This insight also applies to design practitioners, where the last mile of detailed design makes or breaks the user experience.

Detailed design play outlines the phases you need to go through to produce designs that are ready for engineering. This play will help you build effective and quality designs by iterating rapidly and testing the experiences before investing significant engineering effort and resources into engineering.

Why Do You Need the Detailed Design Play?

This play will allow your business to:

→ Make the design process iterative;

→ Understand and navigate the different variables of design;

→ Remove ambiguity and churn on product functionality and content;

→ Test the product with end users before rolling out the final version to the engineering team.

who Are the key players in the Detailed Design Play?

ROLE	WHO'S INVOLVED	RESPONSIBILITIES
DRIVER	• Experience practitioners (interaction experience designer, visual experience designer, content experience designer, user experience researcher)	• Identify and solve design problems; • Rapidly iterate on designs to reach the outcome; • Document behavior and interaction notes; • Design visual experiences and prototype.
CONTRIBUTOR	• Product manager	• Provide feedback on designs; • Help recruit users for testing; • Sign off on final designs; • Work with the engineering team on engineering scope.
	• Engineering team	• Understand the functionality and behavior of the product; • Look for the scope and development effort.
	• Experience strategist	• Track whether all key design problems are solved and outcomes are met.

Detailed Design

INTENT

→ What are the user, business, and product problems that you are trying to solve?

→ What are the user and business outcomes that you are trying to achieve?

→ What are the design problems that you are trying to solve?

→ What are the design opportunities that you need to go after?

→ What are the content problems that you are trying to solve?

CRAFT

Interaction Design

→ What are the variables that you need to consider during interaction design?

→ What are the framework level items you need to consider? e.g. navigation, search, user assistance, dashboard.

Visual Design

→ What are the variables that you need to consider during visual design?

→ What typography, color, iconography, illustrations, motion guidelines that you will be using in your visual design language?

→ What are all the platforms/devices and respective grid system that you need to consider for your users?

Content Design

→ What are the variables that you need to consider during content design?

→ What content need to be created in order to achieve your goals?

→ What will be your tone and voice in the content?

FIDELITY

→ What are the different ways of fidelity you need to be mindful of ?

→ What are the tools you need to create the artifacts?

RATIONALIZATION

→ What are the different ways you converge for the right solution?

→ How do you prioritize solutions?

TRACEABILITY

→ Did you solve the all the user, business and product problems?

→ Did you achieve user and business outcomes?

→ Did you solve all the design problem and opportunities?

→ Did you meet all the goals that are identified?

THE HOW

To run an effective detailed design play, you need to be mindful of:

1. The INTENT

Before investing time into detailed design, take the time necessary to understand:

→ Your users, experiences, and scenarios that need to be designed;
→ The user, business, and product problems you need to solve and the user and business outcomes you intend to achieve (Chapter 33: "Experience Design Brief Play");
→ The systemic relationships in the entire ecosystem and how design decisions affect each other (Chapter 18: "Experience Ecosystem Play");
→ The goals that you are trying to achieve, the design problems that you are trying to solve, and the design opportunities that you need to pursue (Chapter 34: "Design Problems and Opportunities Play");
→ Your brand's personality that you want your audience to perceive.

2. The CRAFT of Digital Experiences

There are three important crafts involved to make the magic of great digital design experience stand out:

→ Interaction design;
→ Visual design;
→ Content design.

Each of these three crafts require the practice of consistent ideation and inspiration-gathering. Maintain an environment in which practitioners have the freedom and psychological space to think widely. They should not be confined to a short-term-focus state of mind ("What do I put on the screen for tomorrow's review?" vs. "What would be an excellent solution to the design problem?"). Fostering this creative environment will help practitioners develop quality ideas within each of the three crafts. Moreover, in order to give a great experiential product to the user, all three crafts and their practitioners should work hand in hand, not be relegated to design silos.

HERE'S A TIP!

Start the visual design and content design processes in parallel with interaction design, in order to have shared common understanding.

Interaction Design: Is all about the functional behavior of the product experience. It focuses on creating engaging experiences that determine how your user interacts with your product in varying scenarios.

In interaction design, you need to think about and ideate on:

→ Framework-level items such as navigation, search, user assistance, notifications, and settings;
→ Components and patterns based on the need and problem you are solving;
→ Layouts across the product, information hierarchy, and alignment between sections;
→ Consistency at a layout, component, and pattern level, creating templates that can be reused;

- → Screen states such as "Zero," "Loading," "None," "One," "Some," "Too Many/Overflow," "Incorrect," "Correct," and "Done";
- → Accessibility;
- → Behavior and interaction documentation.

While doing interaction design, consider the design problems and design opportunities you want to solve (Chapter 34: "Design Problems and Opportunities Play," Chapter 39: "Workflow Design Play"). Collect inspirations for all the DPs. Then, begin creating low- and mid-fidelity designs, and get sign-off from stakeholders.

Visual Design: Once you establish the functional framework of the product, establish its form. Specifically, start the visual design process in parallel with interaction design: perform visual conceptualization while functionality is being built. Visual design establishes both desirability and personality for the product by focusing on aesthetics and ease of use. It also communicates your brand's personality, creates delight, and sets your product apart from your competition. Visual design can't be done in a silo as it affects the entire user experience. It should go hand in hand with interaction and content design.

In visual design, you need to think about and ideate on:

- → Foundation:

    - → Typography;
    - → Colors;
    - → Iconography;
    - → Imagery;
    - → Illustrations;
    - → Motion guidelines.

- → Layout and hierarchy;
- → Alignments and consistencies;
- → Readability and accessibility;
- → Composition and spacings;
- → States for all the components and patterns.

While doing visual design, consider your goals, your product's functionality, and the design problems you want to solve. Collect inspirations for all the visual design problems. Then begin creating high-fidelity designs, and get sign-off from stakeholders.

Content Design: Is the process of crafting a clear, consistent, and relatable narrative within the product, a narrative that works seamlessly with the brand design. A great content design will guide the user through the product in an intuitive manner. In content design, you need to think about and ideate on:

- → The different types of content necessary to achieve your goals;
- → Content guidelines:
    - → Tone and voice;
    - → Semantics used across the product;
    - → Writing style based on the locale;
    - → Internationalization (I18N) and localization (L10n) needs.
- → Incorporating empathy in the copy.

> **"Design is not just what it looks like and feels like. Design is how it works."**
>
> *– Steve Jobs*

HERE'S A TIP!

To quickly generate a range of ideas, perform this timeboxed exercise: Take a sheet of paper and divide it into six squares. Identify the design problem you want to solve and then start a timer for six minutes. In these six minutes, sketch out a solution for the design problem in each of the squares.

Content design is utilized in areas such **as labels, taxonomy, success and error messages, notifications, error pages, instructions, and descriptions.** Begin designing by identifying the user and business outcomes, as well as the problems you want to solve. Collect inspirations for all the content design problems, and complete the content guidelines. Start writing the content in the last stage of mid-fidelity design, incorporate it in your high-fidelity designs, and get sign-off from stakeholders.

3. The FIDELITY of Designs and Prototypes

Leverage the power of these three crafts and create the most effective fidelity of designs in accordance with the phase and need of the project. To do that you need to understand the various fidelity options.

→ Low-fidelity designs;
→ Mid-fidelity designs;
→ High-fidelity designs;
→ High-fidelity prototypes.

FIDELITY TYPE	WHAT THEY ARE	WHAT THEY DO	WHEN TO USE THEM	TOOLS
Low-fidelity designs	Rough sketches	Communicate the concepts and convey ideas	Early Iterations: during brainstorming and conceptualizing phase	Pen, pencil, and paper
Mid-fidelity designs	Refined digital wireframes with details	Demonstrates functionality and layout, patterns, and content system	Once initial high-level concepts are finalized and for early testing, communicate functionality to all stakeholders	Digital wireframing tools such as UXPin, Balsamiq
High-fidelity designs	Visually enhanced designs	Showcase the static version of the final design with finalized look and feel	Once the functionality and the layouts are finalized and to communicate designs to the front end team	Visual design tools such as Figma, Sketch, Adobe
High-fidelity prototypes	Interactive visual design; closest version to the final product	To provide the feel of the final product by adding interactivity before going into dev	To test with end users and while handing it over to engineering and QA teams	Prototyping tools such as UXPin, Figma, InVision

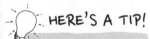

HERE'S A TIP!

Iterate...Iterate...Iterate... Good to Great is made possible by early and often iterating before the deadline.

Most designers don't sketch; they directly jump into wireframing. Every iteration in later stages costs effort, time, and money. Iterate early to ensure perfection later.

"There's a way to do it better—find it.

– Thomas A. Edison

Summative testing should be done at various fidelities. When you're ready to test a design, whether it's a sketch or a visually refined prototype, identify the key scenarios that you want to test. Recruit users and run a usability test. Based on the insights you get from the usability test, incorporate their feedback into the designs. Once the designs are finalized through testing and iterations, make sure all interactions are appropriately documented in a way that's easy for others to understand. This documentation will be helpful when handing off or presenting to various stakeholders, including product managers and engineers (Chapter 42: "Design System Play").

4. The RATIONALIZATION of Design Decisions

As the detailed design process is iterative and you will do numerous variations for numerous problems, you need to have a clear and strong rationale for every design decision you make. **Not having a rationale for design is like building a high-rise tower without a solid foundation: It will not stand.** Once you have the rationale for all the variations, converge the variations for the right solution. Here are few important ways that you can converge and prioritize solutions:

→ Identify the feasibility of the variations and their concepts;
→ Take into consideration the best practices of design and usability;
→ Set design principles as your north star;
→ Avoid biases like confirmation bias and the false consensus effect;
→ Always ground design decision in your research insights;
→ Test your product with users.

HERE'S A TIP!

As an experience practitioner, you always need to communicate design rationales for making the design process objective and aligning all stakeholders.

5. TRACEABILITY of Design Solutions

Make sure that every design decision is attributed directly to why you did it, what problem it solves, what outcomes it achieves, what requirements it is addressing, and what variations were performed. You should be able to map from one variable to the next and back again. This way, you can always trace the entire design back and forth. For example, you can trace forward from the design problems to the final design and the final design back to the design problems. You can also trace back from design problems to user, business, and product problems to answer why the design problem is even there.

A traceability map includes:

→ User and business insights;
→ User, business, and product problems;
→ User and business outcomes;
→ Goals;
→ Design problems;
→ Design opportunities;
→ The final design solution—this can be solved in a workflow or as a detailed design;
→ Validation (whether or not the solution works with real users).

The experience strategist owns the responsibility of ensuring the intended outcome is achieved in a highly traceable manner.

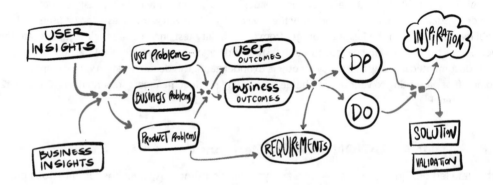

Traceability Builds Credibility

We partnered with a client who had previously worked with another design consulting firm. They had terminated this engagement because the firm didn't generate enough impact for the business. This time, they wanted to get it right, and their CEO and senior leadership team wanted to be involved closely to see how things were progressing.

In one of the design review meetings, they asked the design team a pointed question on why we solved a particular problem this way and not in the way that their competition had done. Since we had a clear process of traceability starting from insights to final solutions, we were able to rationalize our decision. Overall, across all of the reviews, we could go back and forth to address all their questions. In one case, however, we realized that we were solving the wrong design problem—a mistake traceable to a misunderstood business problem—so we went back and iterated on this new information. Together, we and our clients were able to rapidly close the information gaps rapidly and deliver the product on time. This helped them get another round of funding and increased the credibility of our experience design process.

IN ORDER TO MAXIMIZE THE VALUE OF THIS PLAY

→ Don't worry about being exact; let your mind and ideas flow! Remember: ideas before details. When converging, be open to the possibility that modifications or a new option may come out of the discussion.

→ Use standard design conventions and patterns to reduce cognitive load, maximize ease of use, and prevent confusion.

→ Maintain a component and pattern library, and reuse them whenever necessary.

IN SUMMARY

Creating detailed designs will help you build effective, high-quality experiences. Iterate rapidly and test the experiences that are going to be built before investing significant effort and resources into development. Detailed design requires all the crafts to come together to build a seamless and delightful experience for the user.

RELATED PLAYS

Chapter 18: "Experience Ecosystem Play"
Chapter 33: "Experience Design Brief Play".
Chapter 34: "Design Problems and Opportunities Play"
Chapter 39: "Workflow Design Play"
Chapter 42: "Design System Play"

EXPERIENCE DESIGN REVIEW PLAY

How should an experience design review be run?

Poorly run experience design reviews cause unnecessary churn, missed deadlines, and the delivery of a subpar and ineffective solution. This play will empower practitioners and collaborators to get the most out of these reviews, thereby maximizing the effective usage of both time and resources.

Why Do You Need the Experience Design Review Play?

This play will allow your business to:

→ Arrive at the most optimal design that solves your user, product, or business problems;

→ Align and collaborate effectively to design and deliver a high-quality experience;

→ Reduce unnecessary churn among teams;

→ Deliver a great experience for your user on time.

Who Are the Key Players in the Experience Design Review Play?

ROLE	WHO'S INVOLVED	RESPONSIBILITIES
DRIVER	• Experience practitioner	• Prepare and facilitate experience design reviews; • Frame the conversation to focus on user, experience, and design problems and opportunities.
CONTRIBUTOR	• Collaborators	• Provide relevant and constructive feedback on proposed design solutions.

MINDFUL CANVAS

Experience Design Review

PREPARATION

- What is your desired outcome?
- Who are your collaborators?
- What stimuli will you be sharing?

STRUCTURE

How will you structure the review?

Context-setting:
- Who is the user? What is their intent?
- What is the larger experience your design supports?
- What were the prior agreements and goals of this review?

Problem:
- What is the user, business, or product problem and insight?
- Why is this problem important?
- What Design Problems are you addressing?

Process:
- How will you go about solving the problem?
- How does the design solve the DPs and DOs?
- How will you know you've solved them?

Dialogue:
- How can you foster two-way dialogue that yields productive feedback?

CONVERGENCE

- How will you reach convergence?
- What are the agreed-upon decisions?
- What are the next steps?

THE HOW

To run an effective experience design review, you need to be mindful of:

1. Doing the Right PREPARATION

Prepare for the upcoming experience design review by thinking through the following:

→ **Outcome**: What is the ideal outcome of this review? What are you looking to achieve during this meeting? Your outcome will vary based on the problem as well as where this review falls on your product experience plan (Chapter 35: "Product Experience Planning Play").

Outcomes for an experience design review typically (although not exclusively) fall into two categories:

CATEGORY	SAMPLE OUTCOMES
Alignment	• I want the collaborators to review the user insights, so they can help prioritize the next steps; • I want the collaborators to empathize with how much time it takes to resolve a problem.
Feedback	• I want the sponsor of the project to provide timely feedback on the design phase we are in; • I want collaborators to help converge on specific design variations.

Clearly define your outcome. It will serve as a target as you facilitate the meeting, bringing people back to your original intent if the discussion veers too far off course.

HERE'S A TIP!

Try to limit the number of collaborators to seven to eight to avoid the inefficiencies that come with a large group. Assign a designated note-taker so all feedback is clearly captured at the end of the meeting.

→ **Collaborators** : Who are the collaborators you need to involve for this review? What role do they play? What questions do you anticipate them asking? Make sure all of the right and necessary parties are included and present to provide the feedback you are seeking. In addition, proactively anticipate curveball questions, both to avoid derailment and to ensure you can achieve your intended outcome.

Typical collaborators include (but are not limited to):

1. Project sponsors, leaders;
2. Product stakeholders;
3. Internal collaborators;
4. External collaborators;
5. Experience practitioners;
6. End users.

→ **Stimuli:** Stimuli are the artifact(s) that you want your collaborators to react to during the experience design review. What stimuli will you be presenting? Pick the best stimuli that will elicit the feedback you need and help you achieve your intended outcome.

Typical stimuli include (but are not limited to):

1. Design briefs;
2. Experience ecosystems;
3. Experience roadmaps;
4. Storyboards;
5. Vision-types;
6. Workflows;
7. Wireframe variations;
8. Visual explorations.

2. Deciding How to Best STRUCTURE Your Review

The traditional (ineffective) way of presenting design is for practitioners to show a specific artifact or screens to their collaborators and make it a free-for-all, share-any-feedback session.

The feedback, unfortunately, tends to be haphazard and "small-design" focused:

"Why did you left align?" "Can you add this field on the screen?" "I don't like this color." "XYZ company does it another way," "Can you move this button to the top?"

The reviews often are subjective, unstructured, and ultimately ineffective because collaborators don't know how to react to the presentation.

In order to run an effective experience design review, follow this structure:

→ **First, set the context.**
Address the reframed design problem (DP) or design opportunity (DO) that you have been solving (Chapter 34: "Design Problems and Opportunities Play"). Who is the user, and what outcomes are you looking to achieve? If you have already begun meeting, anchor on what was discussed in the previous session and provide an overview of what was agreed. Remember: If the collaborators themselves are not aligned on the user, their problems, and the outcomes, it actually creates unnecessary churn to hold a review. Foundational alignment must be addressed first.

→ **Second, share your approach and proposed solution/design and stimuli.**
Walk your collaborators through your design process by discussing the following:
a. How did we go about solving the problem?
b. How does our design solve the DP or DO?
Cite any relevant metrics that you gathered during user research or that you plan to collect to prove that the root user, business, or product problem has been solved. Answer the question: How did we know we solved it?

HERE'S AN EXAMPLE!

At UXReactor, we frame the discussion by saying, "We prioritized this DP (i.e. HMW make it evident where the user should start their workflow?) to tackle first, addressing it in the following three ways, each with varying complexity ..."

→ **Third, start the dialogue.**
An experience design review is not a one-way presentation; it's a two-way dialogue between the designers and the collaborators. A back-and-forth can happen during any of the above steps for alignment, clarification, and feedback. Always ground your conversation in the user, the DPs and DOs, the metrics, and a solution to the problem, versus in a "pretty screen. " This will focus the dialogue on solving the experience problem at hand.

Let your collaborators know what feedback you'd like them to provide in today's review. This helps ground everyone on the user and ensures the team delivers a great overall experience, even when the proposed design solution may just be a small piece of the larger experience puzzle.

HERE'S A TIP!

Always review and align on the problem before sharing designs. Revisit the problem if stakeholders don't agree.

HERE'S A TIP!

Where possible, conduct reviews in person and print out your artifacts onto a poster-sized paper (invest in a plotter). It's difficult for collaborators to see the bigger picture, connect the dots, and actively engage with the solution when they're looking at it on a small computer screen. Hard-copy artifacts and in-person reviews will mitigate those risks.

If you are a participating collaborator, you have an important role in the review, pick one of the following questions or statements to kick-start the dialogue:

a. Broad, high-level questions in the initial discovery phrase.

HERE'S AN EXAMPLE!

What assumptions are we making about the user?

b. Questions and statements that spur idea generation in the ideation and iteration phrase.

HERE'S AN EXAMPLE!

What if … How might we… Yes, and… What about …

c. Statements of intent and clarifying questions to explore ways to achieve the intent during design review sessions.

HERE'S AN EXAMPLE!

"I want to make sure the visual brand has been consistently applied across all steps along the workflow" vs. "I don't like this blue here."

This structured approach serves three purposes. First, collaborators are realigned on the bigger picture. Second, stating the underlying problem allows collaborators to attack the solution to the problem versus providing unguided or subjective feedback to the design. Lastly, this approach propels the conversation forward by allowing everyone to work together and identify a magical solution for the problem.

3. Guiding Stakeholders towards CONVERGENCE

HERE'S A TIP!

Before the end of the review, verbally run down the key decisions made and ask for agreement from all stakeholders. Then, document your key decisions.

The experience design review cannot be wholly effective without convergence. Convergence indicates reaching an agreement. It can take many forms, including:

→ Aligning on key decisions made;
→ Having clearly agreed-upon action items, such us getting more data;
→ Deciding on a path forward based on the best information available at a given time;
→ Arriving at a single design solution that solves the user and business problem.

There are two helpful ways to facilitate convergence.

1. Does this solution solve the intended user, business, or product problem? The best solution is not necessarily the prettiest one. Constantly refer back to this question, not only to drive convergence, but more importantly to ensure that you deliver an experience that meets the needs of your user.

2. What do our experience design principles mandate? Your experience design principles are your organization's benchmark about the experiences you plan to craft for your users. All experiences need to follow these principles. Use them as a guide to drive consensus. (see Chapter 42: Design Systems Play)

Examples of design principles include:

→ Key flows should be accessible within one click;
→ Data should be meaningful and actionable.

Taking a Page from Home Renovation Projects

Before your next experience design review, think about how an HGTV home renovator walks their clients through a home they're remodeling. They don't point at the kitchen counter and start asking for feedback on its color or placement. Instead, they bring it back to the original insight or challenge their clients shared with them as they surveyed the house before the remodel. The renovator says something like, "You told me one of the biggest challenges you have in your house is not having enough space to prepare large meals for family gatherings and dinner parties. So we decided to ..." And they go through this process for each new room design or addition to the house.

In other words, the renovator has extracted insights from the homeowner and from those insights, derived the design problems to tackle. In the end, they present a solution that is grounded in the user's experience and the original problems as stated by the homeowner.

Try facilitating your next experience design review the way that HGTV home renovator does.

IN ORDER TO MAXIMIZE THE VALUE OF THIS PLAY

→ Talk experiences, not user interface. When presenting early conceptual designs, be sure to focus on the entire experience, journey, and outcome, rather than on the small details on the screen. This will frame the discussion around the overarching experience instead of pigeonholing the team on tactical details.
→ Conclude all presentations with key decisions made and next steps. Summarize any action items and set proper expectations for when your audience will see the next iteration of artifacts.

IN SUMMARY

Leave behind the old way that you've been conducting experience design reviews. Shift away from reviewing screens or artifacts. Instead, treat the review as a two-way dialogue where you, the experience practitioner, are a user-experience steward. You are responsible for framing and guiding the conversation to focus on the larger experience and identifying a solution to the underlying user, business, or product problem.

RELATED PLAYS
Chapter 35: "Product Experience Planning Play"
Chapter 40: "Detailed Design Play"

DESIGN SYSTEM PLAY

How do I build and scale experience designs with high consistency and quality?

A quality design system empowers design and engineering teams. But while most people understand the impact and value that design systems bring, they don't know how to create them. Rookie practices write up a style guide and call it done. There is much more to a design system.

This play will help you understand and build an effective design system that enables all your stakeholders to build consistent and quality experience designs.

Why Do You Need the Design System Play?

This play will allow your business to:

→ Elucidate the design principles that drive your design;

→ Build a product with efficiency and consistency;

→ Build scalable products;

→ Increase productivity by decreasing redundant work.

Who Are the Key Players in the Design System Play?

ROLE	WHO'S INVOLVED	RESPONSIBILITIES
DRIVER	• Experience practitioners (interaction designer, visual designer)	• Document the design principles that will drive the design; • Document the templates at a screen level and describes their anatomy; • Document the visual foundations, components, and patterns with their behavior and interdependencies; • Specify the designs; • Create an inventory of all the deliverables and the final readout for hand-off.
CONTRIBUTOR	• Product manager	• Scope the effort according to the roadmap; • Mutually define guidelines for updating the design system with experience practitioners; • Review and sign off on the design system.
	• Engineering team	• Review and use the design system; • Comment on any changes or new requirements.

MINDFUL CANVAS
Design System

CONTEXT

→ Who are the users ? What are their experiences?
→ What are the principles that the entire system is built on ?
→ What are the frameworks that engineering team will use?
→ Who are the audience for the design system?

SPECIFICATIONS

→ What foundations do your product need? e.g. color, typography, iconography, illustrations, grids & layouts
→ What components do your product need? e.g. CTA's, forms, selection controls
→ What patterns do your product need? e.g. tables, navigation, search
→ What are the behaviors of components and patterns?
→ What are the elements that need to be spec'd in the workflows? interdependencies, etc.
→ What are the elements that need to be spec'd in the prototypes?
→ What are the elements that need to be spec'd in the Visuals?

SOCIALIZATION

→ How the design system is created and maintained?
→ How will you notify the product and engineering team about new changes and updates?
→ What are all the artifacts that need to be included in the inventory?

GOVERNANCE

→ How frequently will you update the design system?
→ What are the versioning guidelines and who are the stakeholders that need to be aware?

THE HOW

To build an effective design system, you need to be mindful of:

1. The CONTEXT

Before starting to build and activate your design system, you need to deeply understand the user, the product, the organization, and its related context. This includes the experience vision, the larger interconnected ecosystem, and the skills and capabilities of the engineering and product teams.

The design system is an effective tool for the engineering team to help build the product experience. More importantly, it also acts as a centralized source of truth for the product and the experience design teams, providing context for overall design decisions (for example, why one typography was picked over another).

2. What SPECIFICATIONS to Include

Specifications should be provided at both the framework and experience levels and be documented in the design system. Framework-level specifications describe exactly what to build and how. Experience-level specifications explain why things are built the way they are and how they connect to each other in the broader system.

Framework-level Specifications: To specify at a framework level, understand the relationship between three elements in the design system: foundations, which make up components, which make up patterns.

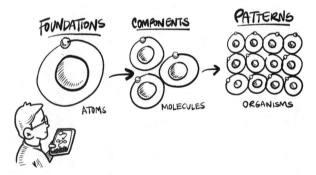

→ **Foundations:** Foundations are the building blocks for design and should align with any existing brand guidelines. Foundations include:
   → **Colors:** The primary, secondary, and other additional color palettes that you will be using across the product. Define where and when colors can be used.
   → **Typography:** The typography suite, including the hierarchy and styles used for different situations such as headers and body text.
   → **Iconography:** The overall style of iconography and the icons themselves, in all different sizes. Define where iconography should and should not be used.
   → **Illustration:** The overall style of illustrations—for example, line vs. filled. Define standard sizes and usage, laying out specific rules across the product.

→ Grids and layouts: The overall grids and layouts used across the product in different platforms such as web, mobile, and tablet, with their respective dimensions. Define where and when they can be used.

→ **Components:** Are the reusable functional elements that make up the foundation. Components meet a specific interaction or interface need, and include:

- → Call to action (CTA);
- → Form input fields;
- → Selection controls (checkboxes, radio buttons, dropdowns, etc.);
- → Accordions.

Identify and document all of the components in your product. Include descriptions, redlining, rules, and usage. Document the component behaviors:

- → States such as "Loading," "Zero," "One," "Some," " Too Many," "Incorrect";
- → Various interdependencies between components and patterns;
- → Changes that happen when the screen resolution is changed;
- → Changes due to role-based access (if applicable).

→ **Patterns:** Are made up of a combination of foundations and components. They standardize designs and make them consistent across the product, enabling product scalability. Patterns help users achieve their goals via the following tools:

- → Tables;
- → Navigation;
- → Search;
- → Filters;
- → Modal windows;
- → Widgets, such as calendars.

Identify and document all the patterns in your product. Include description, redlining, rules, and usage. Document all pattern behaviors, including:

- → States such as "Loading," "Zero," "One," "Some," " Too Many," "Incorrect";
- → Various interdependencies between components and other patterns;
- → Changes that happen when the screen resolution is changed;
- → Changes due to role-based access (if applicable).

With the framework level specifications in place, building and improving any future experiences will become easier, faster, and more efficient, and consistency between experiences will increase.

Experience-Level Specifications: Are the key for the engineering team to understand the intent behind the experiences you've designed. To make this seamless, provide the engineering team with the following:

→ **The context:** A brief summary of the key user needs, the design problems, and the goals the experience is intended to address. This also includes the design principles: the universal guideposts that have informed the design at large.

→ **A consolidated workflow:** Lays out the overall breadth and depth of the product. It also shows the interdependencies and error cases that will enable the engineering team to understand how to handle the happy path and the edge cases.

→ **High-fidelity designs with specifications:** Final, unique designs that give a clear picture of how the relevant foundations, components, and patterns come together. Ensure specifications are provided for the colors, typography, padding, assets, and so forth, used for each screen. Fortunately most of the modern design tools can auto-generate these specifications. There are several design tools that do this automatically. Animations also should be specified and given to the engineering team as they build delight into the product.

→ **Prototypes and interaction notes:** Prototypes with their corresponding workflows will help the engineering team see how the actual product should work. All interactions should be documented appropriately in a way that's easy for others to understand.

3. Proactively SOCIALIZING the Required Documentation to Build Out Designs

Proactively and clearly socialize the design system at regular intervals before handing off artifacts to the engineering team.

Before an experience is formally handed over to engineering to build, ensure there is agreement on:

→ How the design system will be created and maintained.
   For example: What tools will be used? Who will have access?

→ The process by which the design system is updated.
   For example: Who needs to approve changes and be informed?

→ How updates to the design system and final designs will be communicated.
   For example: Will the hand-off take place in a formal meeting, in a daily stand-up (DSU), or as a message on a chat channel?

Create an inventory for all the experience design deliverables, including the experience design brief, workflows, sketches, and prototypes. The inventory should be searchable, centralized, and organized and accessible from the design system.

4. Implementing Proper Systems of GOVERNANCE

Working with the peer practitioners determine versioning guidelines and update frequency for the design system. Versioning will give all stakeholders visibility into any changes and their impact on their work and the product. Ensure that those who need to be informed of design system updates are rightly informed in a timely manner, through the most appropriate communication channel.

Design System Saves the Day

UXReactor partnered with an organization on a few product suites. As we started working, we found many inconsistencies in their designs: multiple styles, iconography, interaction patterns, and navigation models were littered across all the suites. For example, we discovered 40 shades of the same color and more than 10 font families. One of our main jobs was to clean up the designs and create a comprehensive system. When we finished building the design system, inconsistencies and quality level issues had decreased by approximately 87%. In a few months, once all the teams got into a rhythm using the design systems, the inconsistency issues dropped to nearly zero, and a drastic increase in productivity was noticed.

IN ORDER TO MAXIMIZE THE VALUE OF THIS PLAY

→ Document, document, document! Explain every element in the design system with its intent and use.

→ Design systems should evolve. If it is not evolving, your design system is getting obsolete.

→ Perform regular audits of your product and update the newer elements into the design system.

IN SUMMARY

Investing time in building a comprehensive design system with richer documentation exponentially increases efficiency and enables high productivity for your teams. It also gives stakeholders experience-level visibility into why the designs are the way they are.

RELATED PLAYS

Chapter 36: "Cross-Functional Collaboration Play"
Chapter 39: "Workflow Design Play"

CHAPTER 43

DESIGN QUALITY ASSURANCE (QA) PLAY

How do I test the quality of the designed vs. engineered experience designs?

Engineering a product experience that deviates from the designs that have been delivered always results in a subpar product. This play will help you incorporate more rigor by being mindful of a design QA process within your organization. It will ensure that the engineering team has implemented the actual experience designed, maintaining product quality and consistency.

Why Do You Need the Design QA Play?

This play will allow your business to:

→ Identify the gaps between the delivered designs and the engineered product;

→ Prevent cascading experience debt;

→ Prioritize and plan for changes in the engineered product.

Who Are the Key Players in the Design QA Play?

ROLE	WHO'S INVOLVED	RESPONSIBILITIES
DRIVER	• Experience practitioners	• Compare the designs delivered and engineered product; • Identify the deltas; • Define the severity and prioritization of issues; • Review delta documentation report with product manager and engineering team; • Track the changes.
CONTRIBUTOR	• Product manager	• Review and approve delta documentation report; • Review the severity and prioritize the issues; • Assign to the engineering team; • Track the changes.
	• Engineering team	• Review delta documentation; • Make sure issues are resolved.

MINDFUL CANVAS
Design Quality Assurance (QA)

CONTEXT

- What are the design problems that you solved?
- At what stage of engineering process are you doing the quality check? e.g. after flow is built, interface is built
- For which experiences and scenarios you want to do a quality check?

EVALUATING

- How will you define the severity of the issue?
- How will you determine which issues should be prioritized?
- Which of the issues will you focus on first?

IDENTIFYING

- What is the test plan for the quality check? e.g. objectives, schedule, deliverables, and resources required
- What are the workflows that need to go through quality check?
- What are your defensive steps (steps taken to mitigate the errors cases), and are they covered in the design?
- What are the visual flows that need to go through quality check?
- What are the elements in visuals that need to be considered?
- What are all the platforms/devices catered to users that need to go through quality check?
- What are the data and content in the design that need to go through quality check?

COLLABORATION

- What is the plan for implementation—design level and engineering level—deadlines, releases etc.?
- Where will the issues be stored and tracked?
- What are all included in the experience debt?

THE HOW

To run an effective design QA, you need to be mindful of:

1. The CONTEXT

To catalyze an effective design QA process, first recall the design problems you set out to solve. This will help you to keep an eye out for them while doing the QA. Then, identify the experiences and scenarios you want to perform the quality check on. Determine when the quality check takes place in the engineering process: for example, after the framework is built, after a particular flow is built, or after the entire end-to-end product is built. This will help you define your scope and allocate resources better. Investing time in a frequent and progressive design QA will save subsequent time and resources.

Socialize the process with the peer practitioners to ensure there is awareness of what will come, and to ensure you have access to the latest build.

2. IDENTIFYING the Issues

Create a plan for the quality check that describes the objectives, schedule, milestones, deliverables, resources required, and so forth. Be sure to review the entire engineered product and use it once before the QA. This will give you a high-level understanding of the issues that are present in the product. Keep the design system in hand as a source of truth for the intent and specifications of the design (Chapter 42: "Design System Play").

Start doing the quality check on both a **system and a design** level.

The system-level quality check includes reviewing experiences, journeys, workflows, and the steps that users should follow to achieve their intended goal.

Quality checks should be performed for different scenarios and contexts. You typically will see three types of issues:

→ **Experience:** Key context and friction points have not been addressed.
→ **Flow:** Incorrect linkage of flows, mostly from screen to screen.
→ **Usability:** The designed solution is not intuitive, learnable, or efficient.

The design-level check includes reviewing colors, padding, asset sizes, error states, and data and content types used.

Quality checks should be performed on all of the different platforms and devices catering to your users. You typically will see two types of issues:

→ **Components and patterns:** Inconsistencies in components and behavioral design patterns.
→ **Aesthetic:** Inconsistencies in colors, typography.

Ensure all the issues are appropriately documented in a way that is easy for stakeholders to understand and prioritize. Include a detailed description of the issue, an image, and any relevant links.

3. EVALUATING the Issues

As you identify and document the issues, determine their severity. Severity defines the impact of the issue on the system and user. Severity can be at various levels. If you identify an issue that should be fixed before launch, such as uncompleted flows where users might get stuck and not know what to do next, mark it as high severity. If the issue causes irritation and users can find a workaround, or if the issue is cosmetic, mark it as medium severity.

Once you determine the severity, prioritize the issues using a 2x2 decision matrix, where frequency and severity are the two variables. This will allow the collaboration trinity to anticipate the scope of changes and make an implementation plan. Once prioritization is done, share your findings with all the stakeholders, highlighting which priorities must be fixed before the product goes live.

> **When users might get stuck and not know what to do next, mark it as high severity."**

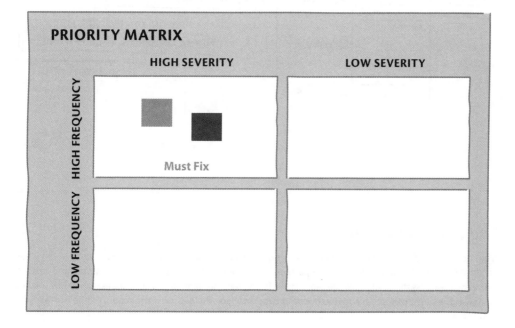

4. COLLABORATING with Stakeholders

Coordinate a timeline for rectifying issues with the product manager and engineering team. Ensure the findings and agreements are recorded in a way that can be tracked.

There will likely be some technical challenges during implementation. Support the engineering team with alternate designs that achieve the same outcomes. At times, constraints such as release dates or competing product engineering plans may mean that every issue can't be fixed immediately.

De-prioritize issues that create less positive impact on the experiences for the user, but document them as experience debt (unresolved flow-, pattern-, and aesthetic-level issues). Once the engineering team fixes the issues, do a second round of quality checks, testing the initial improvements while also keeping an eye out for any new issues that may have arisen.

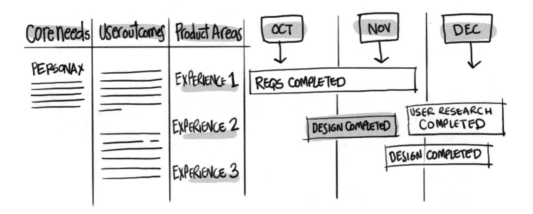

Fix It before You Launch It

In our practice at UXReactor, design QA is a non-negotiable part of the process. As part of an engagement when we ran the design QA for one of our client partners, we identified more than 500 flow-, pattern-, and aesthetic-level issues across the product. While most of the issues were not high on severity, that said 500 low severity issues was the surest way to a "death by thousand cuts," as users would assume the product to be not ready for prime time.

Interestingly none of the issues came up as part of the engineering QA process, as the product worked as functionally intended.

Nonetheless we collaboratively prioritized the issues with the product manager and engineering lead, and nearly 300 issues were fixed before the launch. The remaining 200 remained on the experience debt to be solved on a later date.

IN ORDER TO MAXIMIZE THE VALUE OF THIS PLAY

→ Make a note of all issues, irrespective of size or severity.

→ Create a design QA checklist, so you don't miss a thing.

→ As you go through the product identifying and evaluating issues, progressively disclose your findings to your shareholders to help set expectations about the extent of the delta. This also will help them get a head start on resolving some issues.

IN SUMMARY

Having a delta between the experience designed and engineered is very common. Many businesses have a QA team to do a quality check on code and functionality. However, incorporating an additional design QA process is a deliberate shift that allows you to check the build against design intent. Investing time in doing design QA will help your business build consistency and quality across your products, and avoid accruing experience debt.

RELATED PLAYS

Chapter 42: "Design System Play"

EXPERIENCE DESIGN DOING PROGRAM PLAY

How do I run an effective Experience Design Doing Program?

Businesses that prioritize product experience or experience transformation cannot succeed without a well-structured experience design doing program. This program helps build structure and rigor around all aspects of design doing so the practice can consistently design high-quality experience solutions.

Why Do You Need the Experience Design Doing Program Play?

This play will allow your business to:

→ Establish a sustainable process around all aspects of design doing, within the organization;

→ Consistently deliver tangible outcomes of good design focused on an experience;

→ Improve your organizational efficiency by leveraging a thorough detailed design process.

Who Are the Key Players in the Experience Design Doing Program Play?

ROLE	WHO'S INVOLVED	RESPONSIBILITIES
DRIVER	• Experience strategist	• Identify the right people and skills needed on their team; • Establish, govern, and improve the process; • Foster an environment with the right mindsets.
CONTRIBUTOR	• Cross-functional teams	• Provide input when needed.

Experience Design Doing Program

PEOPLE

→ What skill mix do you need?
→ Who will lead the experience design doing program?

PROBLEMS

→ What are you users' problems?
→ What are you business problems?
→ How will you prioritize which problems to solve?

PROCESS

→ What other experience design doing plays will you need?
→ What will your workflow include?

EXPERIMENTATION

→ What experiments will you run on your design to validate it?
→ How can you test your process to ensure it's helping drive value?

TOOLS AND COLLABORATION

→ What tools will you need to create design solutions?
→ How will you use these tools to communicate solutions to experience partners?
→ Who will you collaborate with among your experience partners?
→ How will you collaborate with your experience partners?

GOVERNANCE

→ What experience metrics will you measure?
→ When will you improve your experiences?

THE HOW

To build an effective experience design doing program, you need to be mindful of:

1. Determining the PEOPLE and Skills That Will Drive You to Success

The people who make up your team are one of the cornerstones of how you structure your experience design doing program.

When building your team for a design doing program, be mindful about hiring:

→ An **interaction designer** to solve workflow, framework, and interaction behavior related design problems (DPs)
→ A **visual designer** to solve visual related DPs
→ A **content designer** to solve content related DPs
→ A **user researcher** to help facilitate user research experiments
→ **Peer practitioners** who are collaborating with the above experience practitioners.
→ An **experience strategist** to establish and govern the processes with a focus to drive the user and business problems

2. Identifying the PROBLEMS You Want to Solve

Make sure that the program is working with and solving the most relevant design problems identified through the product thinking process. (Chapter 34: "Design Problems and Opportunities Play")

If you're thorough, you will end up with an incredibly large list of problems to solve. But unfortunately you can't solve every problem. Once you've identified the pool of possible problems to solve, prioritize them and work toward a manageable scope for you and your team.

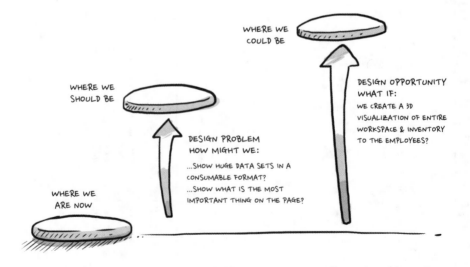

3. Defining Your PROCESS

A rigorous design process is critical for designing high-quality digital experiences. It needs a **systemic, collaborative, and highly traceable** approach for crafting solutions for a variety of design problems.

When establishing your experience design doing process, always start with an ecosystem system level perspective to ensure that you do not get blindsided by a myopic solution. Regardless of your focus, try not to cut corners from a process standpoint, you will always need to run the following structure:

→ **Ecosystem/workflows:** Ensure that you understand and optimize the overall system, its inter-relationships, before getting into the details.

→ **Detailed design:** Ensure iteration in the actual design, from sketches to visual experience. The devil is in the details (interaction/visual/content), so make sure that you allocate enough time for collaboration and iteration.

→ **Design system:** Establish the source of truth for all relevant design specifications, making development consistent and scalable. Try not to solve the same design problems in different contexts, leverage the design system to bring efficiency throughout the process.

→ **Design QA:** Enable the experience practitioner to frequently review whether functionality is impacting as designed. Allocate frequent and consistent time to QA the solution as it is being built.

4. Validating Experience Design via EXPERIMENTATION

As you are iterating and designing solutions for the various design problems, think through how you'll validate the solutions to those experiences: What do you need to discover? What kind of tests will you run, and when? What stimuli will you need? By testing hypotheses through experiments you will mitigate business risk, and above all get data to further improve the designs.

Most effective experience design doing programs consistently experiment by leveraging some type of summative method (Chapter 25: "Picking a Research Method Play"), typically in the form of a usability study where a user's actions are actively observed, or in the form of an A/B test.

Make sure the program has experimentation built out to ensure that the designs get from good to great through user feedback.

5. Identifying the TOOLS You Need to Succeed and Who to COLLABORATE With

Due to the increasing impact of user experience design in business transformation, a ton of tools are being created and introduced in the market, and are fairly affordable.

Identify the tools that work in your organization and be consistent in leveraging them across your design process.

Some of the tools that you would need to be aware of in your design doing process would include (but are not limited to)

→ **For design definition/workflows:** Miro, Mural, Whimsical;
→ **For detailed design:** Figma, Sketch+Abstract, AdobeXD;
→ **For prototyping:** UXPIN, Justinmind, Principle;
→ **For experimentation:** UserTesting, Userlytics, Great Question.

Make sure that all the tools are available and accessible for the practitioners involved in the process.

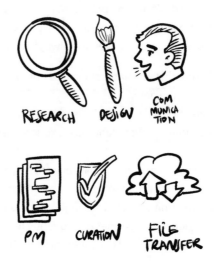

6. Continuously Providing Value through GOVERNANCE

Ensure and govern that the rigor of the program is not diluted by focusing on the right people, problem, process, tools, and experimentation in your design doing program.

Remember that solving user and business problems through experience design is an ongoing process. Over time, your solutions may lose their effectiveness or new technologies or design standards may develop that will affect your experience design. Make sure that you are always tracking your existing and previous solutions for the DPs so you identify which ones are continuously driving value and which ones are not.

Finally, always be aware of the experience debt that is being accrued in the organization, a debt that comes by not solving the right user problems or not solving the problem to the fullest extent. Make sure you keep your experience debt below a level that is unnoticeable to the user.

Trust the Process

At UXReactor, we take on design problems with a wide variety of focuses. Sometimes we are focused on design problems related to simplifying a UI hierarchy of a screen and to contrast it, sometimes we may also be focused on building a brand new platform where multiple products are being brought together in a seamless experience.

Every practitioner follows the same rigor of design regardless of the complexity of the problem in hand; this ensures that we deliver consistently high-quality results.

Interestingly each and every time a practitioner or a client-partner has tried to shortcut the process (for example: by directly getting into detailed visual design with the engineer), we have noticed that it has a direct impact on the final outcome generated, typically due to lack of a deliberate thought process from the system level to the screen level.

Our hard earned lesson is: Trust the process and the rest will ensue.

IN ORDER TO MAXIMIZE THE VALUE OF THIS PLAY

→ When you map out the people on your team, identify the experience partners and how they might impact your experience design. They may be able to provide different perspectives or they may be required to sign off on your solutions.

→ Don't be afraid to run everything as an experiment. Capture adequate insights at the right stage of the process through proper experimentation. This way, you won't make workflow-level changes in the visual design stage, or create similar levels of churn elsewhere.

IN SUMMARY

A successful experience design doing program is essential for ensuring high-quality experience design solutions. Always make sure to have the right people, problems, process, experiments, and tools, in your program to enable the high-quality value creation for your users and business.

RELATED PLAYS

Chapter 23: "Experience Transformation Program Play"
Chapter 30: "User Research Program Play"
Chapter 37: "Product Thinking Program Play"

PART N°3

GAME PLANNING

> "HE WILL WIN WHO KNOWS WHEN TO FIGHT AND WHEN NOT TO FIGHT."
> —SUN TZU

A BUSINESS LEADER'S GAME PLAN

Contrasting the journey of two leaders in different business contexts

To illustrate the power of the UXD Playbook, let's go through some scenarios inspired by real life that **business leaders** in two different contexts have to deal with and discuss how they both can leverage this Playbook to get to their intended outcome.

Chris leads AltEdukation, the small but highly effective organization that was introduced in Chapter 1. Kathy leads LivPharma, a large, publicly traded multinational organization.

AltEdukation: Innovate or Perish

AltEdukation is a well-established company providing after-school enrichment programs in multiple physical locations to K–12 students across the West Coast. Its story begins in 2017. Under CEO Chris, this successful brick-and-mortar education company had built a loyal customer base, and its brand was well known within the local community. The business was profitable with reasonable margins, and steady growth was coming as it launched new locations.

However, AltEdukation's acceleration was limited by the capital they had available to reinvest in opening these new locations. Chris had been doing research on digital transformation and also had observed an influx of online training programs such as Coursera and Udemy. He knew that he needed a less capital-intensive way to accelerate his business and a way to expand the brand nationwide. He also understood that although digital transformation was a huge opportunity, it would take an investment of a few million dollars.

Chris was concerned about risking his limited resources. While AltEdukation had a small design and development team, they were predominantly leveraged for marketing, instruction design, and IT needs.

How might Chris leverage the UXD Playbook? And crucially, how would his actions affect AltEdukation's ability to navigate the 2020 pandemic that nobody saw coming?

AltEdukation: Chris's Game Plan [2017–2020]

It's 2017. After studying the UXD Playbook, Chris adopts the user-first approach and believes that he can leapfrog the competition by building the best digital learning experience. He further recognizes the need to assess and evolve the people, process, environment, and mindsets at AltEdukation. The best part is that Chris realizes that he can start experimenting without a lot of investment; he sees a way to crawl, walk, and then run. And while he himself has become highly attuned to user-centricity, he wants to bring someone in to help catalyze this transformation across his organization.

He leverages the hiring play (Chapter 21: "Hiring Play") and hires an experience strategist to drive the immediate next steps, giving them clear accountability to create customer-centric experiments.

Chris then does the following:

→ **He sets up monthly check-ins** with the experience strategist to discuss curated research insights based on learning from the experience transformation program play (Chapter 23: "Experience Transformation Program Play").
→ **He reviews and prioritizes the key experiences** revealed by the research and uses them to create an experience roadmap for every user that matters to AltEdukation (Chapter 19: "Experience Roadmap Play").
→ **He defines an experience vision** based on the above data (Chapter 20: "Experience Vision Play").
→ **He engages a researcher to validate the vision** with the users to ensure they have solved the right problems (Chapter 25: "Picking a Research Method Play").

By now, it's 2018. Once the vision is defined and shared across the organization, Chris brings the leadership together to define the user and business metrics that he wants to observe and adopt over the next two years (Chapter 28: "Experience Metrics Play"). They commission a technology vendor to build the product as laid out in the experience vision. The experience strategist, in collaboration with the technology partner, creates a product experience plan so the design team can collaborate to design and build the digital transformation with the users' experience in mind (Chapter 35: "Product Experience Planning Play").

By the time 2020 comes around, Chris's organization has evolved significantly. They have in place the relevant people, processes, and products to go fully digital. In fact, they have spent more than 12 months perfecting their users' experience of their digital product, and AltEdukation sees 100 % growth of active users on a monthly basis—during the pandemic.

> Chris leverages the hiring play and hires an experience strategist to drive the immediate next steps, giving them clear accountability to create customer-centric experiments.

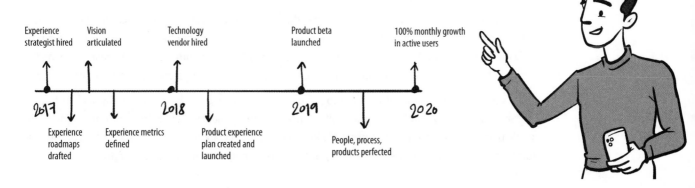

LivPharma: Seeding Tomorrow's Growth

Kathy takes over as CEO of LivPharma, a 40-year-old pharmaceutical company. LivPharma has more than 3,000 employees globally, and their very successful antiviral drugs on the market give them significant cash revenues in the near term. Kathy is determined to lead LivPharma into its next act of growth. She has an engineering background and strongly believes that leveraging the latest technology is the way to make LivPharma lean and mean. Many of its systems and practices are decades old, adding inefficiency in operating in the new digital world.

An avid reader, Kathy comes across a Harvard Business Review book curating 10 must-reads on design thinking. After going over the various case studies, Kathy decides she wants to leverage a user-and-technology-first strategy for LivPharma.

She knows that her firm is making a significant impact on different patients and their families through the drugs that they have put on the market. Kathy wants to build a sustainable and healthy organization that can innovate, accelerate, and evolve aggressively in the next decade—but she isn't sure how to operationalize the new culture in her organization.

In this context, how can Kathy leverage the UXD Playbook?

LivPharma: Kathy's Game Plan

As Kathy reads the UXD Playbook, she realizes that becoming a user experience-centric organization will be a slow and steady marathon. As a first step, Kathy decides to get her whole leadership team to read the Playbook and become sensitized to its concepts. Needing someone to take responsibility for this transformation, Kathy requests her head of strategy, Rohan, to lead the charge as an interim CXO.

Kathy's immediate goals for Rohan are to increase LivPharma's place on the empathy scale (Chapter 17: "Shared Empathy Play"), and curate all the user insights (Chapter 29: "Insights Curation Play") in a single place. She realizes that her organization has very low awareness and understanding of the customers they serve, and although some insights are available, they are not easy to find.

Within six months, Rohan's efforts are showing significant success. It has become evident as they begin to understand the users they serve, more people in the organization, from grassroots to the board room, have a renewed sense of purpose.

Kathy then realizes she needs a single accountable owner to drive this initiative. She promotes Rohan to full-time CXO, formalizing the experience practice under him and increasing his budget and team allocation.

Rohan's group does the following:

→ **Their empathy work had revealed an insight:** Employees were having difficulty using internal tools to do their work, which directly affected the customer's experience. So they expand the definition of "users" to focus on internal users at LivPharma, including employees in sales, support, production, R&D, marketing, and operations, as well as on end users.
→ **They identify the experience roadmap** (Chapter 19: "Experience Roadmap Play") for each user, and articulate a related vision for each of them (Chapter 20: "Experience Vision Play").
→ **They identify relevant business metrics** and correlate them with user experience metrics (Chapter 28: "Experience Metrics Play").
→ **They prioritize and execute on the product experience plan** (Chapter 35: Product Experience Planning Play).

Kathy further decides to create a quarterly business review (QBR) to review activities and progress based on the tenets laid out in the experience transformation program (Chapter 23: "Experience Transformation Program Play"). This includes governing various aspects of people, processes, environments, and mindsets.

In the next few quarters, as the organization starts focusing on investments based on deep customer insights, LivPharma runs a lot of experiments. Some succeed; some fail. But through this process, more initiatives start seeing the light of day:

→ A new patient community experience;
→ A new employee intranet experience;
→ A new drug formulation simulator experience;
→ A global physician collaboration experience.

In 24 months, LivPharma is adding delight and efficiency for its customers as well as for its internal users. The shareholders love the buzz in the market, increasing the stock price by over 150%. And the best part for Kathy and Rohan is that this is just the beginning.

> As Kathy reads the UXD playbook, she realizes that becoming a user experience-centric organization will be a slow and steady marathon.

Interim CXO designated — Month 1

Empathy scale increased

Experience practice established

Experience roadmaps and vision drafted

Experience metrics defined — Month 12

Product experience plan created and launched

QBRs established

New initiatives launched — Month 24

A DESIGN LEADER'S GAME PLAN

Two journeys: Mature bv.d vs. Immature bv.d

To continue illustrating the power of the UXD Playbook, let's go through a couple of real-life scenarios that **design leaders** in different contexts would have to deal with and how they should leverage this Playbook to get to their intended outcome.

Joe leads a small design team in a health care company. Isaac is part of a large organization and wants to make a larger impact on his business.

Joe: Leading Small design to BIG DESIGN

Joe is a design leader in a mid-sized (500-employee) health care payments company. His original training and background were in graphic design, and he has very strong creative and visual skills. He initially joined the company as a marketing visual designer; over time, as the company continues to grow, he has evolved to support product design. Last year, he got promoted to UX design manager, with responsibility for two full-stack designers (individuals who are responsible for the full range of design skills). His team's primary goal is to ensure that the engineering teams are being "fed" constant design specifications, in accordance with the product requirements prioritized by the product managers, so they can build the product without the loss of engineering cycles.

Recently, a new manager of product management was hired into the company. This person believes in leading the product roadmap with a user-centric focus. In his first meeting with Joe, she mentions that she would like to move forward with a user-first approach vs. the team's existing inside-first approach, and she wants Joe to be more involved and collaborative in bringing this shift. While Joe is excited about the possibility, he is struggling on how to go toe-to-toe with this new product leader without stumbling in the process.

The new manager gives Joe a copy of the UXD Playbook. Joe reads the book and realizes that although he has been doing a lot of UI design, he has a limited understanding of the business and user impact of his team's work. Given that Joe has limited resources, his first order of action is to introduce his team to the five mindsets (Chapter 8: "Mindsets of a User-Centric Organization"), along with a user-first approach (Chapter 5: "Business Insanity"). This ensures that he and his team are aligned.

Next, he starts building a body of user insights (Chapter 29: "Insights Curation Play") that can inform his team's design and the product roadmaps. To kick-start this, he hires an intern to help conduct a few summative research studies, the insights from which are distilled and communicated across the organization. From there, Joe does the following:

→ **He facilitates a new collaboration process across the product, design, and engineering teams** (Chapter 36: "Cross-Functional Collaboration Play"). The impact of this is noticeable as teams work together seamlessly and camaraderie is high.

→ **He facilitates the creation of the first experience roadmap** (Chapter 19: "Experience Roadmap Play") by coordinating a workshop including the team's key stakeholders.

As the word spreads, Joe and the product management leader are asked to present this roadmap to the leadership team. It's a grand success—the first time there's been cohesion on multiteam activities and prioritization of the user and their experiences. The leadership team agrees to invest more in this user-first approach and allows Joe to triple his team (Chapter 21: "Hiring Play") and **build a dedicated research program** (Chapter 30: "User Research Program Play").

With the insights from this program, which everyone from interns to the CEO leverage, the organization become attuned to its users and their needs, increasing shared empathy across the company.

Joe slowly and steadily builds the experience transformation program (Chapter 23: "Experience Transformation Program Play"). Within 30 months, his team achieves the following wins:

→ They conceptualize and design a net new product focused on dental practices (Chapter 20: "Experience Vision Play").

→ They increase the organization's empathy to a level 5 (Chapter 17: "Shared Empathy Play").

→ They run a mature design process with clear and deliberate plans (Chapter 35: "Product Experience Planning Play").

> Joe reads the book and realizes that although he has been doing a lot of UI design, he actually has a limited understanding of the business and user impact of his team's work.

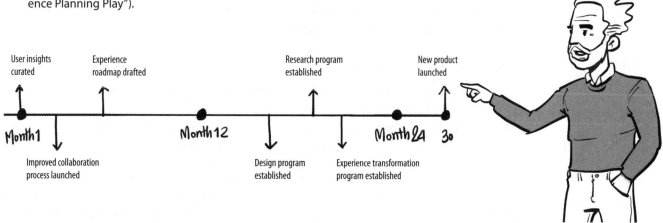

A Practical Playbook to Fuel Business Growth | **277**

Leading the Business: Isaac's Game Plan

Isaac is the design manager of a UX team at a publicly traded supply-chain company whose backbone is a proprietary software technology. Isaac's role reports under the CIO's organization. His team, which consists of a user researcher, an interaction designer, and a visual designer, supports the engineering releases by providing designs and summative user testing. They are responsible for the design and research for maintaining the software, as new features are constantly being added to this powerful platform. Isaac's team has built a collaborative rhythm within the software development organization.

One day, Isaac listens in on the quarterly earnings call presented by the CEO. He can sense a certain amount of defensiveness in the CEO when market analysts ask him why the competition's technology is much easier to use and much more user experience–centric. The CEO doesn't have much of a rebuttal, and the analysts are catching on to it.

Isaac wonders if there is something that he could do.

Isaac asks his researcher to conduct an experience benchmarking exercise (Chapter 32: "Experience Benchmarking Play") for the existing product.

Once the exercise is complete:

→ **He facilitates a workshop where his team analyzes the insights.** This allows them to articulate the difference between their user experience and the competition's.

→ **He takes these insights to the CIO** and shares the opportunities and relevant problems his team has identified (Chapter 34: "Design Problems and Opportunities Play").

Appreciating how the information is presented, the CIO asks Isaac (along with product and engineering) to come up with an **experience vision** (Chapter 20: "Experience Vision Play") for each user. Over the next quarter, Isaac leads this initiative and his team creates **experience roadmaps** for all key users.

After multiple rounds of iterating the experience vision with user feedback, Isaac is invited to the CEOs executive leadership team (ELT) to share the updated experience vision. Given a positive response to his presentation, he shares the root cause of incremental software innovation: **The organization doesn't deeply understand its users.** Isaac advises the ELT to make a deliberate effort to shift the organization from the status quo. The ELT registers that this is a significant gap and empowers Isaac and the CIO to keep investing in a user experience–first philosophy

With the ELT's support, Issac starts making bigger strides:

→ **He deploys the shared empathy play** (Chapter 17: "Shared Empathy Play") to increase empathy in the organization.
→ He makes sure that the **experience visions and roadmaps** are directly informing the product roadmaps and execution plans (Chapter 35: "Product Experience Planning Play").
→ **His team defines experience metrics** (Chapter 28: "Experience Metrics Play") so they can clearly demonstrate their impact on their users' experience. This impact also shows a significant correlation to increased customer retention and upgrades.

In just 24 months, Isaac's team grows by a factor of five, and he is promoted to the new role of CXO, directly reporting to the CEO. More important, Isaac gets his first opportunity to be physically present in an earnings call to address any questions about the company's user-centric practices.

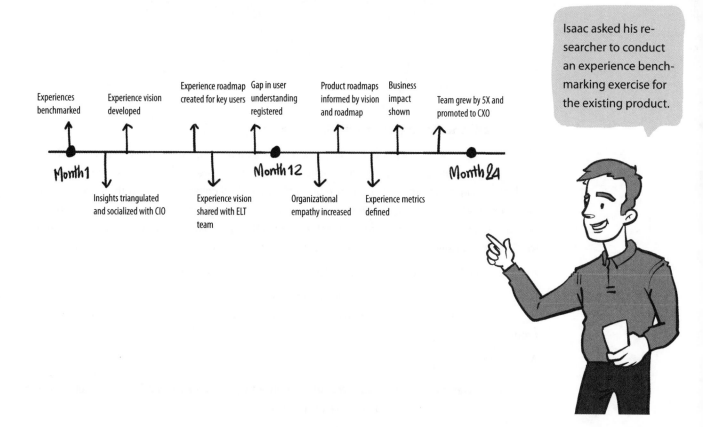

Isaac asked his researcher to conduct an experience benchmarking exercise for the existing product.

A DESIGN PRACTITIONER'S GAME PLAN

A journey of a successful experience strategist

Over the past decade, the user experience design profession has been a melting pot of backgrounds and perspectives. Although this has helped strengthen the field, it also has created a large cohort of professionals who have three to five years of experience in designing digital products but don't know how to become strategic players in their organizations.

Here is the scenario of one such practitioner. Ali is a member of a design practice and wants to leverage his skills to make a strategic impact on the business.

From Practitioner to Strategist: Ali's Game Plan

Ali is a senior interaction designer in a six-person UX design team in a networking software technology company. In this role, he has been working in a highly structured software development process. Product managers provide the product requirements, and Ali collaborates with them to create and iterate on wireframes before handing them off to the visual designer. As the most senior practitioner on the team, he aspires to grow further in the organization. His manager has told him multiple times to think strategically to assert his influence, but Ali isn't sure how or where to start.

As Ali reviews the UXD Playbook, he decides to put several plays into action.

Using his knowledge of the product, Ali creates an **experience ecosystem map** (Chapter 18: "Experience Ecosystem Play") that enables him to understand and articulate the company's different users, products, and services.

As next steps:

> **1. He reviews all the available reports provided by his user researcher,** to understand the insights that were collected over the last few years.

2. He composes a first draft of the experience roadmaps (Chapter 19: "Experience Roadmap Play") for his company's two primary users. This exercise reveals that the migration tools are a big problem for the user—in fact, they are so intimidating that users don't move forward with the product. Further analysis reveals that the migration tools are owned by the customer success team; they are not under the product team's purview.

Ali brings this insight back to his design and product group. The team then brainstorms ways to solve this issue, especially given the business consequences of not having good migration. In less than a week, the team puts together a storyboard laying out a vision of how their user's experience would evolve if the organization could work more seamlessly across units (Chapter 20: "Experience Vision Play"). The team researcher tests this vision-type with users to gauge their response and gain additional feedback that could be factored into the next iteration.

Implementing the feedback from user research, Ali adjusts the experience vision and shares it with the larger leadership team. Needless to say, they love what they see—and they really love their users' reactions.

The leadership team asks Ali to spearhead the design of the trial and onboarding experiences across all the company's products and promote him to experience strategist. Within a year, Ali has identified the need for an improved migration experience, designed and iterated on it, and created a vision that is well received by customers.

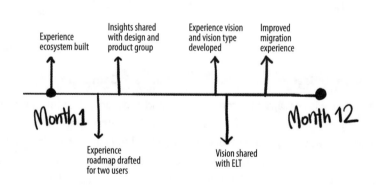

This exercise reveals that the migration tools are a big problem for the user.

A NEWBIE PRACTITIONER'S GAME PLAN

CHAPTER 48

The successful career transitions of an architect and a communication graduate

User experience practitioners have rewarding careers: They get to have a big impact on people's lives, while enjoying a high level of intellectual and creative challenge. In addition, demand for UX practitioners has been growing globally: More than 100,000 are needed in the next few years. Needless to say, there is a huge opportunity for people with the right aptitude and mindset to make a shift into this new career path. Here are the scenarios of two newbie practitioners. Scott is an architect who wants to build a career in interaction experience design. Janet is a college intern at an e-commerce business who wants to make an impact.

From Communication to User Research Practitioner: Janet's Game Plan

Janet is a recent graduate with a major in communication and sociology. She's intrigued by how people communicate and interact in different contexts and appreciates ethnography as a method to build insights. In her junior year at college, Janet worked at a technology company as a marketing intern. She helped create a few different campaign messages and could see the direct impact of messaging and human behavior on a marketing site. This intrigued Janet. As she wrapped up her internship, she started to look into user research as a career option and discovered the UXD Playbook.

As she nears graduation, Janet approaches the head of product at the firm where she interned to see if she can help with user research. She shares some ideas she had jotted down as she read the UXD Playbook. Janet lands an internship to conduct user research for an in-house product the organization wants to release as an SaaS application later in the year.

Since Janet is aware of the **six attributes of conducting effective research** (Chapter 27: "Research Quality Play"), she approaches the process deliberately.

She does the following:

→ **She collaborates with the product manager to identify the users and key research questions the team wants to further understand.** This helps her select an effective method from the playbook (Chapter 25: "Picking a Research Method Play").

→ **She recruits relevant users** (Chapter 26: "Research Recruitment Play") who would find value with the product.

→ **She conducts research with these users and collects valuable insights** (Chapter 29: "Insights Curation Play").

In parallel:

→ **She investigates how other competitors are solving similar problems.** She benchmarks the users' experiences (Chapter 32: "Experience Benchmarking Play") to define what would be minimally acceptable and what would go above and beyond in providing users with functionality and delight.

→ **She further creates design problems and design opportunities** (Chapter 34: "Design Problems and Opportunities Play") that she prioritizes based on all the work done so far.

At the end of her six-month internship, Janet presents her insights to the product and engineering teams. The managers are impressed with the quality of insights and, unsurprisingly, want a similar rigor for their product lines.

To her delight, Janet is offered a full-time role to join the team as a user research practitioner. While her peers are working in entry-level jobs, she joins the company as someone who has created a deliberate strategy informed by quality user research.

> Since Janet is aware of the six attributes of conducting effective research, she approaches the process deliberately.

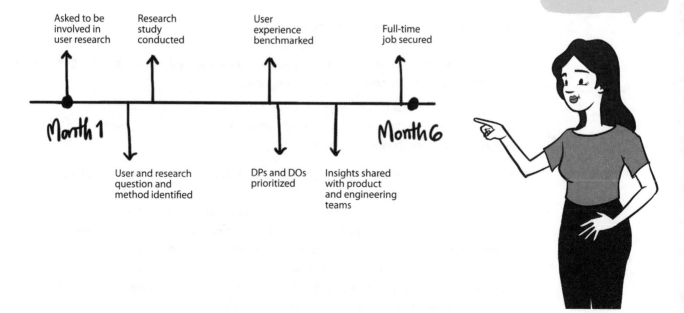

From Architect to Interaction Experience Practitioner: Scott's Game Plan

Fascinated by architectural design and how it surrounds and affects people, Scott studied architecture in college and practiced for a few years after graduation. However, he became concerned by what he saw as a cookie-cutter and top-down approach to design in practice. He wanted to be in the profession of DESIGN, but he wanted a career where he could actively iterate based on real feedback from those experiencing his designs.

While searching online, Scott discovered the career of user experience design. He has come to believe that there are many parallels between the BIG DESIGN of architecture and the BIG DESIGN of digital systems. He just needs to build skills specific to the new field.

Scott reads the UXD Playbook to understand the experience design profession and its impact on users and businesses. He's eager to try some plays out and approaches his friend, a software developer in the initial stages of founding a start-up venture around college students. His friend eagerly accepts Scott's offer to take on the design, as there is a lot to do.

Scott decides to create a quick discussion guide (Chapter 27: "Research Quality Play") to interview college students so he can empathize with them and understand their pain points (Chapter 14: "User Empathy Play"). Research insights in hand:

→ **He frames the user and business problems that should be prioritized** (Chapter 33: "Experience Design Brief Play").

→ **He gathers inspiration** on multiple approaches to solving the prioritized problems.

→ **He starts a workflow** (Chapter 39: "Workflow Design Play") of the various experiences and scenarios the college students will encounter in the product he is designing. He realizes several inefficiencies in how the existing workflow is structured and optimizes it to as few steps and interactions as possible. This is informed by the knowledge of industry standards he gained and the notable experiences he identified during his inspiration gathering.

→ **He starts wireframing** (Chapter 40: "Detailed Design Play") all elements in the flow, such as the screens, texts, emails, and alerts, **while ensuring that he solves the identified design problems** (Chapter 34: "Design Problems and Opportunities Play"). He iterates on wireframes until he has a prototype that he takes back to users for feedback, ensuring that he has resolved his original experience metrics.

Using his updated designs, Scott works with his friend to start developing the software. He verifies the experience design at regular intervals of the build to keep true to the intended experience (Chapter 43: "Design Quality Assurance (QA) Play").

When Scott's friend releases a beta version of the product on a select few college campuses, students love what they see, as it solves key problems: What initially took 10 steps now is optimized to two. Similarly, information that was hard to comprehend is now much easier to access and understand. The product soon has a wait list of potential users.

Given the buzz the product creates, venture funds reach out to Scott's friend to fund the start-up—with the caveat that the user experience continues to be the focus. Scott's friend asks him to be his cofounder. Scott realizes that the simple but powerful plays that he employed transformed him into an innovator, and he is loving every moment of it.

Scott reads the UXD playbook to understand the experience design profession as a whole and its impact on users and businesses.

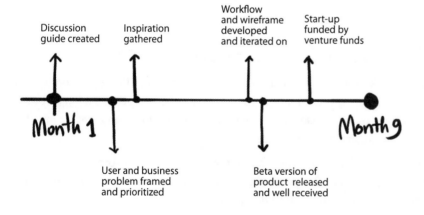

Discussion guide created

Inspiration gathered

Workflow and wireframe developed and iterated on

Start-up funded by venture funds

Month 1

Month 9

User and business problem framed and prioritized

Beta version of product released and well received

A DESIGN COLLABORATOR'S GAME PLAN

A product manager and an engineer's journey in becoming awesome collaborators

It takes collaborators in multiple departments—product, engineering, sales, customer service, and others—working in alignment to deliver the best user experience.

Anita is a product manager and Tom is an engineering lead in the same organization. Let's discuss how they can leverage the UXD Playbook to collaborate effectively with the experience practice.

From Coworkers to Collaborators: Anita and Tom's Game Plan

Anita and Tom are coworkers at a small e-commerce company with a successful track record selling perfumes online. Anita is the senior product manager, and Tom has been the senior engineer for the past couple of years. Recently, their company got a significant cash infusion from a private investor with a vision to create a global brand in personal care.

Along with the expansion came a big shift in the organization's philosophy. The organization began building a high-quality user experience design practice with specialized roles, including interaction designers, visual designers, user researchers, and a design manager.

Neither Anita nor Tom are used to collaborating with a mature design practice, as they usually work with a consultant who handles UI design tasks. Moving forward, they want to ensure that they can effectively engage with this new design practice and, more important, collaborate to meet the aggressive goals the business has set.

As Anita reads the UXD Playbook, she realizes that working with an experience design team is a highly collaborative process. She also realizes that she can rely on the team in ways she is not used to; she can have a true "partner in crime."

As the experience design team is being built, Anita is actively involved in hiring. As an interview panelist, she wants to make sure she is hiring based on mindsets as well as on the candidates' quality of impact on the experience value chain. In fact, Anita wants to make sure that candidates applying for the user researcher role can help drive key elements of (Chapter 21: "Hiring Play"). In fact, Anita wants to make sure that candidates applying for the User Researcher role can help drive key elements of the following:"

→ **User empathy** (Chapter 14: "User Empathy Play");
→ **Experience benchmarking** (Chapter 32: "Experience Benchmarking Play");
→ **Insights curation** (Chapter 29: "Insights Curation Play").

As the team coalesces, Anita is ready to collaborate (Chapter 36: "Cross-Functional Collaboration Play") with this new group and looks forward to the magic they can make happen together.

As Tom reviews the UXD Playbook, he likewise begins to understand that there are many ways to engage with the new design team. He realizes that he needs his engineering team to work more collaboratively (Chapter 36: "Cross-Functional Collaboration Play") with this new experience design practice and that a research team can increase empathy for and understanding of users.

Tom also understands how to leverage and collaborate on artifacts such as:

→ **Workflows** (Chapter 39: "Workflow Design Play") so that his team can actively identify the data models needed to deliver the best UX;
→ **Wireframes** (Chapter 40: "Detailed Design Play") so that his team can understand interactions and required components;
→ **Design systems** (Chapter 42: "Design Systems Play") so that he can bring consistency across all the products being built at the firm.

Overall, Tom has a much better understanding of what he can expect from an experience design practice and how he should collaborate with his colleagues to deliver the best experiences possible.

> Moving forward, Anita and Tom want to ensure that they can effectively collaborate to meet the aggressive goals the business has set.

READY, SET, GO

"THE HEIGHT OF YOUR ACCOMPLISHMENTS WILL
EQUAL THE DEPTH OF YOUR CONVICTIONS."

– WILLIAM F. SCOLAVINO

THE MANIFESTOS

As you come to the end of this book, I hope you've built a deeper understanding of the power of experience design in a rapidly digitally transforming world. I also hope that you've been able to identify a few relevant plays to leverage within your organization. Just remember that this journey is not going to be easy, as you're going against the laws of inertia, and therefore it will take you a few iterations to get it right.

To better enable you in this pursuit, I've distilled the essence of this book into two aspirational manifestos: one for practitioners to enable them in their journey in designing the best experiences, and the other for business and design leaders to enable their teams and organizations to drive business value through user experience design.

The 10 commitments in each manifesto are meant as reminders of the effort required to get it right. I would encourage you to print the relevant manifesto and display it in your work environment so you and your team are constantly exposed to it.

If you'd like to print this out you can go to www.UXDPlaybook.com, where you'll find a version to share within your organization.

THE EXPERIENCE PRACTITIONER'S MANIFESTO

A PRACTITIONER'S COMMITMENT TO DESIGNING AN AWESOME USER EXPERIENCE

1. I will walk in my user's shoes and immerse myself in their journey before designing anything.

2. I will not let my organizational structure get in the way of a great experience design.

3. I will be accountable to my user FIRST before others.

4. I will perfect the craft of experience design while remaining anchored to the intent of fueling business growth.

5. I will design experiences, not screens.

6. I will diagnose before I prescribe.

7. I will collaborate and push my peers to achieve the best outcomes for our users and business.

8. I will catalyze innovation and bring about cultural change through deep customer empathy.

9. I will operate as a partner and always have an experience vision to guide the future state of business decision-making.

10. I will drive business growth through the toolkit of experience design.

THE LEADING BY EXPERIENCE MANIFESTO

A leader's commitment to driving business value through user experience design

1.
I will build an organization with deep empathy for the users we serve.

2.
I will not let my organizational structure get in the way of delivering great experiences.

3.
I will be accountable to the user FIRST before others.

4.
I will lead an organization that will force-multiply business outcomes.

5.
I will eat, sleep, and drink experience metrics.

6.
I will hire and manage an experience-centric team with a healthy diversity of mindsets.

7.
I will cultivate an environment of user-centric experimentation, where a failure is celebrated by what we learn.

8.
I will track and effectively manage experience debt in my organization.

9.
I will give freedom and responsibility to my team to drive experience outcomes.

10.
I will lead from the front.

WHERE TO GO TO LEARN MORE?

Congratulations on making a sizable dent in your experience transformation journey. It's been a joy sharing my life's work with you. If you enjoyed reading this book and are itching to get started or learn more, allow me to offer a few suggestions.

What If I Want to Follow This Topic and Keep Myself Updated?

www.uxdplaybook.com is our dedicated site for this book. It offers a wealth of resources that include extra plays that are not in the book, instructional videos where we walk you through a real-life application of a play, templates to share with your teammates, assessments to help you understand where you fall on the maturity model, my advice to each persona covered in the book, and much more. It also has access to a community of fellow practitioners who are in a similar pursuit as you.

What If I Want to Get More Hands-On Support?

For those of you who want more hands-on training and coaching, be on the lookout for tailored training courses to enable you to lead with more confidence and be more successful in your professional journeys.

For organizations looking to transform with user-centric experiences, we also offer custom consulting engagements designed to help you fuel your growth and leapfrog your competition. You can find more information about our enablement courses and custom engagements at www.uxreactor.com.

uxdplaybook.com   **uxreactor.com**

THE PLAYERS BEHIND THE PLAYBOOK

| PRASAD KANTAMNENI | JAMIE YOO |

I am in the business of experience design because...

…I strongly believe that user experience design is the new currency of success for businesses.

I am also sick and tired of business building tons of features in the garb of digital transformation and getting it wrong.

…It is where we can converge around users to apply reason to creativity.

Products are made to be used by people who need a problem solved. This means every product should have a clear reason for existence, but it can address the problem in any multitude of ways.

Your favorite play and why

The shared empathy play:

When deployed well, the transformation is very visible in all aspects of people, process, and environment. For instance, it affects how the organization behaves, hires, incentivizes, and makes decisions.

The experience metrics play:

This play makes the user the focal point of how success is measured in a company, and only good things happen when a company measures success by their user's success.

Tips on how to fuel business growth through design

Experiment! Take one of the plays and try it, learn from it before moving to the next play.
You can only win or lose the game if you play it. :)

Know thy user.

LinkedIn

| ELINOR CHANG | VINAY DRAKSHARAM | SARAH KHALID |

…Experience preserves what makes us human in an age of rising automation.

Humans still crave to be understood, cared for, and empowered in a digital world. Experience fills the void that technology isn't programmed to deliver by first understanding the person and then crafting the experience we are born to seek.

…Experience design can help businesses reach their desired goals, while keeping their users happy.

Additionally experience design is not just looking after the end users, it's a triangulation between users, business, and technology.

…Experience design—good and bad—has an impact on how we move through and interact with the world. I've seen and experienced what happens when there is negligence in experience design, and I'd like to be part of the solution. :)

The culture design play: Culture is the bedrock of an organization and defines how successful your organization will be in the long term. This play primes organizations to be user- and experience-first by helping organizations build the right cultural pillars.

The experience ecosystem play:

This play allows you to see the forest before focusing on the individual trees. Helps see the big picture before diving straight into design.

The design problems and opportunities play:

The correct identification of the problems to solve is paramount. This play also emphasizes tracing a design problem from conception to design solution to validation. It's oh-so-satisfying to be able to trace solutions to problems and then govern the effectiveness of the solution.

It's a marathon, not a sprint.

Focus on building sustainable systems to achieve your outcomes.

Iterate … iterate … iterate …

Take the time to understand the unmet needs of your users. Find that sweet spot of what's really important for them to get done but they have trouble doing.

| **KALYAN GUMMADI** | **JONATHAN HWANG** |

I am in the business of experience design because...

...I believe that design can make people's lives exciting and better and opens up disruptive market opportunities for businesses.

...Thinking about design through the lens of experience is to think holistically. It gives us a deeper understanding of ourselves and the world around us.

Your favorite play and why

The culture design play

Culture is the most important in any organization. A user-first culture delivers great experiences for anyone in the organization ecosystem.

The experience benchmarking play

The concept of different levels of inspiration is not only pragmatic, it is incredibly fascinating and empowering to be able to connect dots that previously seemed like they had no relation.

Tips on how to fuel business growth through design

Get your hands dirty and be ready to learn a lot of new things in the process.

Make sure you are solving a need and not just providing the product or service you *think* people want.

LinkedIn

ACKNOWLEDGMENTS

Throughout the process of putting this book together, one thing that became clear to me was that curating an effective body of work like this is much easier imagined than done. This book is the result of many individuals who have encouraged, influenced, and contributed.

There are quite a few people to acknowledge in this journey, and I would like to recognize a few of them.

THE SYSTEM

Foremost. I would like to acknowledge my cofounder (and brother) **Prasad Kantamneni,** without whom UXReactor would just have been a pipe dream. A little more than 20 years ago he was the first person to introduce me to a nascent field of study called human factors. Both of us eventually earned graduate degrees in the discipline, and it transformed us into human-centered problem solvers.

In addition, there's the awesome **team at UXReactor**, which has steadily grown to more than 60 practitioners across three continents. It's not uncommon to hear phrases such as, "Is there a play for this?" or "We should write this as a play" in the team's day-to-day conversation. The plays shared in this book have been created, tested, and evolved through the team's constant pursuit of improvement in all aspects of our practice. I would like to acknowledge the leadership team of **Vinay Draksharam, Kalyan Gummadi, Jamie Yoo, Sarah Khalid, Elinor Chang, and Camilo Rendon Gomez**, who on a daily basis direct key aspects of the people, process, mindset, and environment at the firm.

It would not have been possible for the Playbook to evolve and strengthen over the past seven years without the lessons we've learned through our dynamic collaboration with our client-partners. Their belief in our philosophy and process has been our pillar of strength. I would like to thank **Kurt Van Etten** at RedSeal; **Guru Sankararaman** and **Jay Vijayan** at Tekion; **Nabil Bukhari, Carla Guzzeti,** and **Shyam Pullela** at Extreme Networks; **Randy Sieffert, Amy Lokey,** and their team at ServiceNow; Lewis Black and his leadership team at Actian; **Greg Petroff** and his team at Compass; **Rizwan Pirani** and his team at DataCore; **Steven Miller** at 8x8; **Michael Homeier** and **Barry Hill** at Nokia; and **Balaji Parimi** at CloudKnox/CloudPhysics.

THE BOOK

The process of producing this book involved support from quite a few contributors that I would like to acknowledge.

Apart from the core contributing team listed in the previous section ("The Players Behind the Playbook") I would also like to acknowledge my teammates **Grace Ang** and **Padmaja Maddala**, who spent significant time contributing to and reviewing this book.

We were also fortunate to have some very capable volunteers, representing the various personas this book was written for, reviewing and providing feedback in true user-first fashion. I would like to acknowledge **Lalatendu Satpathy, Kelly Patchet, Uday Gajendar, Justin Hou, Mukul Bhist, Kate Vyvial, Saibaba Attelli, Wendy Kastner, Nithya Lakshmanan, Kurt Van Etten, Steve Venkateshan, Sridhar Machiroutu,** and **Peter Wohlsen** for their effective and timely feedback.

This book went through multiple iterations and it is a much better product because of the editorial support we got throughout this process. Foremost to acknowledge is **Richard Narramore** from Wiley, who first believed in publishing a book that focused on the power of user experience design fueling business growth and subsequently set the initial structure and narrative. I would also like to acknowledge **Emily Moberg Robinson** and **Bryn Mooth**, who spent significant time editing and providing feedback to improve this book.

Finally, achieving the ambitious goal of having a highly visual finished product would not have been possible without the awesome illustration skills of **Dario Bolivar** and layout skills of my teammate **Diana Sánchez.**

THE FOUNDATION

On a personal front, this book is a result of my decades of experience in various environments and situations that directly influenced my philosophy, mindset, and passion for driving business value through design.

I would like to acknowledge **Dr. Sundaram Narayanan** and **Dr. Ray Rothrock,** who nurtured my inquisitiveness during my graduate studies at Wright State University; **Dr. Nuray Aykin** who was my first non-academic manager at Siemens (to a naive intern); **Chris Rockwell** at Lextant, who gave me my first opportunity to be a full-time teammate and nurtured me to think in a system-thinking way; **Darren Beyer** at Wildcard Systems (FIS), who created an environment for me to dabble in product management; **Corey Bernardo** and **KC Teis** for enabling my transition into design leadership at PayPal; **Catherine Courage** for providing me the support and empowerment to build design teams at scale at Citrix; and **Dasaradha Gude**, who helped mentor us in our early days of UXReactor.

I would also like to acknowledge the awesome faculty of the **General Management Program** at **Harvard Business School**, who have deeply influenced and enabled my business acumen.

My late father **Col. KLK Prasad** (Ret'd.) who as an officer in the Indian Army exposed me to the soldier's ethos of esprit-de-corps and always leading from the front.

Last but not least I would like to acknowledge my dear mother **Ratna Kantamneni**, who helped instill in both Prasad and me the fundamental philosophy of pursuing what we believe is right in life and not focusing too much on the fruits of labor. Without this philosophy we would not have taken the path of delayed gratification by leveraging UXReactor to finesse and evolve the Playbook.

REFERENCES

PART 1 - PLAY TO WIN

Chapter 1 - Case Study of AltEdukation

Li, Cathy, and Farah Lalani. "The COVID-19 pandemic has changed education FOREVER. This is how." World Economic Forum, April 29, 2020. https://www.weforum.org/agenda/2020/04/coronavirus-education-global-covid19-online-digital-learning/.

Chapter 2 - Introduction

"The value of design." Design Management Institute, n.d. https://www.dmi.org/page/DesignValue.

Sheppard, Benedict, Hugo Sarrazin, Garen Kouyoumjian, and Fabricio Dore. "The business value of design." McKinsey & Company, April 28, 2021. https://www.mckinsey.com/business-functions/mckinsey-design/our-insights/the-business-value-of-design.

"The 100 largest companies in the world by market capitalization in 2021." Statista, September 10, 2021. https://www.statista.com/statistics/263264/top-companies-in-the-world-by-market-capitalization/.

Böringer, Jochen, Brett Grehan, Dieter Kiewell, Soenke Lehmitz, and Philipp Moser. "Four pathways to digital growth that work for B2B companies." McKinsey & Company, October 31, 2019. https://www.mckinsey.com/business-functions/marketing-and-sales/our-insights/four-pathways-to-digital-growth-that-work-for-b2b-companies.

Chapter 3 - The User Experience Problem

Hajro, Neira, Klemens Hjartar, Paul Jenkins, and Benjamim Vieira. "What's next for digital consumers." McKinsey & Company, August 16, 2021. https://www.mckinsey.com/business-functions/mckinsey-digital/our-insights/whats-next-for-digital-consumers.

"IDC reveals 2021 worldwide digital TRANSFORMATION predictions; 65% of global GDP digitalized by 2022, driving over $6.8 trillion of DIRECT DX investments from 2020 to 2023." IDC, October 29, 2020. https://www.idc.com/getdoc.jsp?containerId=prUS46967420.

Sheetz, Michael. "Technology killing off corporate AMERICA: average life span of companies under 20 years." CNBC, August 24, 2017. https://www.cnbc.com/2017/08/24/technology-killing-off-corporations-average-lifespan-of-company-under-20-years.html.

Chapter 5 - Business Insanity

Sheppard, Benedict, Hugo Sarrazin, Garen Kouyoumjian, and Fabricio Dore. "The business value of design." McKinsey & Company, April 28, 2021. https://www.mckinsey.com/business-functions/mckinsey-design/our-insights/the-business-value-of-design.

CB Insights. "Why startups fail: top 12 reasons L CB insights." CB Insights Research. CB Insights, September 16, 2021. https://www.cbinsights.com/research/startup-failure-reasons-top/.

Syal, Rajeev. "Abandoned NHS IT system has cost £10bn so far." The Guardian. Guardian News and Media, September 17, 2013. https://www.theguardian.com/society/2013/sep/18/nhs-records-system-10bn.

Chapter 6 - Two Case Studies of Experience Transformation

Morris, Charles. "The waiting list to buy a Tesla is growing rapidly." InsideEVs. EVANNEX, August 28, 2021. https://insideevs.com/news/529446/tesla-waiting-list-growing-quickly/.

"Customer experience study identifies expectation gap between dealers consumers." Driving Sales, March 31, 2015. https://www.drivingsales.com/drivingsales/blog/20150331-driving-sales-customer-experience-study-identifies-expectation-gap-between-dealers-consumers.

Boudette, Neal E. "In electric car market, it's Tesla and a jumbled field of also-rans." The New York Times, July 22, 2020. https://www.nytimes.com/2020/07/22/business/tesla-electric-car-audi-polestar.html.

DeBord, Matthew. "The Tesla Model 3 interior sets a radical new standard for auto design." Business Insider, July 20, 2018. https://www.businessinsider.com/tesla-model-3-interior-is-a-gamechanger-pictures-2018-2#so-there-you-have-it-the-model-3-teslas-minimalist-masterpiece-for-the-masses-12.

Hayes, Tyler. "Hidden Tesla tricks every EV fan should know." PCMAG, March 16, 2021. https://www.pcmag.com/how-to/hidden-tesla-tips-every-ev-fan-should-know.

Livescault, Jonathan. "7 Pillars Shaping Tesla's Corporate Culture." Braineet, June 7, 2021. https://www.braineet.com/blog/tesla-innovation-culture.

Loveday, Steven. "Tesla Model Y 2.0: what changes will come later this year?" InsideEVs, April 22, 2021. https://insideevs.com/features/502871/tesla-modely-updates-late-2021/.

"Great big beautiful tomorrow: the futurism of Walt Disney." YouTube. CM Films, January 9, 2016. https://www.youtube.com/watch?v=pwLznNpJz2I.

Dickerson, Joseph. "Walt Disney: the world's first UX designer." UX Magazine, September 9, 2013. https://uxmag.com/articles/walt-disney-the-worlds-first-ux-designer.

Kinni, Theodore, and The Disney Institute. "Be our guest: perfecting the art of customer service." The DISNEY Institute, 2020.

Sijwang. "Disney's Mymagic+: transforming the theme park experience." Digital Innovation and Transformation, April 6, 2017. https://digital.hbs.edu/platform-digit/submission/disneys-mymagic-transforming-the-theme-park-experience/.

Carr, Austin. "The messy business of reinventing happiness." Fast Company, April 15, 2015. https://www.fastcompany.com/3044283/the-messy-business-of-reinventing-happiness.

"Disney: making magic through digital innovation." Capgemini Consulting, n.d. https://capgemini.com/consulting/wp-content/uploads/sites/30/2017/07/disney_0.pdf.

Barnes, Brooks. "Disney reimagines its stores to be more like a vacation." The New York Times, September 26, 2017. https://www.nytimes.com/2017/09/26/business/media/disney-stores.html.

Richwine, Lisa. "Disney tests new store design as shoppers go online." Reuters. Thomson Reuters, September 26, 2017. https://www.reuters.com/article/us-disney-stores/disney-tests-new-store-design-as-shoppers-go-online-idUSKCN1C10NR.

PART 2 - 27 PLAYS TO PRACTICE

USING THE PLAYBOOK

Chapter 14 - User Empathy Play

Ross, L., D. Greene, and P. House. 1977. The "False consensus effect: an egocentric bias in social perception and attribution processes. Journal of Experimental Social Psychology.

Bach, Deborah. "Plugged in: Microsoft Story Labs." Plugged In | Microsoft Story Labs, May 16, 2018. https://news.microsoft.com/stories/xbox-adaptive-controller/.

Chapter 15 - Experience Strategy: Introduction

Porter, M.E. 1996. "What is a strategy?" Harvard Business Review (November–December): 61–78.

EXPERIENCE STRATEGY

Chapter 16 - Culture Design Play

"How design thinking transformed Airbnb from a failing startup to a billion dollar business." First-round review. Accessed July 15, 2021. https://review.firstround.com/How-design-thinking-transformed-Airbnb-from-failing-startup-to-billion-dollar-business.

Grant, Adam. "How to build a culture of originality." HBR's 10 Must Reads on Building a Great Culture, 2019, 139–39.

Razzetti, Gustavo. "Airbnb culture design canvas." Fearless Culture, February 9, 2020. https://www.fearlessculture.design/blog-posts/airbnb-culture-design-canvas.

Sinek, Simon. "How to make a cultural transformation." YouTube, 2020. https://www.youtube.com/watch?v=N9d0NqSztWA.

Thomke, Stefan. "Optimizely partner story: HBS Professor Stefan Thomke on experimentation." YouTube, 2018. https://www.youtube.com/watch?v=5sklu7J5r90.

Chapter 17 - Shared Empathy Play

"Memorable onboarding for new hires, the Zappos way," Zappos, January 28th, 2020. https://www.zappos.com/about/stories/memorable-onboarding-new-hires.

"A company of holiday helpers," Zappos, December 19, 2017. https://www.zappos.com/about/stories/holiday-helpers.

"Coursera 2020 impact report: serving the world through learning," Coursera, July 26, 2021. https://about.coursera.org/press/wp-content/uploads/2020/09/Coursera-Impact-Report-2020.pdf.

"Learner stories," Coursera Blog, Coursera. https://blog.coursera.org/stories/.

Jon Wong, "The Coursera Make-A-Thon" Coursera Blog, May 25, 2018. https://blog.coursera.org/the-coursera-make-a-thon/.

"Jennifer Ruzek Liebermann," Linkedin, July 26, 2021. https://www.linkedin.com/in/jenniferruzek/.

"The Garfield Innovation Center: a legacy of innovation lives on," Kaiser Permanente Careers, accessed July 26, 2021. https://www.kaiserpermanentejobs.org/garfield-innovation-center-history.

Chapter 18 - Experience Ecosystem Play

Nielsen, Jakob. "Mental models." Nielsen Norman Group, October 10, 2010. https://www.nn-group.com/articles/mental-models/.

Chapter 20 - Experience Vision Play

"Apple knowledge navigator VIDEO (1987) - YouTube." YouTube. Mac History, March 4, 2012. https://www.youtube.com/watch?v=umJsITGzXd0.

Spool, Jared M. "The experience vision: a self-fulfilling UX strategy." Medium, August 16, 2019. https://jmspool.medium.com/the-experience-vision-a-self-fulfilling-ux-strategy-ce4cdb58227e.

USER RESEARCH INSIGHTS

Chapter 25 - Picking a Research Method Play

Rohrer, Christian. "A landscape of user research methods," 2015. https://www.xdstrategy.com/wp-content/uploads/2013/03/Landscape-1440x1080.jpg.

Chapter 26 - Research Recruitment Play

"Lotteries law and legal definition." USLegal, Inc., n.d., 9

"Elements of an anti-corruption policy." Ethisphere, n.d. https://ethisphere.com/wp-content/uploads/Model-Policies-7.2.18.pdf.

"General Data Protection Regulation (GDPR) Compliance Guidelines." GDPR, n.d. https://gdpr.eu/.

"Guide to the UK General Data Protection Regulation (UK GDPR)." Information Commissioner's Office, n.d. https://ico.org.uk/for-organisations/guide-to-data-protection/guide-to-the-general-data-protection-regulation-gdpr/.

"O que muda com a nova lei de dados pessoais" International Association of Privacy Professionals, n.d. https://www.lgpdbrasil.com.br/.

Chapter 30 - User Research Program Play

Rohrer, Christian. "A landscape of user research methods," 2015. https://www.xdstrategy.com/wp-content/uploads/2013/03/Landscape-1440x1080.jpg.

PRODUCT THINKING

Chapter 31 - Product Thinking: Introduction

Emmer, Mark. "95 percent of new products failed. Here are the 6 steps to make sure yours don't." Inc., July 6, 2018. https://www.inc.com/marc-emmer/95-percent-of-new-products-fail-here-are-6-steps-to-make-sure-yours-dont.html#:~:text=According%20to%20Harvard%20Business%20School,is%2070%20to%2080%20percent.

Chapter 36 - Cross-Functional Collaboration Play

Casciaro, Tiziana, Sujin Jang, and Amy C. Edmondson. "What cross-silo leadership looks like." Harvard Business Review, November 24, 2020. https://hbr.org/2019/05/cross-silo-leadership.

Chapter 37 - Product Thinking Program Play

Fernandes, Thaisa. "DACI framework: a tool for group decisions." Medium, n.d. https://medium.com/pm101/daci-framework-a-tool-for-group-decisions-665bd71585cf.

EXPERIENCE DESIGN DOING

Chapter 42 - Design System Play

Frost, Brad. "Atomic design." Brad Frost, n.d. https://bradfrost.com/blog/post/atomic-web-design/.

PART 3 - GAME TIME

GAME PLANNING

Chapter 48 - A Newbie Practitioner's Game Plan

"Mind the gap: a report on the UK's technology skills gap." Hired, n.d. https://hired.com/whitepapers/skills-gap-report-download.

INDEX